THE CLASSICS
OF WESTERN
SPIRITUALITY

THE CLASSICS OF WESTERN SPIRITUALITY
A Library of the Great Spiritual Masters

THE TALMUD
SELECTED WRITINGS

TRANSLATED BY
BEN ZION BOKSER

INTRODUCED BY
BEN ZION BOKSER AND BARUCH M. BOKSER

PREFACE BY
ROBERT GOLDENBERG

PAULIST PRESS
NEW YORK • MAHWAH

Cover art: From David Goldstein's *The Ashkenazi Haggadah* (Harry N. Abrams, Inc., 1985), fol. 7b. Permission granted by The British Library.

Library of Congress Cataloging-in-Publication Data

Talmud. English. Selections.
    The Talmud : selected writings / [selected] by Ben Zion Bokser,
Baruch M. Bokser.
        p.   cm.—(Classics of Western spirituality)

    ISBN 0-8091-3114-5 (pbk.)
    1. Talmud—Introductions.   I. Bokser, Ben Zion, 1907–
II. Bokser, Baruch M.   III. Title.   IV. Series.
BM499.5.E5B65   1989
296.1'250521—dc20   89-36560
                                                                              CIP

Published by Paulist Press
997 Macarthur Boulevard
Mahwah, New Jersey 07430

Printed and bound in the United States of America

Contents

BEN ZION BOKSER, born in Poland, in 1907, and died in New York, in 1984, was a graduate of City College of New York, the Jewish Theological Seminary of America, and Columbia University, from which he received his Ph.D. in 1935. He served as an active pulpit rabbi for more than fifty years as well as pursuing an academic career, teaching at the Jewish Theological Seminary of America, the Hebrew University, Jerusalem, and Queens College of the City of New York, where he was an Adjunct Professor. Besides editing and translating into English the Daily, Sabbath and Festival Prayer Book and the High Holy Day Prayer Book, he authored thirteen books and numerous articles on the history of Jewish thought, with special interest in Jewish law, philosophy, and mysticism: some of these works were translated into Hebrew, Italian, Spanish, and Japanese. Among his books are: *Pharisaic Judaism in Transition*, *Wisdom of the Talmud*, *The World of the Kabbalah*, *The Legacy of Maimonides*, *Abraham Isaac Kook*, and *Judaism: Profile of a Faith*.

BARUCH M. BOKSER, Professor of Talmud and Rabbinics and Director of the Program in Ancient Judaism at the Jewish Theological Seminary of America, New York, was born in Waltham, Massachusetts, in 1945. He is a graduate of the University of Pennsylvania, the Jewish Theological Seminary of America, and received his Ph.D. from Brown University in 1974. He is the author of three books and numerous articles on rabbinic thought and literature and the history of Judaism in Late Antiquity, most notably, *The Origins of the Seder: The Passover Rite and Early Rabbinic Judaism* (1984).

Author of the Preface
ROBERT GOLDENBERG is Associate Professor of Judaic Studies at the State University of New York at Stony Brook. He holds degrees from Cornell and Brown Universities, and was ordained by the Jewish Theological Seminary of America. Professor Goldenberg has published one book and articles on numerous aspects of Talmudic religion and literature.

Foreword

The Talmud reflects the thinking of those Sages who shaped Judaism in the first to sixth centuries C.E. and who created Rabbinic Judaism. The Talmud has been compared to a sea in its size and complexity, requiring proper navigation to be traversed. This metaphor may be extended to convey the notion that the Talmud, like the sea, may be viewed from many different angles and may therefore be described from divergent perspectives. In presenting the spiritual dimension of the Talmud, which is often not portrayed in the secondary literature, the present volume aims at exposing a new vista to the readers as well as sensitizing them to appreciate this component when they directly read and study the Talmud.

The Introduction discusses what the talmudic concept of spirituality entails and how it affected rabbinic views on the world and God. The selections from the Talmud, forming the bulk of the book, enable an individual to encounter the Talmud in its own idiom and to gain a sense of the Talmud's vast expanse.

Publishing this volume weighed heavily on my father before he died in 1984. The original plan was to reprint an earlier work, *The Wisdom of the Talmud* (1951). Then the project was redefined, making the book into an anthology capturing the spirituality of the Talmud. For this my father culled from the Talmud the relevant portions, translating them afresh. In the Note to the anthology he discusses the criteria he employed in making those selections. He further supplemented and reworked the original material—which has become the Introduction—but before completing the final revisions, he passed away.

1

FOREWORD

I acknowledge the assistance of several individuals who helped me in completing the revisions as well as in putting the volume into final form: Mr. David Szonyi and Ms. Miriam Ruth Caravella (my sister), who assisted in the editing and proofreading; Mr. Lorne M. Hanick, who checked the footnotes; and Dr. Trudie Grace, who typed the revised Introduction. I also thank Ms. Shirley Tendler, who typed the original manuscript for my father. I am grateful as well to Ms. Kallia Halpern Bokser, my mother, who from the very beginning showed a commitment to bring to publication my father's unpublished manuscripts, and to Ms. Ann F. Wimpfheimer, my wife, who urged me to take up this task, gave me encouragement as I tried to fit it into my own busy schedule, and offered critical comments on many points. I am further appreciative of Dr. John Farina of the Paulist Press, who not only remained ᾽interested in the manuscript but who showed great patience while the project was being completed, and Ms. Georgia Christo, editor at Paulist Press, who guided the volume to its final publication.

The volume is dedicated to the memory of my father. "The words of the righteous are their memorial."

Preface

No book in the history of Judaism, not even the Bible, has had the formative influence of the Talmud. Everything in the history of Judaism that predates the Talmud seems incomplete and unfinished, while everything that comes after the Talmud seems a mere supplement to it. This situation came into being because the Talmud was produced by a self-conscious elite that managed, despite the absence of a stable structure of governance, to preserve its dominance over Jewish life for over a thousand years. This remarkable achievement, the fruit of unusual political resiliency combined with charismatic religious leadership, meant that for all this time a single religious text could both supply practical guidance to the leaders of the community and serve as the basis of their ongoing authority.

To put the point another way, the Bible speaks in the voices of many different types of religious leadership—priests, prophets, kings—and was produced under a great many different regimes, from the period of pre-monarchic anarchy through the four centuries or so of the independent kingdoms down to the period of Persian and even Greek sovereignty over the Land of Israel. This rich variety is one of the sources of the Bible's power, but for Jews and Christians alike it has given rise to constant dispute over what the Bible wishes to say, over what it might mean to base one's life on its message. Both Talmuds, however, were produced by a single religious movement, that of the "Sages" or the early rabbis, men who had a consistent though not monolithic vision of what Jewish life ought to be, men who for centuries did everything they could to bring it about that the people of Israel would embody that

3

vision in their communities and their personal lives. The embodiment thus created has been called "Judaism" ever since.

As a result of the rabbinization of Judaism, if it may be called that, certain features of the Talmud stamped themselves on all later forms of Jewish life. The earliest rabbis served primarily as judges (or officials more generally) and teachers rather than as liturgical performers, wandering miracle-workers, or inspirational holy men; some rabbis might individually attract attention in these latter roles, but they did not provide or reflect most people's idea of what it meant to be a rabbi or a Sage. The rabbis' communal functions thus required them to cultivate their intellects, to learn how to argue and prove a point, and to master a great body of received teaching; it was much less necessary for them to perfect techniques of introspection or express deep religious feeling. Jewish religiosity in the Middle Ages and beyond, despite important individual exceptions, continued to share those preferences. The rabbis' legal training taught them to consider the observed consequences of an act ahead of the putative motives that gave rise to it, and Judaism preserved its "legalistic" character into the modern world. (This is not the place to examine the parody of "legalism" that has underlain much anti-Judaic polemic over the last hundred years, or to trace what has actually happened to that character in recent generations.) The rabbis' argumentative, lawyerly discourse likewise shaped the Jewish folk character, and attached a set of connotations to the word *talmudic* that have persisted to our own time.

The focus of the present volume, however, is not rabbinic culture but rabbinic spirituality; the purpose of this collection of texts is to shed light on the early rabbis as the shapers of a religion. Assembled by a respected scholar who was both steeped in rabbinic learning and a distinguished leader of the modern rabbinate, the materials in this book uncover for the modern reader the early Sages' fundamental beliefs concerning God, the world, and the human condition. Jewish religious life has been constructed on the foundation of these beliefs for the better part of the last two thousand years.

There is only one point on which I would like to amplify Dr. Bokser's presentation. Almost at the very end of his long Introduction, Dr. Bokser remarks that talmudic Judaism "asserts that in doing God's will—in study, ritual, and the performance of moral acts and righteous acts—one draws closer to God." That is true, but not the whole story. Early rabbinic Judaism in fact developed a kind of two-level spiritual universe, one level for those who "do" God's will, as Dr. Bokser correctly states, but another for those—namely, the rabbis themselves—who actually help to determine it. In case after case, the careful study of talmudic legal discussion reveals that there is no real law at all, and thus no useful statement of God's will, until the rabbinic authorities have decided what the law is to be. Scripture commands that Israel observe the Sabbath, for example, but the Talmud needed two whole tractates, running to 260 double-sided folio pages, to articulate in detail how the Sabbath was in fact to be observed. The deservedly famous story at Baba Mezia 59a–b, included by Dr. Bokser in this anthology, raises this observation to the level of consciousness: The collective of the Sages, and no one else, now determine the meaning of Torah. The Torah is no longer "in heaven"; even its heavenly Giver can no longer interfere in the process of interpreting it, applying it, and expanding its scope.

However, this story excludes on two sides: God must allow the learned to do their task, and so must the unlearned. The latter, by "doing God's will," can "draw closer to God" as Dr. Bokser has written, but only the rabbis themselves, by stating God's will, can *become more like God:* They can do what God does, they can increase the World's knowledge of Torah. The rabbinic act of teaching is a kind of divine revelation. Like Moses himself at the original revelation on Mount Sinai (Ex 19:24, 20:18; Dt 5:5), the Sage stands between the people and their God; with respect to God they are as the people, but with respect to the people they are like God.

The awareness that they stood in this exposed position produced in the early rabbis a heady mixture of extreme self-confidence as they built a brand new form of Jewish religion and equally extreme deference toward the tradition in the name of which they were building it. A number of rabbis took pride in the claim that they had never taught their students anything new or original. The very implausibility of this claim, and the odd spectacle of a scholar refusing to be original, suggests that we are close here to the very center of the rabbis' relationship to the Torah. This is the heart of the talmudic spirituality, the distinctive feature that marks it off from other religious world views of its own time or ours.

The texts in this collection record the teachings of religious leaders who understood their role in the way just described. Under their leadership the people of Israel could achieve its destiny of living as the Creator wished them to live. By allowing rabbinic instruction to shape their communities and their lives, the Jews could become the "kingdom

Introduction
The Spirituality
of the Talmud

The Talmud represents one of the most comprehensive types of spirituality. While compelling an individual to remain a part of the world, it offers him constant opportunities to draw closer to the transcendent. It is the purpose of this Introduction to discuss what this spirituality entailed for the rabbis of the Talmud. I will assess how their notion of spirituality affected not only their teachings about achieving closeness to God, but, more broadly, their whole conception of God, human nature, and society as a whole.

The talmudic conception of spirituality assumes that ultimate reality resides in a person's heart, the locus of the soul or spiritual dimension. By drawing on his inner spiritual awareness, one senses a personal connection with God and begins to build links to the divine. For the talmudic rabbis, this was done not by escaping from the world, as in some other mystical traditions, but by being aware of the manifestations of the divine and by relating to every situation as a potential encounter with God.

> [The editors of the Talmud] did not think that the quest for closeness to God was dependent on experiencing a direct encounter with God, to which mystics were drawn. . . . Instead of seeking direct encounters, they channeled their mys-

7

tical quest through the study of Torah, but this study was pursued not to gain knowledge. The Torah and the commandments were rather seen as a ladder by which a person might reach the higher goal of cleaving to God. Indeed, subsequent developments in Jewish mysticism were often to move in this direction.[1]

The talmudists' approach proved formative for all subsequent Jewish spirituality and mysticism. In medieval and later times the talmudists' commitment to study and to the performance of commandments as the primary means of achieving a *direct encounter with God* became normative and was cultivated by specially gifted individuals. This perspective contrasted with that of antiquity, when Jewish spiritual leaders believed that *nearness to God* was available to all Jews in the course of their mundane activities.

The idea that one can sanctify the everyday is articulated throughout the Book of Leviticus. In Leviticus 19, which covers a wide range of personal and cultic situations, God commands Israel to be holy, "for I am holy." In leaving it to Israel to effectuate the sanctification of life, the Bible views the world as a stage on which humans can manifest and "direct" manifestations of the divine. Israel in particular can impart holiness to the world. Not only is no sphere foreign to the holy, but all human qualities are associated with it. A person's heart and mind, his emotions and intellect, all are aspects of the divine image implanted in creation.

Rabbinic Judaism also emphasized the importance of the conscious expression of human will. The talmudic rabbis viewed reality not as material existence, but as the meaning that undergirds and suffuses the material. The Psalms are permeated by the belief that man can constantly experience manifestations of God in nature, history, and human acts. This belief in a closeness of God to the world, and to certain conscious human actions, was beautifully articulated by Abraham Joshua Heschel:

> Life passes on in proximity to the sacred, and it is this proximity that endows existence with ultimate significance. In our relation to the immediate we touch upon the most distant.

---

1. Ben Zion Bokser, *The Jewish Mystical Tradition* (New York: Pilgrim Press, 1981), p. 48.

INTRODUCTION

Even the satisfaction of physical needs can be a sacred act. Perhaps the essential message of Judaism is that in doing the finite we may perceive the infinite. It is incumbent on us to obtain the perception of the impossible in the possible, the perception of life eternal in everyday deeds.[2]

■ THE TALMUD AND THE BIBLE ■

The Talmud embodies approximately a thousand years of Jewish religious thought. Made up of teachings from Palestinian and Babylonian scholars, it exists in two versions, one edited in Palestine, 350–400 C.E., and one edited in Babylonia, ca. 500–600 C.E. While historically each reflects different societies, in world view they are quite similar and traditionally have been seen as one essence.

Their roots go back to the Bible, which was recognized as the Word of God, communicated to the people of Israel at Sinai through the mediation of Moses, and amplified later through the teachings of the prophets. Even after the biblical canon was formally adopted in several stages through the end of the Second Temple Period, the voices of divine inspiration needed outlets for their writings and teachings, both legal and imaginative. Much of this copious teaching, which was mostly oral, was eventually recorded and then redacted. Ultimately, what resulted was the Talmud—a vast encyclopedia of teachings, comprising sixty-three tractates with many commentaries and supercommentaries.

The Talmud may be viewed as both a supplement to the Bible, which it interprets and clarifies, and a second revelation from God. As time went on the supplementary dimension gained in prominence. The Talmud applies the Bible's basic teachings on the human condition to its own age; it offers procedures for dealing with problems that challenged the Jews in the new historical circumstances they faced. Its foundations supposedly were laid by Ezra and his associates, who had come from the Babylonian exile and who inaugurated the second Jewish commonwealth in Palestine during the middle of the fifth century B.C.E. Little is known, however, regarding these figures. One group, the Pharisees, apparently placed great stress on extending the holiness

---

2. A. J. Heschel, *Man Is Not Alone* (New York: Farrar, Straus and Young, Inc., 1951, 1966), p. 265.

9

of the Temple into the people's daily lives by requiring them, for example, when eating their common food in their homes, to adopt the procedures that priests followed when eating consecrated food in the Temple. Our knowledge of the Pharisees comes largely from the rabbis, who viewed them as their intellectual and spiritual forebears.

The Talmud's period of greatest flowering came in the centuries that followed the disastrous Jewish war against Rome in 70 C.E., after which the rabbis emerged as a distinct group. Their teachings are in the Talmud's two basic strata, the Mishnah and the Gemara. The Mishnah (the word is derived from *shanah*, to "repeat" or "study") states explicitly the teachings of the rabbis; it weaves together diverse opinions into a single whole. Written in a lucid, succinct Hebrew, the Mishnah consists of six main sections that in turn are subdivided into sixty-three tractates. These are further subdivided into chapters, and the chapters into individual *mishnayot*, or paragraphs. The Mishnah was edited in the form we have it today in the early third century of the Common Era.

The Mishnah was supplemented by extended discussions during subsequent centuries, which ultimately were edited and presented under the term *Gemara* ("teaching" or "study" in Aramaic). It exists in two versions—Palestinian and Babylonian. The Mishnah, which might be thought of as the core text to which the Gemara is a supplement, is the same in both versions of the Talmud.

The Talmud's style reflects the rabbis' view of themselves as only partly grounded in the biblical world. In contrast to the authors of such earlier postbiblical works as the Pseudepigrapha and the Qumran scrolls, the rabbis formulated their thoughts and preserved their teachings through nonbiblical literary genres. Even when they supplemented scriptural texts, their writings sought to bridge what was an unmistakable gap between biblical and contemporary contexts. For example, they cite a biblical verse and apply to it their own comment. Similarly, they articulate an opinion and cite a verse as a proof-text. The rich literary flowering of the Talmud was conceived as a means of extending or implementing biblical teachings, sometimes in bold new ways. It was an implicit statement that God's word was not final, and that man can, and should, exercise some initiative in adapting it to the world.

The extent to which God's word could be supplemented, and the manner in which it was done, was an issue about which conservative and progressive schools of Jewish thought debated for centuries. The

INTRODUCTION

Bible, after all, had spoken out against man's tampering with the word of God in such verses as Deuteronomy 4:2: "You shall not add to the word which I command you, nor shall you take anything from it." But spokesmen for bold supplementation also found ample justification for their efforts in the Bible. Apparently presupposing the need for supplementation and even projecting an institution to accomplish it, the Bible depicts Moses, during the time he and the Israelites were still in the desert, as establishing a judicial system with a supreme court to resolve legal problems the lower courts could not resolve. As Deuteronomy 17:8–12 states: "If there arise a matter too hard for thee in judgment . . . then you shall come to the priests and the Levites and to the judges who shall be in those days; and you shall inquire and they shall declare to you the sentence of judgment. . . . According to the law which they shall teach you . . . you shall do." The religious leadership thus was mandated to address whatever disputes over legal doctrines or fine points might arise.

The rabbis of the Talmud believed that ultimate authority could not be found in fixed texts or apodictic teachings but only in a living interpretation of those texts. The texts are sacred, but, given the finitude of the human condition and the pressures of the new historical circumstances, they also must be seen as a source of wisdom to which we turn for general principles in seeking guidance for new situations. One talmudic master put it this way: "If the Torah had been given in fixed and inimitable formulations, it would not have endured. Thus Moses pleaded with the Lord, Master of the universe, reveal to me the final truth in each problem of doctrine and law. To which the Lord replied: There are no pre-existent final truths in doctrine or law; the truth is the considered judgment of the majority of authoritative interpreters in every generation."[3]

The Talmud's lack of systematization, and what to the novice may appear as its disorderly discussion, reflects its creators' belief that the essence of Judaism entails carefully weighing the applicability of traditional principles in encountering daily dilemmas. As Robert Goldenberg notes: "The Talmud is a scholastic text. *Its chief purpose is to preserve the record of earlier generations studying their own tradition and provide materials for later generations wishing to do the same.* It is a book produced

---

3. Yerushalmi Sanhedrin 4:2.

11

by and for people whose highest value was the life of study."[4] While the Talmud later became a guide for practice and *halakhah*, its debates and discussions provided a model for Jewish study during the medieval period.

The masters who participated in these discussions were known as "rabbis," a title that did not exist in biblical times. The religious leadership of the Jewish people was then in the hands of the priests, while prophets occasionally were moved to voice new visions, proddings, and teachings.

With the destruction of the Second Temple in 70 C.E., the priesthood ended and a new Jewish religious leadership began to emerge: the scholars. They interpreted Scripture less as experts in reading the text, as their ancestors had done, than as individuals who offered direction for the law's implementation in the new realities of the post-Temple period. The word *rabbi*, which was used to identify this new group of scholars, who were also ordained members of the rabbinic group, derives from the Hebrew word meaning master.[5]

While the rabbinic group's early history, in the first and second centuries, is not fully known,[6] it clearly consisted of a religious elite that viewed itself as having the responsibility to teach that all facets of life could be permeated by spiritual striving. In the early period in particular, when they lacked strong social bonds and significant political power in the community, the rabbis acted as judges in religious matters. Appointed as community judges by the Jewish lay political leaders, the Patriarch and the Exilarch (who served under the Romans and the Iranians in Palestine and Babylonia respectively), the rabbis wielded actual authority even over what we now call "religious matters" when they involved the courts. Their impact was particularly strong in Babylonia, where the Exilarch relied heavily on the rabbis to staff the courts and to supervise commerce in the marketplace.

The relationship between rabbis and lay leaders varied throughout the early centuries of the Common Era. Generally the Patriarchs, especially in the second to mid-third centuries, were closely allied with the rabbis. R. Judah the Patriarch, the editor of the Mishnah, was the

---

4. Robert Goldenberg, "Talmud," in *Back to the Sources*, ed. Barry Holtz (New York: Summit, 1984), p. 156; italics in the original.

5. This is first attested in Mark 10:51 (*ribbon*).

6. Michael J. Cook, "Judaism. Early Rabbinic," s.v. *Interpreter's Dictionary of the Bible. Supplementary Volume* (Nashville: Abingdon, 1976).

INTRODUCTION

leading lay and religious figure during this period. Tensions arose when the rabbis competed with the Exilarchs and Patriarchs as to who was the true descendant of King David, the "Shepherd of Israel."[7] The rabbis were motivated by both their individual perspectives and their desire for communal consensus. They taught and served the community by adapting the teachings of their predecessors, and at times sought clarification from other Sages to resolve difficult issues. Because the rabbis believed in the individual's obligation to study a complex issue and to grapple with and attempt to decode the divine will, they staunchly resisted subservience to another's intellectual or spiritual authority.

Midrash, a word derived from the verb to "search out" (*darash*), refers to the body of literature created during the talmudic period that explains and imaginatively expands on biblical texts for homiletic purpose.[8] In the Midrash, the exegetical underpinning of a passage is presented as the basis for the positions the passage expresses. Some talmudic discussions were preserved in a complementary work called *Tosefta* ("supplement"). The editor of the Tosefta found that the Mishnah either omitted some material that he thought should be preserved, or included material that needed elaboration.

Talmudic discussions are subdivided into two categories, *halakha*, or "law," and *haggadah* (or *aggadah*), the nonlegal material that is the narrative and often homiletical and ethical teaching. However, the Talmud presupposes no sharp distinction between the legal and spiritual: The former incarnates the latter, while the spiritual can only be "implemented" in daily life via the legal.

The Talmud, second in importance only to the Bible, has had an enormous impact on Judaism. Talmudic teachings have shaped the thinking and behavior of Jews and the talmudic text has provided a model for study as a means to obtain practical information and as an end in its own right.

One of the most significant results of the central role of Talmud study derives from the Talmud's process of inquiry, which inculcates a

---

7. See, e.g., Jacob Neusner, *History of the Jews in Babylonia*, 5 vols. (Leiden: E. J. Brill, 1966–1970); Lee Levine, *Caesarea under Roman Rule* (Leiden: E. J. Brill, 1975); and idem, "The Jewish Patriarch (Nasi) in Third-Century Palestine," *Aufstieg und Niedergang der Römischen Welt*, 2.19 (Berlin: de Gruyter, 1979) 2:649–88.

8. The term *midrash* may refer to the unit of exegetical analysis or to the title of the book in which this analysis occurs. The plural, *Midrashim*, generally designates the book.

critical intellectual approach that uses the mind to evaluate the significance and appropriateness of ideas. Because Torah study was deemed
to provide a means to achieve a nearness with the divine and to uncover
God's will, divine revelation was therefore obtainable through reason,
reflection, and rational discourse. Hence these activities became the
means to approach life, to imitate God, and to become holy. The
midrashic Bible expositions, which make use of the imaginative faculty
as well as the rational, likewise inculcate these traits, for even interpretations and homilies are grounded in Scripture and often withstand a
process of questioning and challenge.

Since in medieval times the Talmud became an authoritative religious guide in all spheres of life, diverse genres of commentaries,
digests, and codes emerged to explain and apply the Talmud, and the
mastery of its text became the highest form of piety and status. Accordingly, the Talmud's accounts of biblical and post-biblical events and
individuals rivaled the biblical record in shaping the perception of the
past. Similarly, the Talmud's symbols and ideas affected the way Jews
were to experience and describe reality.

Due to the significance of the Talmud, its mode of spirituality
remained formative in post-talmudic times, though those who later
evolved alternative modes of piety recast the norms of study and practice. As mentioned above, the Talmud had considered study—like the
rites and rituals—a commandment incumbent on *all* Jews to draw them
closer to the divine. Later spiritual thinkers with a philosophical or
mystical tendency believed that their new perspectives on Judaism
could also be found in the Scripture and the Talmud and Midrash.
Hence, *select* devotees employed diverse hermeneutical principles or
keys, many of which were based on talmudic and midrashic methods
of exegesis, to unlock these deeper meanings, to read the new values
into the text, and to explain God's nature and role in the world.

On the one hand, those who interpreted the Bible to confront
external reality reworked with symbols the talmudic legal and narrative traditions. While they devoted much effort to the contemplation of
texts, their study was geared to acting so as to induce divine harmony.
They claimed that their study and practices had cosmic significance,
for example, in affecting the Godhead. They found precedents for
their approach in the Talmud and its system of commandments, and
perhaps inspiration in several amoraic traditions that describe how
performing the *misvot* had an impact on God. Clearly emphasizing
action over thought, they further standardized details of rites previ-

ously not prescribed. On the other hand, those seeking direct encounters with the divine and spiritual perfection, either to contemplate God's presence or to achieve mystical union, used allegory. While their notion of the significance of religious acts is related to earlier rabbinic ideas on the theological importance of *every* person's fulfillment of the commandments (which could be termed *theurgical*), making the ascent dependent on expert knowledge of the talmudic tradition and precise acting-out of its norms rendered the path traversable only by an elite. Some mystics combined both of the above approaches in differing degrees.[9]

Paradoxically, while for the mystics determining the exactly correct procedure gained increased importance, emphasizing study as a commandment in its own right made the act of searching out Torah more important than uncovering a text's original truth. The stress on contemplation in philosophical spiritual circles likewise resulted in the heightened importance of the act of Torah study.

Accordingly, the Talmud left a heritage of method—to study; a challenge—to treat all of life in all contexts and to try to experience the divine presence; a rich set of symbols and full repertoire of stories and characters—to shape one's imagination and perception of reality; and sets of laws, practices, and prayers—to guide one's actions. Later spiritualists adapted these features of the Talmud to their divergent perspectives, holding that the select could employ the earlier traditions and methods in their new sense to obtain greater knowledge of God and induce divine harmony or to gain a direct encounter with the divine. Hence, even those who ostensibly concentrated on interpreting Scripture were challenged by and responded to the Talmud.

■　　THE INDIVIDUAL BEFORE GOD　　■

Rabbinic spirituality is unique in asserting that the individual can repeatedly encounter a transcendent deity. The challenge of faith, then, is to sanctify one's mundane activities. In this regard, the rabbis held a simple belief in God as the Creator of life, the Lord of history, the Lawgiver, and the Architect of human destinies.

---

9. On these two types, see Moshe Idel, *Kabbalah: New Perspectives* (New Haven: Yale University Press, 1988).

INTRODUCTION

The talmudists desist from any formal effort to prove God's existence. Yet some passages in their writings, following the logic of the Greek philosophers, reason from nature the "first cause" of all existence. Such reasoning is imputed by the rabbis to Abraham, as they trace his odyssey from idolatry to monotheism. According to one account, Abraham inferred the existence of God by contemplating on the universe, as one may infer the existence of an architectural master when viewing some brilliantly illuminated palace. According to the rabbis, Abraham asked, "Can it be that the universe and all that exists within it is without a directing intelligence?" In the course of his speculation, he felt God's presence as the reassuring response to his quest. "The Lord looked upon him and said: 'I am the master of the universe.' "[10]

The rabbis, like the authors of the Bible, spoke of God anthropomorphically, that is, as though he were a person with bodily attributes. It is clear, however, that such references were meant figuratively, so as to make vivid God's active presence in the world. "We borrow terms from His creatures in order to aid our comprehension." Another Midrash noted: "Great is the daring of the prophets who ascribe attributes to the Creator by analogy to attributes of His creatures."[11] Thus, in the story of God's revelation at Sinai, as related by R. Yose, one talmudic master, "Moses never ascended to heaven and God never descended on earth." Revelation here referred to an inner transformation that brought man and God closer to each other. The biblical narrative is to be taken as a poetic elaboration of the doctrine that God's revelation comprised the basis of the teachings that Israel pledged to uphold at Sinai.

The rabbis repeatedly insisted that God has no tangible form and occupies no specific area in space. Indeed, one of the ways he is referred to in the Talmud is *Makom*, "Place." God is the "place," the locus of creation; the universe exists in Him, not He in the universe. In the words of one master: "The Holy One, praised be He, is the place of His universe, but His universe is not His place."[12]

The assertion that God is invisible made it difficult for people accustomed to a concrete and tangible reality to conceive of Him. The rabbis, however, exalted an intangible deity. Thus, it is related in a

---

10. Midrash Genesis Rabbah 39:1.
11. Mekilta on Exodus 19:18; Genesis Rabbah 27.
12. Genesis Rabbah 68:10.

16

INTRODUCTION

talmudic anecdote that the Emperor Hadrian once said to R. Joshua ben Hananyah: "I desire to behold your God." R. Joshua explained that this was impossible. When the emperor persisted, the rabbi asked him to stare at the sun. When the emperor found it too strong, the rabbi exclaimed: "You admit you cannot look at the sun, which is only one of the ministering servants of the Holy One, praised be He; how much more beyond your power of vision is God Himself." Rabban Gamaliel compared the reality of God's presence in the universe to the presence of the soul in a person. We do not know the soul's specific abode, and may have no direct experience of it, yet we still intuit its reality.[13]

If not visible, God is accessible. Although humans cannot comprehend his ultimate essence, they may observe manifestations of divine activity in creation and in the dynamics of history and society. The talmudic rabbis viewed the universe as an area of continual dynamic activity: "The universe is pervaded by the might and power of God. . . . He formed you and infused into you the breath of life. He stretched forth the heavens and laid the foundations of the earth. . . . He causes the rain and the dew to descend, and causes vegetation to sprout forth. He also forms the embryo in the mother's womb and enables it to emerge as a living being."[14]

■ HUMANITY'S PURPOSE ■

Why did God create people? He did so, so that people might glorify their Maker through the cultivation of virtue and the continued perfection of the soul and of behavior. Of course, the acquisition of a virtuous character and the attainment of perfection hardly come easily. One must work hard and persistently for them, knowing one will achieve only partial success.

God, however, has given each person certain attributes that drive and guide him. These include the impulse toward self-interest—the *yezer ra*, or "evil impulse" as it is sometimes called. When taken beyond its legitimate limits, this self-preoccupation becomes destructive, but in its essential character, it is not more evil than anything else the

---

13. Hullin 59b, Midrash on Psalms to Psalm 103:1.
14. Exodus Rabbah 5:14.

Lord has made. Balancing it is the drive to goodness, the *yezer tov*, which spurs us on to acts of self-denial in furtherance of every noble endeavor. The so-called evil impulse generally dominates life, but as people mature in their development, the good impulse gains ascendancy until the proper balance is achieved between the two basic drives. That this is possible implies the presence and potential of free will. The talmudists pronounce their judgment on the two impulses in a comment on Genesis 1:31: "And God saw everything which He had made and behold it was very good." "Very good," say the rabbis, applies to those two impulses. "But," it is asked, "is the evil impulse very good?" The answer is given that it is: "Were it not for that impulse, a man would not build a house, marry a wife, beget children, or conduct business affairs."[15]

The person who has achieved a sound character has made of the so-called evil impulse a tool for goodness. The Talmud makes this clear in a comment on Deuteronomy 6:5: "Thou shalt love the Lord thy God with all thy heart." "Thy heart" is taken as meaning "with the two impulses—the good and the evil."[16]

■   THE TORAH AND THE COMMANDMENTS:

CONVEYING THE DIVINE CHALLENGE   ■

God did not thrust people into the world to grope entirely on their own for the right course in life. Rather, he gave people a chart by which to steer themselves: the Torah and its commandments. These commandments, the rabbis believed, help each person find his true self and achieve closeness to God.

The talmudists believed that not every person is ready to receive divine revelation. Rather, the chosen few to whom God does reveal himself—his prophets—are to be instruments for disseminating the fruits of revelation among all mankind. The most important manifestation of prophecy was in the people of Israel. The rabbis also saw evidence of prophetic inspiration in the lives of such non-Israelites as

---

15. Genesis Rabbah 9:7.
16. Sifre Deut 6:5.

Balaam and his father, and Job and his four friends.[17] In its highest expressions, however, prophecy appeared solely in Israel.

The important permanent fruit of prophecy was the various books that make up the Holy Scriptures, commencing with the Pentateuch, which is traced back to the authorship of Moses. A famous talmudic statement relates the services of biblical revelations: "Who wrote the Scriptures? Moses wrote his own book and the parables of Balaam (Nm 23:24) and Job; Joshua wrote the book which bears his name, and the last eight verses of the Pentateuch; Samuel wrote the book which bears his name, and the Book of Judges and Ruth; David wrote the Book of Psalms . . . Jeremiah wrote the book which bears his name, the Book of Kings, and Lamentations; Hezekiah and his colleagues wrote Isaiah, Proverbs, the Song of Songs, and Ecclesiastes; the men of the Great Assembly wrote Ezekiel, the Twelve Minor Prophets, Daniel, and the Scroll of Esther. Ezra wrote the book that bears his name and the genealogies of the Book of Chronicles up to his own time."[18]

Even what has become the Written Torah, however, does not fully convey God's word. Intellect and imagination are needed to understand, for God reveals Himself to the prophets not in the fullness of His essence. The limitations of human understanding do not permit the prophet to see the fullness of the divine light. Even Moses, the greatest prophet, for all his near-perfection as a leader and prophet, remained subject to the constraints of his mortality. Thus, one talmudic rabbi states that "the fiftieth level of wisdom," which is the highest level of the knowledge of God, was not revealed even to Moses."[19]

The brightness of the divine truth is further muted when the prophets strive to communicate it to the common people. To do so, they must use widely understood similes and symbols. Their use of anthropomorphisms is what we call analogical language; for the sake of comprehensibility, the Torah speaks of God by way of analogy to man.[20]

The divine plan could not, however, fulfill itself only through individual prophets. It was essential that they be given a particular society that would respond to their call and would be prepared to

17. Megillah 14a; Baba Batra 15b.
18. Baba Batra 14b, 15a.
19. Rosh Hashanah 21b.
20. Midrash Genesis Rabbah 27:1.

implement their ideas. For that special duty, God chose Israel. A talmudic homily relates how God sought the society that would be the best custodian of the Torah.

> When the All-present revealed Himself to give the Torah to Israel, not to them alone did He manifest Himself, but to all the nations. He first went to the sons of Esau, and said to them, "Will you accept the Torah?" They asked what was written in it and God told them: "Thou shalt not murder." They replied, "Sovereign of the Universe! The very nature of our ancestors was bloodshed. . . ." He then went to the sons of Ammon and Moab and said to them, "Will you accept the Torah?" They asked what was written in it and He replied, "Thou shalt not commit adultery!" They said to Him, "Sovereign of the Universe! The very existence of this people is rooted in unchastity." He went and found the children of Ishmael and said to them, "Will you accept the Torah?" They asked what was written in it and He replied: "Thou shalt not steal." They said unto Him, "Sovereign of the Universe! The very life of our ancestors depended upon robbery. . . ." There was not a single nation to whom He did not go and offer the Torah. . . . [God selected Israel] because all the peoples repudiated the Torah and refused to receive it; but Israel agreed and chose the Holy One, blessed be He, and His Torah.[21]

Israel was the chosen people in a double sense. Israel had chosen God even as God had chosen Israel.

Israel's function in history, then, was to serve as a witness to the truths of the Torah and to embody its teachings. For the Torah, of which Israel was the custodian, ultimately was intended for all mankind. In promoting the goal of sharing the Torah with the rest of mankind, the rabbis did not call for the conversion of all people to Judaism. They distinguished between a universal element in their faith, which all people must adopt, and a more particular element that applied to specific aspects of Jewish existence. This universal element could be integrated with any culture and with whatever formal reli-

---

21. Sifre Deut 33:2, sect. 343.

gious expression a people had developed. Its provisions, known as the "seven Noachide laws," include the practices of equity in human relations and the prohibitions of blaspheming God's name, idolatry, sexual unchastity, bloodshed, robbery, and cruelty to animals, such as tearing off their limbs while they are still alive.[22]

Proselytes were of course accepted in Judaism—and, until the third century, actively encouraged—when they proved their sincere desire to become part of Israel and to share in its destiny. That conversion was not, however, a prerequisite for earning divine approval, as the rabbis made it clear. "A pagan," declared R. Meir, "who studies the Torah and practices it is equal to a high priest in Israel."[23] By this, he clearly refers to a pagan who practices the universal principles of religion and morality embodied in the seven Noachide laws. If he practiced the Torah in its entirety, he would no longer be a pagan.

Along with the Written Torah, God revealed a second, unwritten one that was orally handed down through the ages, from Moses and Aaron to the prophets to the rabbinic Sages. Although this Torah covered topics not mentioned in the Written Torah, people soon understood it as a supplement and clarification of the Written Torah. This perception heightened the importance of knowing the Oral Torah, which was seen as containing the key to the deeper meanings of the Written Torah. Thus, the notion of Talmud Torah (the study of both the written and oral Torahs) became the central motif of rabbinic Judaism. The exalted place of Talmud Torah builds on the idea, articulated in Deuteronomy 4:5–8, Proverbs 8, and Ben Sira, that the Torah is the highest form of wisdom in the world. While the Torah is in principle a source of wisdom open to all, it is fully accessible only through the rabbinic tradition by learning its teaching or by observing and imitating the actions of the rabbis who embody its truths.

While pre-rabbinic thinkers emphasized the importance of study for the leisurely, or rich intellectuals, the rabbis held that study comprised an ideal that was incumbent on all Jews. With the Temple destroyed, they affirmed that the sacred could still be experienced in the "sanctuary" of the Torah, and not through sacrifices but in the use of one's own divinely endowed intellect. Accordingly, one draws closer to one's own traces of the divine in studying the Torah; in applying its

---

22. Mekilta on Exodus 19:2; Sifre Deut sect. 40; Sanhedrin 56a.
23. Baba Kamma 38a; Abodah Zarah 3a; Yalkut on Jgs 4:1.

teachings, one interacts with God. Study therefore became the highest form of piety. Thus, the rabbis asserted that the divine presence is found among any two who study (Avot 3:2); again and again, they employed metaphors from the revelation at Sinai to describe the experience of students engaged in studying the Torah. The mere attempt at searching for divine truth in the text should not, however; satisfy the spiritually inclined Jew. Hence some rabbis stressed that it was truly important to understand the Torah and to correctly apply its teachings in everyday life. Sensitivity to the divine tolerates no false idols or ideologies. Different rabbinic circles emphasized one or the other of these two complementary approaches—study as a pious act or as a means to derive truth and proper guidance for mundane life.[24]

■ REVERENCE FOR GOD AND HIS CREATION ■

The study of Torah also prompts a person to become reverent of God's holiness and solicitous for his creation. God created man and placed him into this world to enjoy the bounty of nature that is produced through the creative labor of human beings. In many other ways, too, God's providence guides, sustains, and directs a person toward the fulfillment of his destiny. God's providence is not, however, always apparent in the immediacy of a person's life. Often, it reaches him via an indirect path, through various mediating agents and after the passage of time. Thus, the rabbis particularly emphasized *emunah*, faith in God. Even when God's providential care is not readily apparent, a person should trust, believe, and have faith that God's design will eventually become apparent and will work in his behalf.

The call to faith is often sounded in Talmudic literature. According to R. Simlai, all 613 commandments that were communicated to Moses were summed up by the prophet Habakuk in the one admonition "The righteous shall live by his faith" (Hb 2:4). Another sage

---

24. See Saul Lieberman, *Hilkhot haYerushalmi: The Laws of the Palestinian Talmud of Rabbi Moses ben Maimon* (New York: The Jewish Theological Seminary of America, 1947), pp. 34–35 and nn.; David Weiss Halivni, "Whoever Studies Laws . . . ," *Proceedings of the Rabbinical Assembly* 41 (1979): 298–303; Baruch M. Bokser, *Post Mishnaic Judaism in Transition* (Chico: Scholars Press, 1980), pp. 448–49 and nn.; and Jacob Neusner, *Torah: From Scroll to Symbol in Formative Judaism* (Philadelphia: Fortress Press, 1985).

made the following statement: "Whoever has a morsel of bread in his basket, and says, 'What shall I eat tomorrow?' belongs to the people of little faith."[25]

The rabbis saw *emunah* as the distinguishing mark of Jewish heroes. They noted the virtues of Abraham, of whom the Bible repeats that "he believed in the Lord and He counted it to him for righteousness." Among their own colleagues, they idealized Nahum of Gamzu and Akiba. Whatever happened, Nahum would exclaim: "This too (*gam zu*) is for the best," while one of Akiba's favorite adages was "Whatever the All-Merciful one does is for the best."[26]

God's providence, they taught, should also evoke the response of love and fear, which really are one. The Bible includes both love and fear in stating what God expects of man: "Know, O Israel, what does the Lord require of you, but to fear the Lord your God, to walk in all His ways, and to love Him and to serve the Lord your God with all your heart and all your soul, to keep the commandments of the Lord and His statutes which I command you this day for your good" (Dt 10:12, 13). Commenting on the verse in the Shema, "And you shall love the Lord your God" (Dt 6:5), an anonymous rabbi states: "Act [fulfill the commandments] out of love." Action based on love is seen as also associated with the emotion of fear of God. "Love does not coexist with fear, and fear does not coexist with love, except regarding the Omnipresent." As Antigonus of Sokho stated: "Be not like servants who serve their master for the sake of receiving a reward, but be like those who serve their master without expecting a reward; and let the fear of heaven be upon you."[27]

In an assessment of the two basic emotions toward God, one talmudic sage states that one who is inspired by love is greater than one who is inspired by fear. But the Talmud makes it clear that fear adds to love a dimension of humility, great respect, and a recognition of God's grandeur.[28] The caution of Antigonus against serving for the sake of a reward is further developed in this talmudic passage: " 'To love the Lord your God'—beware lest you say, I will study Torah so that I may be rich, or that I may be called 'master,' or that I might receive a

25. Sotah 48b.
26. Taanit 21a, Berakot 60b.
27. Sifre Deut 6:5, sect. 32; Mishnah Avot 1:3.
28. Sotah 31a; Yerushalmi Berakot 9:7.

reward. The text therefore states 'to love,' whatever you do, do it only for the sake of love."[29]

The call to love God is sometimes defined as including the duty of disseminating that love among others. Thus, the Sifre on Deuteronomy 6:5 comments:

> "*And you shall love the Lord your God.*" Spread the love for Him among all the peoples, like your father Abraham of whom it is written: "Abraham took his wife Sarah . . . and the persons that they had acquired [lit. the souls they had made] in Haran." Surely, if the entire world tried to create a single gnat and to breathe life into it, they would be unable to do so. In what sense, then, does it say "and the souls they had made in Haran"? This alludes to the fact that our father Abraham had proselytized them, and brought them under the wings of God's presence.

Faith in God, as well as love for and fear of him, also should inspire the desire to communicate with him. Since God was a loving parent concerned with the welfare of his creation, it was assumed that he hears and is responsive to human prayer. Such prayer was expressed on two levels: one, petitionary, to bring before him our needs and the deepest yearning of our hearts, and, two, praise and adoration.

Originally, God was worshiped in the Temple in Jerusalem to which the people were expected to come as pilgrims during the major festivals to observe and to participate in Temple rites. The main feature of these rites was the offering of priestly sacrifices accompanied by the music of the levitical chorus. The desire for a more personally involved type of worship may have contributed to the establishment of the synagogue, where teaching of Torah and prayer were conducted by the laity. After the Temple's destruction, the synagogue emerged as the major place of Jewish worship.

For many people the destruction of the Temple was a grievous tragedy, but the rabbis gradually worked through the loss and eventually articulated the thought that sacrifices were not indispensable and that the life of devotion inspired by the synagogue also could bring one closer to God. The third-century R. Eleazar ben Pedat declared explic-

---

29. Nedarim 62a.

INTRODUCTION

itly: "Prayer is more vital than the offering of sacrifices."[30] Avot de R. Nathan version A, 4 attributes to Rabban Yohanan ben Zakkai the quotation of Hosea, who said: "I desire mercy and not sacrifices" (Hos 6:6). During the amoraic period, the belief in prayer as a means to create an experience of God became widespread. Still, some rabbis believed that study of Torah was as good as or even preferable to prayer, for it too brought one closer to God's presence.[31]

Observing the commandments also brings one nearer to God. Both negative and positive commandments help us set aside certain spaces and times, which we transform, making them holy or sacred. The commandments also remind us of the divine manifestations in history and in our world. The break from everyday affairs that occurs when we perform a ritual makes us more receptive to its theological message. Similarly, the blessings that precede or follow a ritual act and that state, "Praised be thou, King of the Universe, who has commanded us to . . ." change our consciousness by conceptually framing the experience they refer to. They affect how we go through the act that follows or how we interpret what has just been done. In becoming aware that an object or action results from a manifestation of the divine, we are reminded of the relationship between human beings and God, and so are moved to express gratitude to the source of all life and action.[32]

Several examples of talmudic law present examples of regulations that are intended to deepen a person's consciousness of God. Talmudic law ordains the recitation of the Shema (Dt 6:4), affirming the unity of God, twice daily, morning and evening. It establishes a ritual of daily public and private prayer and formulates the specific texts of benedictions on partaking of various foods. Through these rituals, man is made keenly aware that he is living in God's world and that he must be ever grateful for its manifold blessings. To accept what the world offers him without a thought of what he owes to God for it makes a person an

---

30. Berakot 32b.

31. See Baruch M. Bokser, "Rabbinic Responses to Catastrophe: From Continuity to Discontinuity," *Proceedings of the American Academy for Jewish Research* 50 (1983): 37–61; and idem, "The Wall Separating God and Israel," *Jewish Quarterly Review* 78 (1983): 349–74.

32. See Max Kadushin, *Worship and Ethics* (New York: Bloch Publishing Co., 1963), esp. p. 203; and Baruch M. Bokser, *The Origins of the Seder* (Berkeley: University of California Press, 1984).

ingrate. As the rabbis put it: "It is forbidden a man to enjoy the things of this world without a blessing."[33]

The law governing man's relation to God often serves to prevent the transgression of more fundamental principles or doctrines. The rabbis viewed the basic element of religion and morality as a kind of vineyard that must be fenced in against violators. This was one of the guiding rules of the men of the Great Assembly: "Build a fence around the Torah."[34] The law as a "fence around the Torah" is clearly illustrated in the rules bearing on idolatry. The cult of idol worship was widespread throughout the Roman Empire, and its visible symbols, images of all kinds, dotted city and country alike. Surrounded by these pervasive manifestations of paganism, the Jews were in danger of spiritual contamination.

The danger was met by talmudic law, which declared all idolatry, its symbols, the sites where idols were located, and all activities associated with them out of bounds. Even broken wood or metal that had ever been part of an idol was forbidden. A grove where an idol was situated was not to be entered, even for the purpose of finding shade from the sun. The wine employed in idolatrous offerings was not to be used. Even a drop of it falling into another liquid would render that liquid unfit for consumption.[35]

The desired nature of a person's relation to God and the requirement to "build a fence around the Torah" are illustrated in the law forbidding travel on the Sabbath. The Sabbath was instituted in Judaism to be a memorial to Creation, to recall to us the divine source of all existence, and to serve as a day to rest body and mind in remembrance of the emancipation from Egyptian bondage. Among the many measures by which the Sabbath was to be commemorated was the rule against travel.[36] The spiritual goal of this prohibition was to create a temple in time, a twenty-four hour period during which a person's sensitivity to God's world and experience of the divine would be heightened.[37] The prohibition against traveling on the Sabbath is derived

---

33. Mishnah Berakhot 1:1, 4:3, 6:1; Berakot 28b, 35a.
34. Mishnah Abot 1:1.
35. Mishnah Avodah Zarah 1:3–5.
36. Beza 36b.
37. See Arthur Green, "Sabbath as Temple," in *Go and Study: Essays and Studies in Honor of Alfred Jospe*, ed. Raphael Jospe et al. (Washington: B'nai B'rith Hillel Foundations, 1980), pp. 287–305.

from Exodus 16:29: "Abide ye every man in his place; let no man go out of his place in the seventh day." Originally directed at the gatherers of *manna* in the wilderness, this verse was interpreted as forbidding all movement on the Sabbath beyond one's domicile.

Travel on the Sabbath by riding an animal was also forbidden so as to avoid involvement in incidental labor, such as cutting down a twig in order to prod the animal on its way. The talmudic rabbis also feared that a person who rides an animal might easily move beyond the confines of the *tehum* and so cross the permitted area for movement.[38]

Rabbinic sources offer us two general reasons for this prohibition from labor as well as from anxiety and distraction. The first is expressed in the principle of *tehumin*, the requirement to fix one's domicile in a particular place, and then to limit one's motions within a prescribed radius of it. The Sabbath experience depended on keeping the family within the warm confines of the home, and the home had to be fixed in space, even as the Sabbath was fixed in time.

Originally, the biblical verse was interpreted literally, so that the place of permissible movement was confined to the home and the 2,000 cubits around it. However, the popular tendency to socialize on the Sabbath finally effected a change in interpretation; the "home" was viewed in the widest possible sense, to include one's city, with a radius of 2,000 cubits allowed for additional movement. The terminus of allowed movement could, moreover, be pushed farther back through an *erub*, a conscious designation of a desired place outside the city designed as part of one's domicile, by depositing there some food as a token of home. A traveler who was away from a city at the advent of the Sabbath could, by an act of conscious designation known as *kinyan shebitah*, fix his home anywhere; he was then free to move within the 2,000-cubit radius of that place.

The rabbis did not seek to stifle the free movement of life on the Sabbath. They sought to reject tension and to curb undue exertion. They sought to mold the Sabbath into a day of serenity and relaxation. Thus, they banned the *pesia gasa*, the hurried walk of the busy days of the week. The Tosefta elaborated: "One may not run on the Sabbath to the point of exhaustion, but one may stroll leisurely throughout the day without hesitation."[39]

---

38. Erubin chs. 4–5.
39. Tosefta Shabbat ch. 16.

INTRODUCTION

A person is also obligated to be solicitous toward God's creation. R. Akiba posited the golden rule as the most comprehensive teaching of the Torah. "This is the most fundamental principle enunciated in the Torah: 'Love thy neighbor as thyself' " (Lv 19:18), he taught. Ben Azzai pointed to Genesis 5:1: "This is the book of the generations of man . . . in the likeness of God made He him." Every person's worth, then, is rooted in the teaching that he is created in the divine image, which invests him with some degree of holiness and mandates that he be treated with respect and a deep concern for his well-being.

The relationship between belief in God and the imperative to live a moral life is conveyed in a number of talmudic discussions. According to a well-known homily by R. Simlai:

> Six hundred and thirteen commandments were addressed to Moses—three hundred and sixty-five prohibitions, corresponding to the days of the solar year, and two hundred and forty-eight positive commandments, corresponding to the number of limbs in the human body. David came and reduced them to eleven principles, which are listed in Psalm 15: "Lord, who shall sojourn in Your tabernacle? Who shall dwell on Your holy mountain? He who walks with integrity, and pursues righteousness, and speaks the truth in his heart, who does not slander with his tongue, who commits no evil against a fellow-human, who does not bring shame to a neighbor, who despises a vile person, but honors those who revere the Lord. If he takes an oath to his own heart, he does not change it; he takes no interest on a loan, and does not take a bribe against the innocent." Isaiah came and reduced them to six, as it is stated: "God's providential love will be extended to one who walks in the path of righteousness, and speaks uprightly, who despises profit gained by oppression, and spurns bribes, who avoids hearing of violence, and shuns looking at evil" (Is 33:15). Micah reduced them to three: "What does the Lord require of you, but to do justly, to love mercy, and to walk humbly with your God" (Mi 6:8). Isaiah subsequently reduced them to two: "Thus says the Lord, keep justice and do righteousness" (Is 56:1).[40]

---

40. Makkot 24a.

INTRODUCTION

In becoming aware of one's own spiritual roots and in drawing closer to God, an individual also comes to recognize the presence of the divine in others. As Psalm 15 testifies, living up to such moral standards enables a person to sojourn in God's tabernacle: "Lord, who may sojourn in your tent, who may dwell on your holy mountain? He who lives without blame, who does what is right, and in his heart acknowledges the truth, . . . who has never done harm to his fellow or borne reproach for [his acts toward] his neighbor" (Ps 15:1–3). Rabbinic authorities extended this biblical notion of solicitousness with the concept of *gemilut hasadim*, the doing of righteous acts. Faith, in short, was seen as the impetus for moral behavior.

While the rabbis placed the love of man at the summit of human virtue, they also urged people to cultivate the love of God as the source from which all other virtues flow. This is taught by R. Reuben, who was asked to define the most reprehensible act a man may commit. His answer was: the denial of God's existence, "For no man violates the commandments, 'Thou shalt not murder,' 'Thou shalt not steal,' till he has renounced his faith in God."[41]

The same doctrine is conveyed in a famous homily by Rabbah:

> Rabbah said: when a person is brought for judgment on Judgment Day he is asked, "Did you do your business honestly? Did you set aside time for the study of Torah? Did you raise a family? Did you maintain our faith in the Messianic redemption? Did you pursue wisdom? Did you attain to the level of being able to reason inferentially from one proposition to another?" [If he answers yes,] all this will suffice provided he be a God-fearing man, too, for the fear of God is the treasury in which all else is stored. If [he be] not [a God-fearing man], [the other virtues will] not [prove sufficient].[42]

The realm of spirituality is not limited to interactions between Jews. The Talmud conceives of mankind as one, deriving its character from its common origin and common destiny. The Bible already enunciates this doctrine when it traces the origins of the human race to a single person, who was formed by God in his image. In the Talmud,

---

41. Tosefta Shebuot 3:6.
42. Shabbat 31a.

29

this doctrine reaches its fullest maturity: "Why did the Creator form all life from a single ancestor?" So that "the families of mankind shall not lord one over the other with the claim of being sprung from superior stock . . . that all men, saints and sinners alike, may recognize their common kinship in the collective human family."[43]

Human behavior may be infinitely varied, but the nature that underlies it is essentially the same. Man is both creature of earth and a being infused with the divine spirit. Good and evil reside in varying measure in every individual. But if you probe hard enough, one talmudic maxim advises, you will discover that "even the greatest of sinners" abound in good deeds "as a pomegranate abounds in seeds." On the other hand, the greatest of saints have their share of moral imperfection.[44] In short, all humans are cut from the same cloth; there are no absolute distinctions among them.

The rabbis teach one to be sensitive to others not just as "fellow humans," but as individuals. Each person is both a part of the human race and a unique being with a particular spiritual potential and capacity. Thus, the doctrine of human equality asserts that each individual is distinct. The Talmud explains that "a man strikes many coins from one die and they are all alike. The Holy One, blessed be He, however, strikes every person from the die of the first man, but no one resembles another."[45] Each uniqueness is mental as well as physical; each has a special function to fulfill in the realization of the divine plan. A person thus has a right to feel that "the universe was created for his sake"; the cosmic scheme will be incomplete without him.

From this conception of man's place in the universe comes the sense of the supreme sanctity of all human life. "He who destroys one person has dealt a blow at the entire universe, and he who saves or sustains one person has sustained the whole world."[46] All law, civil and religious, attempts to promote human life; when it ceases to serve that end, it becomes obsolete and should be superseded.[47]

The sanctity of life is not a function of national origin, religious affiliation, or social status. In the sight of God, the humble citizen is

---

43. Tosefta Sanhedrin 8:4.
44. Erubin 19a; Sanhedrin 101a.
45. Sanhedrin 38a; cf. Berakot 17a.
46. Mishnah Sanhedrin 4:5.
47. Shabbat 127a.

the equal of the person who occupies the highest office. As one talmud-ist put it: "Heaven and earth I call to witness, whether it be an Israelite or pagan, man or woman, slave or maidservant, according to the work of every human being doth the Holy Spirit rest upon him." The legal implication of this view required that non-Jews residing in Jewish communities were to share in all the benefits the Jewish community offered its own members. As the rabbis put it: "We are obligated to feed non-Jews residing among us even as we feed Jews; we are obli-gated to visit their sick even as we visit the Jewish sick; we are obligated to attend to the burial of their dead, even as we attend to the burial of Jewish dead." The rabbis base their demand on the ground that these are "the ways of peace."[48]

The divine dimension and spiritual capacity inherent in every human being cannot be forfeited. Even he who has endangered the public welfare by committing a crime must be given a fair trial. Before the law, all are to be treated equitably. Thus, one of two litigants was not to appear in court in expensive robes when the other came in tatters, lest there be a swaying of the juror-judges.[49]

The Talmud particularly sought to protect the accused against a miscarriage of justice in criminal cases. Circumstantial evidence, no matter how apparently convincing, was inadmissible. At least one of the judges was to act as the defense counsel. The juror-judges could reverse a verdict from guilty to not guilty, but not vice versa. The younger members of the court were first to announce their vote, so as not to be influenced by the decisions of their seniors. Whereas in civil cases a majority of one was sufficient to establish guilt, criminal cases required a majority of two. Even when he was found guilty, the con-victed felon did not lose his tie to the human brotherhood. The higher end of safeguarding public welfare might require his execution, but even the punishment inflicted on him must not brutalize him by gratu-itous cruelty, for example, not cutting down the body of a hanged man within a day of his hanging. Talmudists advocated the abolition of capital punishment, and it was agreed that any court that inflicts capi-tal punishment once in seven years exhibits brutality. The execution of even the most violent criminal was viewed as a cosmic tragedy, for he,

---

48. Yalkut on Judges 4:1; Gittin 61a.
49. Shebuot 31a.

31

too, was formed in the divine image and had been endowed with infinite possibilities for good.[50]

■   THE EXEMPLARY TEACHER: MODEST AND ACCESSIBLE   ■

If, in the hierarchy of Jewish values, the knowledge and practice of Torah represented the apex, the master of the Torah was not to hold himself aloof from or superior to other men. From the time that rabbinic Judaism became a prominent social movement, we find widely promulgated the teaching that a teacher of Torah was to be "modest, humble . . . to make himself beloved of men, to be gracious in his relations even with subordinates . . . to judge man according to his deeds. . . . [To show pride in one's learning is to become] like the carcass of a dead beast from which all men turn away in disgust." The true master of Torah is careful not to aggrandize himself over others or to detach himself from the common people. He cultivates his virtues in the privacy of his own home, and teaches and leads others to a nobler way of life. He who has insights that can widen the horizons of his neighbor's life and does not communicate them is seen as robbing his neighbor of his due. The gifts of the spirit, like those of wealth, are a trust to be shared with others.[51]

■   SOCIETY AND THE INDIVIDUAL   ■

For a people to function in a society, the government must recognize their rights to develop with their own internal regulations. Throughout talmudic times the Jews lived under the domination of foreign rulers—in Palestine under the Romans and in Babylonia under the Parthians and Sasanians. Within this framework of the limited autonomy, the Jews developed certain legal and political mechanisms and institutions. The most important was *halakha*, Jewish civil and religious law.

The Talmud first developed the theory that the ultimate sanction

---

50. Tosefta Sanhedrin 8:3; Sanhedrin 43a, 45a; Mishnah Makkot 1:10; Mishnah Sanhedrin 6:5; Sanhedrin 46b.

51. Derek Erez Zuta I; Abot de Rabbi Nathan ch. 11; Sanhedrin 91b.

of law is the consent of the governed. Of course, *all* authority, including that of the rulers and judges, flowed from the divine source of all human wisdom and leadership. However, man also is endowed with free will; he must give his assent to every legal institution that makes moral claims on him. Judges and legislators also must not enact decrees unless a majority of the people can conform to them. Any decree that is resisted by a popular majority has, *ipso facto*, lost its validity and is rendered obsolete. Indeed, the Talmud even traced the authority of the Bible itself not so much to its divine source as to the consent of the people who agreed to live by it.[52] To be sure, in the Mishnah's portrayal of civil order, civil institutions function through the consensus of Sages.[53]

The talmudists participated in the town councils created by the Roman and other authorities, and sought to assure their democratic and just functioning. All who resided in a community for a year or more could participate in the election of the seven town councillors, who oversaw the people's economic, religious, educational, and philanthropic activities. On important issues, town meetings were held at which the will of the people could be ascertained more directly. Certain local officials were appointed by the head of the Jewish community—the Patriarch in Palestine, and the Exilarch in Babylonia—but in the view of many rabbis, the most important requirement in all such appointments was that they meet with public approval. The Talmud instructed: "We must not appoint a leader over the community without first consulting them, as it is said, 'See, the Lord hath called by name Bezalel, the son of Iri' (Ex 35:30). The Holy One, blessed be He, asked Moses, 'Is Bezalel acceptable to you?' He replied, 'Sovereign of the universe, if he is acceptable to Thee, how much more so to me!' God said to him 'Nevertheless go and consult the people.' "[54]

---

52. Abodah Zarah 36a; Shabbat 88a.

53. See Jacob Neusner, *Judaism: The Evidence of the Mishnah* (Chicago: University of Chicago Press, 1981).

54. Berahot 55a; Mishnah Eduyot 1:5; Erubin 13b; Megillah 27a. Cf. Gedalyahu Alan, "Those Appointed for Money," in his *Jews, Judaisn and the Classical World*, trans. Israel Abrahams (Jerusalem: Magness Press, 1977), pp. 374–435.

INTRODUCTION

The social process frequently brings individuals into a position of exercising power over others. In the social theory of talmudic Judaism, it becomes the community's task to develop instruments of social control that will temper that power with moderation and justice. The talmudists thus declared individual property and ownership rights a subject to considerations of public welfare. When it served the public interest, individual rights might be modified or suspended altogether. Basing its action on this principle, talmudic legislation regulated the wages and hours of labor, as well as commodity prices and rates of profit. The rabbis also mandated that it was the obligation of the community to provide facilities for promoting the public welfare, such as public baths, competent medical services, and adequate elementary education for all.[55]

The poor had a claim on the community for support in accordance with their accustomed standard of living. The more affluent members of the community were to share their possessions with the poor, just as members of a family were obligated to share with their own kin. The administration of poor relief eventually was institutionalized to place it on a more efficient and respectable basis. Begging from door to door was discouraged. Indigent townsmen were given a weekly allowance for food and clothing. Transients received daily allowances. Food was stored in synagogues and other public places to help meet their immediate needs. For the poor traveler and the homeless, public inns were frequently built on the high roads. All these amenities were to be maintained from the proceeds of a general tax to which all the residents of a community contributed.[56]

The same concern for humanitarian and democratic values appears in talmudic legislation bearing on various aspects of family life. Since the rabbis believed that no man is self-sufficient, they encouraged and sanctified matrimony to "complete" him. They taught that "the unmarried person lives without joy, without blessing, and without good. He is not a man in the full sense of the term; as it is said (Gn 5:2), 'male and female created He them, and blessed them and called their

---

55. Yebamot 89b; Baba Batra 8b; Sanhedrin 17b.

56. Tanhuma Shemot, ed. Buber, p. 43a; Tosefta Peah 4:8–13; Baba Batra 8a–9b; Sanhedrin 17b.

name man.' " Marriage thus was seen as a prerequisite for spiritual fulfillment. To ensure social good and spiritual fulfillment, the rabbis spoke extensively of and promoted the idea of marriage. However, they also stated that a person should enter freely into a marriage. He or she must not be coerced to stand under the *chuppah* ("wedding canopy"). In the words of the Babylonian teacher Rab, "A man is forbidden to give his minor daughter in marriage without her consent. He must wait until she grows up and says, 'I wish to marry so and so.' " The man's choice, too, should be a voluntary expression of his choice: "A man should not marry a woman without knowing her, lest he subsequently discover blemishes in her and come to hate her."[57]

As the more dominant partner in the family circle, the husband was exhorted to treat his wife with tenderness and sympathetic understanding. "Whoever loves his wife as himself and honors her more than himself . . . to him may be applied the verse, 'Thou shalt know that thy tent is in peace.' " However, in terms of raising and disciplining children, the father and mother were seen as equals who were to be accorded the very same devotion and respect.[58]

There are occasions when a husband and wife cannot reconcile their differences. In these instances, the Talmud then sanctions divorce, as preferable to a life of ongoing bitterness between the parties or the distress of one of them. While realistic about divorce, the Talmud also regards it as a great domestic tragedy, noting, "Whoever divorces the wife of his youth, even the altar sheds tears on his behalf." Divorce could be initiated upon the request of either party. Legally it was always the husband who severed the marriage ties, but the wife could sue for divorce, and if her request was unreasonably blocked or delayed by her husband, the rabbinic court could force him to divorce her. Among the circumstances warranting such action, the Talmud lists the husband's impotence, failure of proper support, denial of conjugal rights, contraction of a loathsome illness, or engaging in a repugnant occupation. The divorced woman also was protected by her *ketubah* (marriage contract), which provided a financial settlement for her maintenance.[59]

---

57. Yebamot 63a; Kiddushin 41a.
58. Yebamot 62b; Kiddushin 30b.
59. Gittin 90b; Mishnah Ketubot 5:6, 7:9, 10; Ketubot 77a; Mishnah Nedarim 11:12; Mishnah Arakin 5:6; Yebamot 63b. See M. A. Friedman, *Jewish Marriage in Palestine*, 2 vols. (Tel Aviv: Tel Aviv University, 1980), vol. 1.

INTRODUCTION

For the talmudists, children are the noblest fulfillment of married life. By bringing them into the world, parents imitate God's role in creation. While it is a person's obligation to the continuity of humanity to bring children into the world and to raise them properly, when conception was likely to prove dangerous to the mother, birth control was recommended. The Talmud specified that "three types of women should employ an absorbent to prevent conception: a minor, a pregnant woman, and a nursing mother; a minor lest pregnancy prove fatal, a pregnant woman lest she have an abortion, and a nursing mother because of the danger to her young infant."[60] Even abortion was recommended when the life of the mother was imperiled. As stated in one Mishnah, "When a woman has difficulty giving birth, the fetus is to be cut up in her womb, and is to be brought out, limb by limb, because her life takes precedence over its life. But if its greater part has emerged, it may not be touched, because we do not set aside one life because of another life."[61]

The Talmud offers detailed advice on how to bring up children. Parents must treat all children equally, without favoritism and without overindulging them. Thus, the talmudists blame the depraved character of Absalom, who led a revolt against his father King David, on his pampered youth. Excessive severity is no less harmful, however. The Talmud cites the case of a child who committed suicide after some petty misdeed because he was in great mortal fear of his father's reaction. The Talmud in turn underscores the respect children owe their parents. This respect includes not only material help, but also the intangibles of tenderness and consideration.[62]

■ FURTHERING THE EXPERIENCE OF STUDY ■

The rabbis enhanced the educational structures because they believed in the importance of learning and in a benevolent God who wanted all Jews to draw close to him through the act of Torah study. The most important institution of higher education was the Sanhedrin

---

60. Kiddushin 29a ff.; Tosefta Niddah 2:6; Yabamot 12b.
61. Mishnah Ohalot 7:6. See David M. Feldman, *Birth Control in Jewish Law* (New York: New York University Press, 1968).
62. Semahot 2:6; Yerushalmi Peah 1:1.

and the various lower courts that functioned under its supervision. Whatever may have been the historical nature of these institutions, in the rabbinic view, their deliberations, like those of the rabbinic court, were made accessible to advanced students who were preparing themselves for ordination; even students were permitted to participate in the discussions. A rabbi's disciples served as apprentices in his court. To witness the day-to-day conflicts between personalities, in the play of minds and the manipulation of dialectic from which the Torah supplementation evolved, represented a vivid and unforgetable educational experience. As we saw above, the editors of the Talmud who constructed such discussions in the Talmud created models that were to influence many individuals in the future. In addition, the leaders of Pharisaic and rabbinic Judaism offered formal instruction in their own homes or schools. The well-known schools of Shammai and Hillel were continued even after their founders had died. Akiba's school at B'nai Brak is said to have had an enrollment of 12,000 students, like a modern metropolitan university.

As the rabbis later conceived it, these schools in early times generally charged tuition fees that were payable on admission to each lecture. Many students made great sacrifices to attend; frequently they worked their way through school. This is vividly illustrated in the famous story of Hillel's struggle for an education. Hillel spent half of his daily earnings for admission to the lectures in the academy of Shemaiah and Avtalyon. One winter day, being out of work, he could not pay the necessary admission charge, and the doorkeeper refused to admit him. Determined not to miss the session, he climbed up to the roof and listened to the discussion through the skylight. On the following morning the room was darker than usual, and, looking up at the skylight, the students saw a human figure. Hillel had been covered up by the snow that had fallen during the night. Fortunately, he was discovered in time and was saved. This admission fee was abolished after the destruction of the Temple, and higher education became free. In addition, lectures were offered in the evening, which facilitated attendance for those who had to work during the day.[63]

Elementary education was originally the responsibility of the home. Children without fathers often lacked a decent education, and in

---

63. Yoma 35b; Berakot 28a; Pesahim 72b.

time early education too was institutionalized. Rabbinic authorities found a precedent for their system of universal education in the actions of earlier masters. As the Talmud relates, "Were it not for Joshua ben Gamla [High Priest during the latter part of the first century when elementary education was supposedly institutionalized], the Torah would have been forgotten in Israel." A centralized school system and then regional "high schools" supposedly were developed but proved inadequate. The Talmud relates that "R. Joshua then instituted schools in each province and town, and children were enrolled at the age of six or seven." Classes generally were conducted in synagogue buildings, although they were frequently transferred to the outdoors. According to the Talmud, there were 394 schools in Jerusalem before its destruction by the Romans in 70 C.E. The curriculum focused on biblical literature, Midrash, and later on the Mishnah.

The rabbis also were devoted to educating the general public. Special lectures in the rabbinic schools were open to lay auditors.[64] The rabbis also tried to influence the service in the synagogue, an institution that attracted large numbers of people. For example, they tried to shape the existing liturgy to reflect their fundamental views on Judaism, to determine the selection of readings from the Torah, and to develop rules for the Aramaic translation that accompanied the Torah reading. Under the auspices of the synagogue, smaller groups of people formed circles that met on the Sabbath to study Scriptures on some other aspect of the tradition. This was later enhanced with the introduction of the popular sermon Friday evening and Saturday morning, and then the special sermons before each holiday.

Because some of the rabbis were not particularly eloquent, it became customary for an orator-commentator to attach himself to the rabbi. In both the academy and the synagogue, the rabbi would communicate his message to the commentator, who then made it the theme of his public oration. Thus, in addition to providing for religious worship, local synagogues also functioned as popular universities by diffusing the knowledge of Torah among the common people.[65]

---

64. For rabbinic higher education, see David Goodblatt, *Rabbinic Instruction in Sasanian Babylonia* (Leiden: E. J. Brill, 1975).

65. Ketuhot 105a; Baba Batra 21a; Yerushalmi Megillah 4:1.

INTRODUCTION

Because spiritual fulfillment required human society, the rabbis valued the well-being of the local and national communities. Each society makes its unique contribution to human history. The talmudists speak of Israel as being particularly creative in the field of religion, whereas other peoples achieved comparable distinction in the arts and sciences. Some of the rabbis admired Roman law, public works, and commerce. Based on the notion that the collective welfare of all humanity is contingent on the welfare of each nation, some rabbis explained that the sacrificial cult of the second Temple, during the Feast of Tabernacles, included seventy offerings so as to invoke God's aid for each of the seventy nations of the world.

Yet in talmudic times, the Jews suffered heavily from the oppression of Roman rule. The talmudists decried this oppression and some encouraged popular resistance to it. At the same time, the talmudists cautioned against lasting hatreds against other nations. They spoke with compassion about the vanquished Egyptians who drowned in the Red Sea in vain pursuit of the fleeing Israelites. In particular, they depict God as silencing an angelic chorus chanting hallelujahs as the Egyptians were dying: "My handiwork is perishing in the sea; how dare you sing in rejoicing!"[65a]

Even in the face of the suffering inflicted on their people by the Romans, the talmudists counseled against hatred. Although individual teachers may have spoken sharply in denouncing Roman tyranny, many notable third-century masters took a quietistic attitude toward Rome. Their approach is echoed in the liturgy, which stresses Jewish self-criticism and tries to explain why an enemy can have an impact against Israel: "It is because of our sins that we have been banished from our land." These rabbis strove toward Jewish communal regeneration as a model for higher moral standards among all peoples. They also foresaw an era of universal peace and independence, a time without conflicts between nations. When "the kingdom of wickedness" will pass away and all mankind will join to form "one fellowship to do the divine will with a perfect heart" (from the liturgy of the New Year,

---

65a. Megillah 10b.

INTRODUCTION

shaped by Abba Arikha, d. 247 C.E.), Israel's centuries-long call for justice would be vindicated.[66]

The talmudic conception of man implied a chain of responsibility from individual people to nations to the larger human community. The unique gifts with which each individual is endowed must therefore be directed to larger human service. Similarly, the responsibilities of service rest on every society. The Talmud called on the Jews to share with the rest of mankind their achievements in religion and morality. According to the Midrash, the Torah was originally revealed in the desert, a land that belonged to no one and everyone, and not in the land of Israel, in order to suggest that its teachings were meant for all mankind.

To fulfill their mission, the Jews of the early talmudic period proselytized extensively throughout the pagan world. Professor George Foote Moore has pointed out that Judaism was "the first great missionary religion of the Mediterranean world." Jewish missionaries did not seek only formal conversions; they also sought to transform Romans into *metuentes*, or "God-fearing men." These sympathizers of Judaism led their lives according to Jewish ideals of personal and social morality, although they did not follow Jewish law and ritual. By reaching out to potential converts, the Jewish people attempted to meet their responsibilities to the larger human community.[67]

■   SPIRITUALITY AND THE DEVELOPMENT OF CHARACTER   ■

The Talmud is concerned with the individual and with the development of his character, not only with the social consequences of his actions. Throughout talmudic literature we thus have descriptions of the ideal human character.

While hoping and beseeching God for a better life, a person should still perceive and appreciate the many manifestations of the divine in the world. Given this abiding, sustaining presence, the rabbis taught that each person should approach life with a confidence that flows directly from faith to God. For if God's providence extends to all

---

66. Megillah 9b; Ekah Rabba 2:17, ed. Vilna 1897; Shabbat 93b; Genesis Rabba 9, on 1:31; Sukkah 55b; Mishnah Nedarim 3:4; Sanhedrin 39b; Tanhuma Mishpatim 12.

67. Abot de Rabbi Nathan II ch. 21, p. 22b, ed. Schecter; Sanhedrin 91b; Tannit 11a; Mekilta on Exodus 19:2; George F. Moore, *Judaism in the First Centuries of the Christian Era* (Cambridge: Harvard University Press, 1927), vol. I, p. 324.

INTRODUCTION

his creatures, then we may rest assured that "whatever the Lord does is the best," as one talmudic maxim puts it. There are occasions when events transpire that seem injurious to our interest, but are in fact really to our advantage, though we may not be aware of it at the time. The Talmud cites an anecdote from the career of R. Akiba that illustrates this: While on a journey, he sought hospitality in a certain town, but was refused, and he had to spend the night in a nearby field. The same night, robbers came and plundered the entire town. "He thereupon said to the inhabitants, 'Did I not tell you that whatever the Holy One, blessed be He, does is for the best!' "[68]

A person should avoid such passions as envy, jealousy, and pride, which block him from seeing God's role in all of creation and his reflection in all creatures. Thus, one rabbi offered the daily prayer: "May it be acceptable before Thee, O Lord my God and God of my fathers, that no hatred against us may enter the heart of any man, that no hatred of any man enter our heart, that no envy of us enter the heart of any man, nor the envy of any man enter our heart."[69] A person should be well disposed toward his neighbor, as is repeatedly stressed in tractate Avot. Two examples: Matthew ben Heresh taught, "Be the first to offer cordial greetings to every man." Ben Zoma was wont to say, "Who is deserving of honor? He who honors other people."[70] Even if one has a genuine grievance toward his neighbor, he should not respond with hatred. There is another way of coping with grievances—to honestly voice one's anger with the goal of bringing about a reconciliation. Indeed, "A love without rebuke is no real love."[71]

It takes much self-control to act with magnanimity toward those who have wronged us, but only in such self-control does true character develop and reveal itself. The true hero, teaches the Talmud, is "one who converts an enemy into a friend."[72] One's good will should be extended even to the sinner, as illustrated in the following anecdote:

> There were some lawless men living in the neighborhood of R. Meir and they used to vex him sorely. Once R. Meir prayed for their death. His wife, Beruriah, thereupon ex-

68. Berakot 60b.
69. Yerushalmi Berakot 7d; Abot 2:16, 4:28.
70. Abot 4:20, 4:1; cf. 2:15, 3:10.
71. Genesis Rabbah, ch. 54, sect. 3; Yerushalmi Nedarim 9:4.
72. Abot de Rabbi Nathan, ch. 23.

claimed: "What do you take as the sanction for your prayer? Is it because it is written, 'Let sinners cease out of the earth'? (Ps 104:35) But the verse may also be rendered to mean, 'Let sin cease out of the earth.' Consider, moreover, the conclusion of the verse: 'And let the wicked be no more.' When sins shall cease, the wicked will be no more. Rather should you pray that they repent and be no more wicked." R. Meir offered prayer on their behalf and they repented.[73]

The Talmud includes many anecdotes to illustrate the importance of interpersonal sensitivity and respect. A famous anecdote about Hillel demonstrates the extent to which one should be patient with difficult people:

Our masters have taught: A person should always be patient like Hillel and not quick-tempered like Shammai. Two men once made a wager that whoever would succeed in getting Hillel to lose his temper would win four hundred zuz. That day happened to be the eve of the Sabbath and Hillel was then washing his head. One of the men came to the door of the house and shouted, "Is Hillel here? Is Hillel here?" Hillel wrapped himself, came out and asked him, "What do you want, my son?" "I have a question to put to you." "Ask it, my son." "Why are the Babylonians round-headed?" "You have put an important question to me," Hillel answered. "The reason is that they have no skilled midwives."

The man left and after a short while returned, shouting, "Is Hillel here? Is Hillel here?" The Rabbi wrapped himself, came out to him and asked, "What do you want, my son?" "I have a question to put to you." "Ask it, my son." "Why are the inhabitants of Palmyra bleary-eyed?" "You asked an important question," Hillel again replied. "The reason is that they live in sandy districts."

The man went away, waited a brief while, and again returned, shouting, "Is Hillel here? Is Hillel here?" The rabbi

---

73. Berakot 10a.

wrapped himself, came out to him and inquired, "What is it, my son?" "I have a question to put to you." "Ask it, my son." "Why are the Africans broad-footed?" "You have asked an important question," Hillel once more responded. "The reason is that they live in marshy districts."

The man said, "I have many more questions to ask, but I am afraid of provoking your anger." Hillel folded the wrap about himself, sat down, and said, "Ask all that you desire." "Are you Hillel whom people call Prince in Israel?" "I am." "If so, may there not be many like you in Israel." "Why, my son?" "Because through you I have lost four hundred *zuz*." The rabbi then told him, "Be careful, Hillel is worthy that you should lose through him four hundred *zuz* and still another four hundred *zuz*. But Hillel will not lose his temper."[74]

A good man is a peace-lover and peace-maker. Hillel tolled the virtue of peace in these words: "Be of the disciples of Aaron, a lover of peace and a pursuer of peace, one who loves mankind and draws them nearer to the Torah."[75] The admiration for the peacemaker is clearly revealed in the following story: "A rabbi was standing in the marketplace when Elijah appeared to him. The rabbi asked him, 'Is there anybody in this marketplace who will have a share in the life of the world to come?' Elijah answered that there was not. Then two men appeared, and Elijah said, 'These two will have a share in the world to come.' The rabbi asked them what they had done to earn such distinction. They answered, 'We are merrymakers; when we see people troubled in mind we cheer them, and when we see two men quarreling we make peace between them.' "[76]

If drawing close to God means imitating his ways, this must include actively pursuing the welfare of one's neighbor. Thus the Talmud expounds: "What is the meaning of the verse, 'Ye shall walk after the Lord your God' (Dt 13:4)? It is to follow the attributes of the Holy One, blessed be He: As He clothed the naked (Gn 3:21), so do you clothe the naked; as He visited the sick (Gn 18:1), so do you visit the sick; as He comforted mourners (Gn 25:11), so do you comfort those who mourn; as He buried the dead (Dt 34:6), so do you bury the dead." The same thought is expressed in the Midrash: "As the All-present is called compassionate and gracious, so be you also compassionate and gracious and offer thy gifts freely to all. As the Holy One, blessed be He, is called righteous (Ps 145:17), be you also righteous; and as He is called loving (ibid.), be you also loving."[77]

Previously, we saw how the idea of *gemilut hasadim*, acts of lovingkindness, was conceptualized as a way of encouraging benevolence. Among the typical acts of lovingkindness mentioned in the Talmud are visiting the sick, offering hospitality to strangers, providing a proper outfit and dowry for a poor bride, and caring for the orphaned. Highest of all are our acts for the departed, such as attending a funeral and comforting the mourners.[78] Talmudic literature abounds in injunctions to relieve the poor in their distress, but acts of benevolence were seen as greater than almsgiving: "Greater is the benevolence than alms in three respects—almsgiving is performed with money and benevolence with personal service or money; almsgiving is restricted to the poor and benevolence applies to the poor as well as to the affluent; almsgiving applies only to the living and benevolence applies both to the living and the dead."[79]

Various stories regarding R. Akiba extol our responsibility for the poor. Thus, for example:

> It was said of R. Tarfon that he was exceedingly rich but did not give to the poor. Once R. Akiba met him and asked, "Would you like me to buy a town or two for you?" He agreed and offered him four thousand golden denarii. Akiba took them and distributed them to the poor. After a while, R. Tarfon met him and asked, "Where are the towns you bought for me?" Akiba took him by the hand and led him to the House of Study; he then brought a copy of the Psalms, placed it before the two of them, and they continued to read till they reached the verse, "He hath dispersed, he hath given to the needy; his righteousness endureth forever" (Ps 112:9).

77. Sotah 14a; Sifre Deut, sect. 49.
78. Shabbat 127a; Ketubot 50a; Nedarim 39b; Megillah 3b; Berakot 18a.
79. Tosefta Pe'ah 4:19; Sukkah 49b.

INTRODUCTION

Akiba explained, "This is the city I bought for you!" Tarfon arose, kissed him, and said, "My master and guide, my master in wisdom, and my guide in right conduct." He handed him an additional sum to distribute as charity.[80]

Another virtue extolled by the rabbis is truthfulness. "Truth," taught R. Hanina, "is the seal of God Himself." Some rabbis rhetorically taught that those who simulate their speech are like idolators. They condemned misleading a person in his opinions as much as they did fraud. They taught, "It is forbidden to mislead a fellow-creature, including a non-Jew." Another talmudic statement notes that "the Holy One, praised be He, hates a person who says one thing with his mouth and is of another opinion in his heart." According to Rabban Simeon ben Gamaliel, truth is of the three pillars on which the world rests; the other two are justice and peace.[81] The rabbis condemned even the innocent lies that parents tell their children, which they thought set an example in untruthfulness that children would imitate. As one rabbi put it: "A person should not promise his child that he will give him something without giving it to him, for thus he teaches him to lie."[82]

The Talmud recounted with much admiration the exemplary honesty of some of its heroes:

> It happened that Phinehas ben Yair was living in one of the cities of the South, and some men who came there on business left two measures of barley in his possession and departed, forgetting all about the barley. He sowed the barley and each year stored the produce. After seven years had elapsed the same men returned to the town and asked for their barley. He recognized them and asked them to take the entire produce. . . . Another incident is related concerning Simeon ben Shetah, who had purchased a donkey from an Arab. His disciples noted a gem hung from its neck, and they said, "O master, in you has been fulfilled, 'The blessing of the Lord maketh rich' (Prv 10:22)." He replied to them: "I bought the donkey

---

80. Leviticus Rabbah, ch. 34, end. Cf. Baba Batra 10a.
81. Sanhedrin 64a; Tosefta Baba Kamma 7:8; Hullin 94a; Pesahim 113b; Abot 1:18.
82. Sukkah 46b.

and not the gem." He then proceeded to return it to its [original] owner. The Arab, on getting it back, exclaimed, "Blessed be the God of Simeon ben Shetah."[83]

■   MODERATION IN LIVING   ■

The rabbis idealized not the ascetic who shuns the world and its pleasures, but rather one who knows how to live with moderation and yet who also knows how to take pleasure in the fullness and richness of the divine creation. The rabbis declared that a person is destined to give account to his Maker for all the good things his eyes beheld that he did not partake of. They particularly commended the person who possessed "a beautiful home, a beautiful wife, fine furnishings," all of which put a person into "a happy frame of mind."[84]

Thus, rabbinic spirituality hardly meant self-abnegation. The rabbis generally decried the ascetic's assumption of voluntary fasts. According to the Babylonian teacher Samuel, he who indulges in fasting "is called a sinner." Another teacher, Resh Lakish, forbade fasting because it weakens one's body and thus lessens a person's service to God. Another teacher suggested giving the food shunned by the ascetics to the dogs. The *nazirite*, whose vow to reject wine is recognized as binding in the Bible (Nm 6:1–4), was held to be a sinner. One authority suggested: "If a person who withholds himself from wine is called a sinner, how much more is one a sinner who withdraws from all of life's enjoyments."[85]

On the other hand, the rabbis were not unmindful of the dangers from indulgence to excess. Because excessive imbibing of wine or other alcohol might loosen moral and mental constraints, they warned: "Do not become intoxicated and you will not sin" and cautioned that "when wine enters, sense leaves, when wine enters, the secret blurts out."[86]

Although the study of Torah was regarded by the rabbis as life's supreme good, some cautioned that no person should avoid regular work. It was thus taught, "Torah is good when combined with a worldly occupation." The Talmud tells of R. Simeon ben Yohai, who

---

83. Deuteronomy Rabbah 3:3.
84. Berakot 57b.
85. Taanit 11a.
86. Berakot 29b; Numbers Rabbah 10:8.

had hidden in a cave for twelve years in order to elude the Romans. When he finally emerged, he noticed the people were going on with their usual affairs, plowing and sowing, and exclaimed: "They forsake the life of eternity and busy themselves with the life that is transitory!" A heavenly voice rebuked him: "Have you left your cave to destroy my world? Go back to it!"[87]

■   CLEANLINESS AND HEALTH   ■

The rabbis' spiritual views encompassed the proper care of the body as an obligation one owes to himself. They believed that cleanliness was a prerequisite to good health. "Rinse the cup before and after drinking," recommended the rabbis, who also warned that "a person should not drink from a cup and hand it to another, for it is dangerous to health." The talmudists lived among people who were particularly troubled with eye disease, still a common affliction in the Mideast. They blamed this malady on the lack of proper sanitary habits. "Better a drop of cold water in the morning, and the washing of hands and feet in the evening, than all the eye salves in the world."[88]

The rabbis viewed the maintenance of bodily health as a religious obligation. After Hillel had finished a session of study with his pupils, "he accompanied them part of the way. They said to him, 'Master, where are you going?' 'To perform a religious duty,' he replied. 'Which religious duty?' they asked. 'To bathe in the bath-house.' 'Is that a religious duty?' they wondered. He answered them: 'One who is designated to scrape and clean the statues of the king which are set up in theaters and circuses is paid for the work and he associates with nobility. Surely must I, who am created in the divine image and likeness, take care of my body!' "[89] Because each person is created in the image of God, he has an obligation to care for his physical well-being.

The Talmud abounds in rules of health, some of which may intrigue the modern reader. The rabbis cautioned against overeating: "Restrain yourself from the meal you especially enjoy, and do not delay answering nature's call." They urged sufficient sleep during

---

87. Abot 2:2; Shabbat 33b.
88. Taanit 27b; Derekh Eretz 9; Shabbat 108b.
89. Leviticus Rabbah 34:3.

regular nighttime hours; late morning sleep was regarded as injurious. Above all they urged general moderation in daily living: "In eight things excess is harmful and moderation beneficial: travel, sexual intercourse, wealth, work, wine, sleep, hot water [for drinking and bathing], and blood-letting."

The rabbis recognized that bodily illness often derives from psychic causes. Thus, they listed fear and sin among the things that "weaken a man's strength." In the event of illness, the rabbis urged that a physician be consulted; they even insisted that "it is forbidden to live in a city that is without a physician."[90] In short, the rabbis took a holistic perspective when it came to personal well-being.

■   THE LAW EXTENDS BEYOND MINIMUM OBLIGATIONS   ■

As described above, talmudic law is characterized by its comprehensive scope in dealing with the full range of human thoughts, attitudes, and deeds. The rabbis divided these into two categories of duties: those deriving from a person's relationship to God and those from a person's relationship to his neighbor. We have discussed the nature of the former, which cover such laws as those of the Sabbath. Yet the person-God laws also affect each person's self-fulfillment within society. A closer look at the latter realm will underscore the degree to which talmudic law both promotes the social contract and responds to God's concerns.[91]

Rabbinic teachings seek to create a just social order that liberates man from impediments to personal growth, but the Talmud is content to keep individuals safely within their personal realms: "One who asserts what is mine is mine, and what is yours is yours, is only of medium [ethical] stature," it states. One rabbi even claims that such a standard is appropriate only to the ethics of the wicked city of Sodom.[92] The rabbis commend a willingness to bend self-interest through acts of helpfulness toward others. Talmudic law does not seek to bal-

---

90. Erubin 65a; Berakot 62b; Abot 3:14; Gittin 70a; Sanhedrin 17b; Yerushalmi Kiddushin 66d.

91. See Moshe Silberg, *Talmudic Law and the Modern State*, trans. Ben Zion Bokser (New York: Burning Bush Press, 1973).

92. Abot 5:10.

INTRODUCTION

ance self-interests. It seeks to move society toward acts of welfare for the common people, particularly for the underprivileged.

The Talmud promotes the ideal of total identification with the needs and aspirations of one's fellowman. The Mishnah notes: "He who says, 'What is mine is thine and what is thine is thine is a *hasid*, a saintly man.'"[93] Although most people cannot realize this ideal, it still played a vital role in rabbinic law by proclaiming that the law in itself does not exhaust moral duty. The recognition that the law did not encompass the highest moral ideal led to a demand that people go beyond its limits in their dealings with each other. This is clearly conveyed in the rabbinic interpretation of the verse in Exodus 18:30, "And thou shalt make them know the path they are to walk in and the work they are to do." According to R. Eleazer of Modi'in, "the path they are to walk in" refers to the law, while "the work they are to do" refers to acts of saintliness "beyond the measure of the law."[94] The rabbis cite various cases in which morally sensitive people act on a higher standard than the law calls for.[95] Those actions "beyond the line of the law" constitute a "free zone" in which individuals freely express their love for their fellowmen. The Talmud views this free zone of moral action as the very foundation of the good society.

A community in which men are content to hew to the strict letter of the law was seen as devoid of the moral cement that gives a social order stability and enables it to survive. According to R. Yohanan, "Jerusalem was destroyed because her people hewed strictly to the letter of the Torah."[96] Ethical conduct beyond the law reflects a vibrant morality and saves the law itself from falling into a soulless formalism.

The standard of saintliness also pushed the law toward new frontiers of human service. The Talmud gives evidence of a continuously growing program of welfare legislation to enhance the welfare of the common man. Thus, the community was to assume responsibility for elementary education and poor relief. The law compelled children to provide for the maintenance of parents, even as parents were compelled to provide for the maintenance of children. It also authorized the supervision of weights and measures and of fair wages and prices, to

---

93. *Ibid.*
94. Mekilta on Exodus 18:20.
95. Baba Mezia 83a; Ketubot 61a, 97a.
96. Baba Mezia 30b.

prevent unethical business practices.[97] A person was obligated to help his neighbor when he would not lose by so doing. Thus, brothers who were dividing land that had come to them by inheritance were to take into account the one who owned land contiguous to the parcel to be divided and give him his share adjacent to his own land. The Talmud generalized: "We coerce against the standard of Sodom." A person did not have the absolute right to be mean.[98]

The growth of talmudic law came about largely through judicial interpretation rather than formal legislation. The rabbis carefully considered the conditions under which it was to be applied. If they felt that the mechanical application of a precedent was in conflict with the demands of equity, they reinterpreted the law by withdrawing the new case from the traditional category into which it fell. The case so decided in turn became a precedent for parallel situations. The judge thus served in effect as a creator of law and not only as its interpreter. This dual role has been duplicated in every system of jurisprudence.

The rabbis did not manage to resolve every conflict between morality and the law. In the case of the *mamzer*, a "bastard" (a child born of an *illicit* relationship between a man and a woman and not an out-of-wedlock child), the old law that a bastard could only marry another bastard, a convert, or a liberated slave, but not a person of normal status in the Jewish community, remained in effect.

A rabbinic text records dismay at the inequity this involved; it is based on a verse in Ecclesiastes: "But I returned and saw all the oppressions that are done under the sun; and behold the tears of the oppressed, and they have no comforter; and on the side of the oppressors there was power, but they had none to comfort them" (Eccl 4:1):

> Daniel Haita applied this verse to bastards. "And behold the tears of the oppressed." If the parents of these bastards committed transgression, why should it affect these poor sufferers? . . . "But on the side of the oppressors there was power." This applies to Israel's great Sanhedrin that came against them with the authority of the Torah and removed them from the community, because it is written: "A bastard shall not enter the community of the Lord" (Dt 2:3). "But they had

---

97. Baba Batra 21a, 8b; Ketubot 49b; Ketubot 65b; Yerushalmi Kiddushin 1:7.
98. Baba Batra 12b.

INTRODUCTION

none to comfort them." Said the Holy One, praised be He: "It is for me to comfort them."[99]

The same verse from Ecclesiastes is used as the basis for an additional statement by Judah ben Pazi to the effect that bastards will have a share in the world to come. We also have a ruling by R. Yose, which won the support of his colleagues, that the disabilities of the bastard will be removed in the world to come.[100]

■ THE NATURE OF LEGAL CONTROVERSY ■

The rabbis' far-reaching judicial interpretations were hardly made with universal concurrence. Considerations of equity are ultimately subjective in character; they will reflect the diversity of the hearts and minds that make them. This is the principal reason for the ubiquitous presence of controversy in the Talmud. The rabbis were not contentious for contention's sake. They were simply offering varying reactions to the problems of life, as a result of their diverse backgrounds and of those diversities of temperament, character, and outlook that naturally divide people. Thus, the decision making capital punishment almost impossible was challenged by Rabban Simeon ben Gamaliel, who defended the old law as an indispensable deterrent to crime. The proposed reform, he argued, would "cause an increase of bloodshed in Israel."[101]

Often those who transmitted traditions juxtaposed one teaching with another teaching that had similar subject matter. Hence, even where they did not actually disagree, their teachings apppeared to conflict. Where masters do disagree they are often influenced by their diverse backgrounds or social classes. R. Eliezer, who was an aristocrat, exempted swords and other arms from the prohibition of carrying unnecessary objects on the Sabbath. He regarded them as ornaments that were worn as a normal part of a person's apparel. His colleagues, representing the point of view of the common people, forbade the carrying of arms on the Sabbath. Citing the prophetic contempt for war and its implements, they branded the wearing of arms a "disgrace."[102]

---

99. Leviticus Rabbah 32:8.
100. Kiddushin 72b.
101. See also Mishnah Sanhedrin 5:1; Sanhedrin 40a.
102. Mishnah Shabbat 6:4.

51

INTRODUCTION

The rabbis who created talmudic law were the religious representatives of the Jewish community; they were not state functionaries. As the rabbis saw it, prior to the destruction of the Temple in 70 c.e., the state was generally under the authority of the Sadducees, the priestly class. However, the Pharisees, the forerunners of the rabbis, had a great moral influence among the people, and exerted moral, legal, and spiritual pressure with which the state had to reckon. Pharisaic supporters report that when Alexander Yannai, a king and high priest, proceeded to perform the Succot ritual in the Temple according to Sadducean ritual, the assembled worshipers demonstrated in protest.

Talmudic law came into its own after the destruction of the Temple. Within the limited autonomy enjoyed by the Jewish community in Palestine and in Babylonia, rabbinic law gradually gained in influence. Those rabbis who received appointments from the Patriarch in Palestine or from the Exilarch in Babylonia were authorized to impose and administer their view of the law in everyday areas. Yet in many cases, the state asserted its sovereignty in superseding the internal law of the Jewish community. The rabbis advised conformity. In response to this, the Babylonian teacher Samuel ruled: "The law of the state is law."[103] This became the basic rule governing the Jew's obligations as a citizen: Jewish law yielded to the law decreed by the state of which he deemed himself a part.

The Talmud drew a line, however, when the state sought to violate basic principles of morality and faith. As the Midrash declared (commenting on the verse: "I counsel thee, keep the king's command and that in regard of the oath of God" [Eccl 8:2]): "The Holy One, blessed be He, said to Israel, 'I adjure you that if the government decrees harsh decrees, rebel not against it in any matter which it imposes upon you, but keep the king's command; if, however, it decrees that you annul the Torah and the precepts, do not obey.' "[104]

The conflict between state law and Jewish law became a serious issue during the reign of the Emperor Hadrian. As part of the Roman Empire, Palestine and her Jewish community became subject to imperial law. According to certain modern scholars, some rabbinic circles later looked back at this period and described how the edict of Rome proscribed all the practices of Judaism on pain of death. The rabbis

---

103. Baba Kamma 113a.
104. Tanhuma Noah, sect. 10.

INTRODUCTION

responded by calling for conformity to the enemy's laws, for the sake of self-preservation, with the exception of three fundamental Jewish laws: those prohibiting idolatry, immorality, and murder. A person was to suffer martyrdom rather than violate these by submitting to the unjust will of the state. R. Ishmael limited the demand for martyrdom to the case of public idolatry. In private, he called for compromise, rather than martyrdom, even in this instance.[105]

■   THE INNER MAN: REPENTANCE   ■

Law prescribes behavior. The rabbis were keenly aware, however, that the inner man is more important than the deed through which he expresses himself: "The Holy One, blessed be He, is concerned above all with what is in man's heart."[106] A person may conform to the demands of the law and remain inwardly corrupt. Similarly, a person may, in the midst of a life of wrongdoing, go through an intense inner change that ultimately leaves him with a noble character. R. Judah the Prince once reflected that "one may earn his place in the world through the efforts of many years, and another earns it in one hour."[107] Indeed, R. Abbahu ranked the penitent even above the man who had never sinned.[108]

In their teachings on repentance, the rabbis distinguished between the relationship of man to God and the relationships between people. Repentance will clear a person for transgressing laws pertaining to the former. In the case of transgressions of the laws of human relations, however, the aggrieved person must be appeased. The Mishnah declares: "Transgressions between man and God may be atoned on the Day of Atonement, but transgressions between man and man will not be atoned on the Day of Atonement until one has appeased his fellowman."[109] It is significant, however, that the rabbis limited the scope of this required appeasement in order not to unduly burden the would-be penitent. Thus, one who had stolen a beam and used it to

---

105. Ketubot 19a; Sanhedrin 74a. See Saul Lieberman, "The Martyrs of Caesarea," *Annuaire de l'Institut de Philologie et d'Histoire Orientales et Salves* 7 (1939–1944) :395–445.
106. Sanhedrin 106b.
107. Abodah Zarah 17a.
108. Berakot 34b.
109. Mishnah Yoma 8:9.

build his house was not required to damage his building by tearing out the beam to return it. He could monetarily compensate the original owner.[110]

The talmudists also demanded that the law reckon with the intention behind a deed. Thus they absolved a person from guilt if he threw a stone that accidentally fell on someone and injured him. Likewise, a person who intended to kill an animal but missed his target and killed a human being was absolved from responsibility for a capital crime. In the case of a person who intended to kill a person and missed his target, killing instead another person, there was a difference of opinion among the talmudists. R. Eliezer regarded the act as murder; R. Simeon did not.

The talmudists allowed for spontaneity when it came to the fulfillment of certain laws. No fixed measure was given for the area on the corner of a field left for the benefit of the poor. There was no fixed measure for the firstfruit offerings brought as gifts for the priest or for the offerings brought to the Temple during the three major pilgrimage festivals, nor was there a fixed measure for the practice of charity or the study of Torah. The most significant allowances for flexibility and spontaneity in talmudic law were made for *minhagim*, or local customs. Local communities, professional groups, and even extended families often adopted measures to govern their religious or social life. The rabbis invested these *minhagim* with authority; indeed, when a law clashed with a deeply rooted custom, they often gave precedence to the latter.[111]

The rabbis envisioned that in messianic times, when men learned and internalized the true lessons of the love of God and the love of man, the law would no longer be necessary. The ritual worship and the structures of justice by which we now administer the law of human relations and express our relation to God will then become obsolete. Human spontaneity, as expressed by a person's noble character, will suggest the right action in every situation without needing the disci-

---

110. Gittin 55a.

111. Mishnah Keritot 3:10; Baba Kamma 41b; Mishnah Sanhedrin 9:2; Ketubot 33a; Mishnah Peah 1:1; Yerushalmi Pesahim 4:3; Pesahim 50a, 53a, 53b, 54b, 55a; Baba Batra 93b; Sanhedrin 23a, 23b; Soferim 14:18; Yerushalmi Baba Mezia 7:1. Rabbi Eliezer also disagreed on the number of sin-offerings required. He demanded one for each act by which the Sabbath was violated. Cf. Ben Zion Bokser, *Pharisaic Judaism in Transition* (New York: Bloch Publishing Co., 1935), pp. 129–44.

pline of law. "The laws," the Talmud declares, "will become obsolete in the hereafter."[112] In the present stage of human development, however, the law is an indispensable guide to action. It is also a preparation for the next stage of civilization, when the law, which has come "to ennoble the lives of men,"[113] will have done its work in giving individuals an awareness of God's continual presence. The rabbis expressed this vision in their conception of the three stages of human history: The first is the stage of "chaos," before the leaven of divine law has begun to work in the world; the second is the stage of "Torah"; the last is the stage of messianic liberation and enlightenment, which will finally bring human beings to their state of highest development and fulfillment.[114]

In conclusion, we can now answer the central questions of all religions: "Where is the divine sought and located? What sort of response should a person make to it?"[115] Talmudic Judaism seeks to increase a person's inner awareness of the divine. It asserts that in doing God's will—in study, ritual, and the performance of moral and righteous acts—one draws closer to God. This approach became basic for all later forms of Judaism; various individuals and movements developed one or another aspect of it. Some mystics believed that a focus on certain rites could lead to an intense interaction with the divine. But the talmudists, some of whom privately or secretly pursued such mystical practices, encouraged Jews to strive for a closeness to God that could be achieved anywhere and anyplace. Thus, rabbinic spirituality encompassed all the spheres of life.

---

112. Niddah 61b.

113. Tanhuma Shemini, ed. Buber, p. 30; cf. also Genesis Rabbah 44:1.

114. Abodah Zarah 9a.

115. To borrow a question posed in a different context by William P. Alston, in "Religion," *The Encyclopedia of Philosophy*, ed. Paul Edwards (New York: Macmillan Publishing Co., 1967, 1972), 7:143.

Note on the Text

This volume presents selections solely from the Talmud and omits the related literature of the Midrashim and the Tosefta. Only one talmudic tractate, Avot (Ethics of the Fathers), is offered in its entirety. Also, I have not drawn on all talmudic tractates, but selected material I thought most relevant to the modern reader, thus focusing on the Talmud's ethical and pietistic teachings, as opposed to those that are more strictly legal.

The format, that of the Talmud itself, is structured in two categories, Mishnah and Gemara (both mean "teaching," in Hebrew and Aramaic, respectively). The Mishnah offers a succinct summation of what different sages thought on a given subject. The Mishnah is the oldest layer of the talmudic text; the Gemara is a kind of commentary on it, elaborating its subject matter, introducing new problems, and citing the view of later authorities. At times, it also tries to decide which of several views cited in the Mishnah should be regarded as more authoritative.

When the Mishnah's editor wanted us to believe that the rabbis reached a consensus in their thinking, their views are presented anonymously. Where a disagreement persisted, the views of each teacher are cited by name. The selections presented here include both the Mishnah and the corresponding parts of the Gemara. Each Mishnah chosen is preceded by an introductory paragraph, which discusses its significance in the context of both its own period and that of today.

All translations, including the biblical passages that are cited in the talmudic text and are often used homiletically, are mine. I have tried to indicate when such biblical verses are used in ways that deviate from their commonly understood meanings.

While the selections are from both the Babylonian and the Palestinian Talmud, those from the former are far more numerous. The tractate from which a particular passage has been taken is indicated. The Babylonian Talmud is identified by tractate and page number, according to the Vilna edition. The Palestinian Talmud's identification is indicated by Yerushalmi ("of Jerusalem"); all references follow the Horeb edition, to which is added in parenthesis the corresponding page(s) in the Venice or Krotoshin edition. All Mishnah references are to the Horeb edition.

The Talmud's pagination involves folio pages, with text on both sides, which are identified as a and b. In the Venice and Krotoshin editions of the Yerushalmi, each side is further subdivided into two columns, that is, the four columns on both sides are identified as a, b, c, and d. The Palestinian Talmud also numbers each Mishnah, so that references are sometimes to a particular chapter and Mishnah.

The names of Sages are cited as they appear in the Talmud. Sometimes no title is indicated. Regarding the titles that do exist "Rabban" designates a Patriarch, "Rabbi" a Palestinian teacher, whose full name was Rabbi Judah the Patriarch but who was known simply as "Rabbi", and "Rav" a Babylonian master who was known by that name. When no title is indicated, the particular Sage probably had not been fully ordained.

I

The Tractate Berakhot

The tractate Berakhot is the first in the Talmud. It belongs to the Order (or Division) of Zeraim (or Seeds). All the sections of this Order deal with agricultural laws. The term Berakhot means blessings or benedictions. The core theme of the tractate is the benedictions of thanksgiving to God a person is obligated to recite on partaking of the different foods grown on the land. It is, however, extended and deals with all natural phenomena illustrating God's wondrous works in Creation—indeed, it deals with prayer generally. The tractate Berakhot is the major source for the discussion of the Jewish liturgy in all its aspects.

There are four major parts in the Jewish liturgy. The earliest, which was already recited in Temple times, is the Shema, "Hear," an allusion to "Hear, O Israel, the Lord is our God, the Lord is one" (Dt 6:4). The Shema consists of the two primary paragraphs, Deuteronomy 6:4–9 and 11:13–21, which set forth the basic teaching of Judaism: the unity of God, the call to love him with heart and soul and might, to heed his commandments, and to study his Torah. To these is added the brief passage in Numbers 15:37–41, which ordains the wearing of a fringe on each corner of the garment as a reminder of God and His commandments. It was around the Shema that there developed the first major rubric of prayer: The Shema was to be recited twice daily, morning and evening. Two prayers were added preceding the Shema and two following it, in the evening, and two preceding and one following, in the morning.

The first prayer preceding the Shema praises God as Author of nature; the second praises Him for His love shown the people of Israel *by giving them the Torah; the prayer following the Shema praises him for the redemption of Israel from Egyptian bondage, and protection from other tyrants who harassed the Jews throughout history. In the evening service the Shema is followed by an additional prayer, which asks for a night of peace.*

The Shema with its rubric of prayers is followed by the second major category of the liturgy: the Shemoneh Esreh, or "Eighteen," because its most common form consisted originally of eighteen benedictions or prayers. This was not a definitive designation, for soon after adoption, the number was increased to nineteen. The eighteen or nineteen, moreover, were only for weekly recitation. On the Sabbath and festivals the number was changed. Petitionary prayers, which are part of the eighteen, were deemed unsuitable for the Sabbath and the festivals, when we ought to think not of what we lack but of God's bounty and his blessings that these days celebrate. The petitionary prayers were replaced by others that express gratitude for the Sabbath and the festivals. Other terms sometimes used to designate this group of prayers are Amidah, which literally means "standing," for this body of prayers—of whatever number—is recited standing; and Tefillah, which means "prayer," because this is the core of the liturgy.

The Shemoneh Esreh includes two categories of benedictions: prayers of thanksgiving to God for His providential love in nature and in history, and petitionary prayers. The Shemoneh Esreh is communally oriented. It speaks for all Israel. The benedictions of thanksgiving express gratitude for God's protecting love shown the patriarchs and later generations of our ancestors; there is an expression of faith that, in some form, life survives after death; and there is an acknowledgment of God's holiness, which stands for His otherness from all other beings and for His perfection.

The petitionary prayers voice our basic needs: knowledge; reconciliation with God; forgiveness of sin; redemption from oppression; healing; a bountiful harvest; the restoration of the dispersed Jewish people in the Holy Land; righteous judges and counselors; an end to arrogant empire; the vindication of those who trust in God; the rebirth of Jerusalem to her ancient glory; the dawn of the messianic age of universal deliverance; God's acceptance of our prayers; the restoration of the Temple in Zion as the central sanctuary in Judaism; the renewal of Zion as a center of God's presence; and climaxing all these, peace.

The term Tefillah is sometimes used in an informal sense, and this is the third category of the liturgy. It refers to voluntary prayers, when a person feels the need of turning to God in any form of devotion. Happy events, times of stress, retiring for the night and rising in the morning, setting out on a journey, or confronting peril are occasions that would elicit this type of prayer.

The fourth category of the liturgy is known as Berakhot, *which is also the title of our tractate. It refers to benedictions to be recited on any occasion when we encounter God's providential work in nature or in history. On eating fruit of a true vegetation grown in the earth, on seeing an unusual phenomenon that illustrates God's wondrous work as Creator, on seeing people who exemplify special wisdom or special talents—special benedictions are prescribed for such occasions. The architects of the tradition were aware that the average person cannot create his own prayers even if he feels inspired, but as the texts quoted from this tractate will indicate, ample scope was allowed for improvisation and spontaneity.*

The delineation of the four categories of the Jewish liturgy is not present in a systematic form in the Talmud, but it is the context in which the talmudic discussions are to be understood.

■   THE SHEMA AND THE TEN COMMANDMENTS   ■

Why are these two chapters in the Bible [the Shema, Dt 6:4–9, and *Vehoya im shamoa,* Dt 11:13–21] recited daily? R. Levi and R. Simeon commented on this. R. Simeon said, Because each of these chapters alludes to the need of heeding God's commandments at the time of retiring for the night and rising in the morning.

R. Levi said, Because the Ten Commandments are implicit in them: "I am the Lord your God" is included in "Hear, O Israel, the Lord is our God." "You shall have no other gods before Me" is included in "the Lord is One." "You shall not take the name of the Lord your God in vain" is implied in "You shall love the Lord your God," because one who loves the King will not take an oath by His name to perpetrate a lie.

"Remember the Sabbath day, to keep it holy" is implied in "that you may remember all the commandments of the Lord and do them" (Nm 15:39). Rabbi [R. Judah ha-Nasi] said, The commandment concerning the Sabbath is so important that it is the equivalent of all commandments of the Torah, for it is written, "You made known to

61

them Your holy Sabbath, and You ordained for them commandments, and statutes, and a law by the hand of Moses Your servant" (Neh 9:14).

"Honor your father and your mother" is implied in "that your days and the days of your children may be prolonged" (Dt 11:21). "You shall not murder" is implied in "and you will fast disappear from the land" (Dt 11:17)—whoever takes life will lose his life.

"You shall not commit adultery" is implied in "you shall not stray after your hearts and after your eyes." Said R. Levi, The heart and eyes are the agents promoting sin, as it is written, "My son, give me your heart, and let your heart observe my ways" (Prv 23:26)—said the Holy One, praised be He, If you give me your heart and your eye, then I know that you belong to me. "You shall not steal" is implied in "and you will gather in your corn" (Dt 11:14)—but not that of your neighbor.

"You shall not bear false witness against your neighbor" is implied in "I am the Lord your God" (Nm 15:41), and concerning God it is written, "The Lord God is the God of truth, He is the God of life and King of the universe" (Jer 10:10).* What is the significance of calling Him "the God of truth"? It is that He is the Author of life and the Sovereign of the universe. Said R. Levi, Said the Holy One, praised be He, If you have testified falsely against your neighbor it is as though you have testified that I did not create heaven and earth.

"You shall not covet your neighbor's house" is implied in "you shall write them on the doorposts of your house"—your house, but not your neighbor's house.

R. Masna and R. Samuel b. Nahman both agreed that by right the Ten Commandments should have been recited each day. Why then do we not recite them? It is because heretics might well have claimed that these alone were communicated to Moses at Sinai.

Yerushalmi 1:5 (3c)

■　　GUIDELINES FOR PRAYER　　■

R. Eliezer says: If a person makes his prayer a fixed routine, then his prayer is not truly devotional.

MISHNAH 4:4

---

*The conventional translation differs from this, but the Hebrew original permits this reading.

THE TRACTATE BERAKHOT

What is meant by "a fixed routine"? Said R. Jacob b. Idi in the name of R. Oshaya, It means a person to whom the prayer seems burdensome. The Sages say: It means a person who does not recite his prayer with devotion. Rabbah and R. Joseph both say: It means a person who cannot add anything new in his prayer.

29b

One should not begin to recite his prayers unless one is in a reverent frame of mind. The pious men of old used to wait [meditating] an hour before beginning to pray in order to be able to focus their thoughts on their Heavenly Father.

MISHNAH 5:1

Said R. Hamenuna: How many important rules can one infer from the verses which describe the prayer of Hannah (1 Sm 1:13–16)! "Hannah spoke in her heart"—this shows that one who prays must direct her heart. "Only her lips moved"—this shows that one who prays must enunciate the words with his lips. "Her voice was not heard"—this shows that it is forbidden to raise one's voice in prayer. "And he [the priest Eli] thought she was drunk"—this shows that a drunkard is forbidden from praying. "And he said to her, How long will you be drunk?" R. Eleazar said this shows that one is obligated to reprove his neighbor if he sees something improper in him. "Hannah answered, and said, No, my Lord." Ulla or, as some say, R. Yose b. Hanina, said: She told him, You are no lord in this matter, nor does the holy spirit rest on you, that you suspected me of this. Some say that she spoke to him thus: You are no lord: The divine presence and the holy spirit are not with you that you judged me harshly and you did not judge me charitably. Did you not know that I am "a woman of troubled spirit, and that I did not drink wine or strong drink." Said R. Eleazar, This shows that a person who is suspected of something of which he is innocent is under obligation to deny it.

31a–b

"And the Lord spoke to Moses, Go, go down." What was meant by "Go, go down"? Said R. Eleazar, the Holy One, praised be He, said to Moses: Moses, go down from your distinguished position. Did I not endow you with greatness only for the sake of Israel. But now that the Israelites have sinned [in making the golden calf], what purpose do I need you for? Immediately Moses felt enfeebled, and he had no stamina to speak. However, when God said, "Leave me alone, and I will destroy them" (Dt 9:14), Moses said, This depends on me! At once he stood up and zealously prayed for mercy. This may be compared to the case of a king who became angry with his son, and he beat him severely. His friend sat before him, but he was afraid to say anything until the king said, Were it not for my friend here who is sitting before me, I would kill you. The friend then said to himself: This depends on me! He immediately arose and saved him.

"And therefore leave me alone, that my anger may turn against them, and I will destroy them, and I will make of you a great nation" (Ex 32:10). Said R. Abbahu, If the text did not say this, it would be impossible to put it this way. It teaches that Moses took hold of the Holy One, praised be He, like a person who seizes his neighbor by his garment, and said to Him: Sovereign of the universe, I will not leave you until you will forgive and absolve them.

"And I will make of you a great nation." Said R. Eleazar, Moses said to the Holy One, praised be He, If a chair with three legs [a people supported by the merit of the three patriarchs] could not stand up before you, when your anger has been aroused, how would a chair hold up by only one leg? Moreover, I would be ashamed of my ancestor, who will now say, See the leader He appointed over them! He only sought greatness for himself, but he did not plead for mercy on their behalf.

"And Moses besought the Lord His God" (Ex 32:11). Said R. Eleazar, This suggests that Moses remained absorbed in prayer until he felt ill [the word for "besought," *vayhal*, suggests the word *holeh*, "sick"]. Rava said, He prayed until he annulled His vow. The term used for "he besought" is *vayhal* and in the admonition that a person who made a vow shall not break his word, the word used is *lo yahel* (Nm 30:3), and a Sage has said, The person who made the vow may not annul his word but others may annul it for him. Samuel said, It is to teach us that he [Moses] staked his life on their behalf, as it is written, "and if not [if you do not forgive them] erase me from the book which you have written" (Ex 32:32).

Said Rava in the name of R. Isaac: This teaches us that he invoked God's attribute of mercy on their behalf.

32a

Certain criminals lived in the vicinity of R. Meir and they subjected him to much harassment, and he prayed that they might die. His wife Beruria said to him: How do you justify such a prayer? Is it because it is written: "Let sinners cease from the earth" (Ps 104:35)? But the word as written means literally "sin," not "sinners." Moreover, consider the last part of the verse: "and let the wicked be no more." When sins will cease, the wicked will be no more. You should rather pray that they repent, and then the wicked will be no more. He prayed that they repent, and they repented.

10a

■　THE EARTH IS THE LORD'S　■

　　The rabbis taught: It is not permitted for a person to enjoy anything of this world without a benediction, and whoever partakes of this world without offering a benediction has committed an act of sacrilege. How can this be redressed? Let him go to a wise man who will teach him to offer a benediction. He is to go to a wise man? What will he do for him? He has already performed a forbidden act! But Rava said, It means that he is to go to a wise man initially, and he will teach him the practice of offering benedictions, and he will not commit acts of sacrilege.

　　Said R. Judah in the name of Samuel, Whoever enjoys anything of this world without offering benedictions, it is as if he had partaken of what belongs to the heavenly realm, as it is written: "The earth is the Lord's and the fullness thereof" (Ps 24:1). R. Levi pointed to a contradiction. It is written: "The earth is the Lord's and the fullness thereof" (Ps 24:1), and it is also written: "The heavens are the heavens of the Lord, but the earth has He given to the children of men" (Ps 115:16). But there is no contradiction. The one statement [that the earth is the Lord's] applies before one has pronounced a benediction, the other, after one has pronounced a benediction.

　　Said Hanina b. Papa: Whoever enjoys anything in this world without offering a benediction, it is as he has robbed the Holy One, praised be He, and the community of Israel [since the community is diminished through the sin of its constituent individuals]. It is thus that we interpret what is written: "One who robs his father and mother and says, It is no transgression, is a companion of one who is a destroyer" (Prv 28:24). "Father" we interpret as applying to the Holy One, praised be He, as it is written, "Is He not your Father, who created you?" (Dt 32:6); and mother we interpret as applying to the community of Israel, as it is written, "Hear my son, the instruction of

65

your father, and do not abandon the teaching of your mother" (Prv 1:8). What is meant by He "is a companion to one who is a destroyer?" R. Hanina b. Papa said, He is a companion to Jeroboam ben Nevat, who undermined Israel's faith in their Heavenly Father.

35a–35b

■   A TREASURY OF PRAYER   ■

After R. Eleazar concluded his obligatory prayers, he added the following: May it be Your will, O Lord our God, that there be in our midst love, and brotherhood and peace, and friendship, that many disciples come to study under our auspices, and that You prosper our latter years and bring the hopes we cherish to fulfillment, and that you grant us a portion in paradise. May you help us grow toward perfection in Your world through good companions and through good impulses. When we rise in the morning may our hearts be stirred with reverence for Your name, and may all that happens to us be for good.

After R. Yohanan concluded his obligatory prayers he added the following: May it be your will, O Lord our God, to take note of the insults we have suffered and the evils that have befallen us, and may You robe yourself in your mercies and invoke your strength and assert Your lovingkindness and Your graciousness. And may Your good and gentle attributes be stirred to actions.

After R. Zerah concluded his obligatory prayers he added the following: May it be Your will, O Lord our God, that we sin not, nor suffer humiliation, nor be disgraced in comparison with past generations.

After R. Hiyya concluded the obligatory prayers, he added the following: May it be Your will, O Lord our God, that we become proficient in the study of your Torah, that we suffer not from anguish of heart or a blinding of the eyes.

After Rav concluded his obligatory prayers he added the following: May it be Your will, O Lord our God, to grant us long life, a life of peace, a life of good, a life of blessing, a life of sustenance, a life of bodily vigor, a life marked by the fear of sin, a life free from shame and reproach, a life of affluence and honor, a life imbued with the love of Torah and the fear of Heaven, a life in which You will fulfill all the aspirations of our heart.

After Rabbi [R. Judah ha-Nasi] concluded his obligatory prayers he added the following: May it be Your will, O Lord our God, to save us from arrogant men and guard me from showing arrogance toward others. Save me from evil men, and from evil mishaps, from an inner inclination to evil, from an evil companion and evil neighbor. Guard me from Satan the destroyer. Spare me from difficult entanglements with the law, and from difficult litigants, whether or not they are children of the covenant. He prayed thus though he was under the protection of a guard.

After R. Safra concluded his obligatory prayers, he added the following: May it be Your will, O Lord our God, to establish peace in the heavenly order above and in the earthly order below and among the disciples who study Your Torah, whether they study it for its own sake, or they do not study it for its own sake. And as for those who do not study it for its own sake, may it be Your will that they study it for its own sake.

After R. Alexandre concluded his obligatory prayers, he added the following: May it be Your will, O Lord our God, to station us in a place of light and not of darkness, and may our hearts be free of grief, and our eyes not be stricken with blindness.

Some say that the above supplementary prayer was recited by R. Hamnuna and that R. Alexandre would say after praying the following: Sovereign of all worlds, It is revealed and known to you that we would like to act according to Your will, but what prevents us? Negative passions, and the oppression of worldly powers. May it be Your will to save us from the grip of their power, and then we shall be penitent and heed the laws which emanate from Your will with a full heart.

After Rava concluded his obligatory prayers, he added the following: O my God, before I was formed I was without worth, and now that I have been formed I am as though I had not been formed. Like dust am I in life, how much more so when I die. In Your presence I am as a vessel filled with shame and confusion. May it be Your will, O Lord my God, that I sin no more, and as to the sins I have committed before You, purge them from me in your great compassion, but not through grievous suffering and disease. This was also the confession recited by R. Hamnuna Zuta on the Day of Atonement.

After Mar, the son of Ravina, concluded his obligatory prayers, he added the following: My God, guard my tongue from evil and my lips from speaking a falsehood. May I be silent before those who abuse me, may I be as the dust to all. Open my heart to Your Torah, and may I be zealous in pursuing your commandments. Guard me from any mishap, from the evil impulse, from a bad woman, and from every evil that may erupt in the world. And as for those who may scheme evil against me, may You speedily frustrate their designs and make their schemes of no effect. May the words of my mouth and the meditations of my heart be acceptable before You, O Lord, my Rock and my Redeemer.

16b–17a

The rabbis taught: What prayer is one to offer on entering the academy? May it be your will, O Lord, my God, that no error occur through me, and that I do not stumble over any aspect of law, that my colleagues take delight in me, and that I shall not pronounce what is unclean to be clean, or what is clean, unclean, that my colleagues shall not stumble over any aspect of law and that I take delight in my colleagues. On leaving what does one say? I thank you, O Lord, my God, that you set my lot among those who frequent the academy, and that you did not set my portion among those who sit on the street corners. I rise early and they rise early, I rise early to engage in the study of Torah, and they rise early to engage in frivolous talk; I labor and they labor, I labor and gain a reward, but they labor without receiving a reward; I run and they run, I run toward the life of the world to come, while they run toward the pit of destruction.

28b

What does one say on entering the academy? May it be your will, O Lord my God and God of my fathers, that I be not overexacting with my colleagues, and that my colleagues be not overexacting with me; that we do not pronounce unclean what is clean, and that we do not pronounce clean what is unclean, and that we do not forbid what is permitted or permit what is forbidden, bringing on me shame in this world and in the next. And what does one say on leaving? I thank you, O Lord my God and God of my fathers, that you have set my portion among those who attend the academy and the synagogue and that you did not set my portion among those who frequent the theaters [where the Roman games took place] and circuses. For I labor and they labor, I am zealous and they are zealous, I labor to inherit Gan-Eden, and they labor to inherit the pit of destruction, for it is written: "For you will not abandon me to the nether-world, you will not assign your faithful to see the pit" (Ps 16:10).

R. Pedat reported in the name of R. Jacob b. Idi: R. Eleazar used to add a prayer after each of the three obligatory prayers [morning, noon, and night]. What did he say? May it be your will, O Lord my God and God of my fathers, that no hatred toward us occur in the heart of any person, and that no hatred toward any person occur in our hearts, that no envy of any person occur in our hearts; that the study of your Torah be our primary pursuit throughout our life, and may the words we speak before you be truly devotional. R. Hiyya b. Abba added to this the following: And may our hearts be wholly directed toward the fear of you, and may you keep us far from all that is hateful to you, and bring us close to all you love; and act mercifully toward us, for your name's sake.

The School of Yannai said: When a person wakes from sleep he should say: Be praised, O Lord, for the renewal of life [lit. "who revives the dead"]. My Master, I have sinned before You. May it be Your will, O Lord my God, to grant me a good heart, a good portion, a good inclination, a good friend, a good name, a good eye, a good soul, a lowly disposition, and a humble spirit. May your name never be profaned because of us, and may we never become an object of gossip among people. May our lives not terminate in sudden destruction, nor our hope turn to frustration. Do not cause us to be dependent on the gifts of mortals, and may our livelihood not depend on creatures of flesh and blood. They are miserly in giving a gift and generous in spreading calumny. May our portion be in the study of your Torah, together with those who heed your will. Restore your house, your Temple, your city, your shrine, speedily, in our time.

R. Hiyya b. Va prayed thus: May it be Your will, O Lord our God, to stir our hearts to full penitence, that we do not suffer embarrassment in the presence of our ancestors in the world to come.

R. Tanhum b. Istablustika prayed thus: May it be Your will, O Lord my God and God of my fathers, to break and annul the bonds of the evil impulse in our hearts. For you created us with this aim, to do your will, and we are obligated to do Your will. You desire it, and we desire it. Who impeded us? The ferment of the evil impulse. It is well known to You that we do not have the strength to withstand it. But may it be Your will, O Lord my God and God of my fathers, to stop its sway over us, and vanquish it, and then we shall do Your will as it is indeed our will with a full heart.

Yerushalmi 4:2 (7d)

Rabban Gamaliel says: Each day a person should recite the Eighteen Benedictions. R. Joshua says: An abbreviation of the Eighteen. R.

THE TRACTATE BERAKHOT

Akiba says: If he is fluent in reciting the prayers he should recite the Eighteen, but if not he should recite an abbreviation of the Eighteen.
MISHNAH 4:3

What is meant by an abbreviation of the Eighteen? Rav says: An abbreviation of each individual benediction, while Samuel suggests the following: Grant us discernment, O Lord our God, that we may know Your ways, and circumscribe our hearts that we may revere You; forgive us, that we may merit redemption, and keep us away from those who afflict us; prosper us in the dwelling places of our land, and gather our dispersed people from the four corners of the earth; bring judgment on those who stray from the knowledge of your truth, and raise your hand against the wicked; and may the righteous rejoice in the rebuilding of Your city, in the restoration of Your Temple, in the renewed glory of the house of Your servant David, and in the shining light of the descendant of Jesse, Your anointed [the Messiah]. Before we call, you will answer us. Be praised, O Lord, who listens to prayer.

29a

The Sages taught: A person who passes a place that is infested with wild animals or with robbers abbreviates the prayer service. What is meant by an abbreviated prayer service?. R. Eliezer said: Do Your will in the heavens above and grant a tranquil spirit to those who revere You below, and do that which is good in your own eyes. Be praised, O Lord, who heeds prayer.

R. Joshua said: Hear the supplication of Your people Israel, and speedily grant their petition. Be praised, O Lord, who heeds prayer.

R. Eleazar b. Zadok said: Hear the cry of Your people Israel and speedily grant their petition. Be praised, O Lord, who heeds prayers.

Others say: The needs of Your people Israel are numerous, and they are impeded in expressing themselves. May it be your will to grant to each sufficient for his sustenance, and to every creature in accordance with its needs. Be praised, O Lord, who heeds prayer. Said R. Huna, the law is in accordance with the "others."

Said Elijah to R. Judah, the brother of R. Sela the pious: Do not fall into a rage and you will not sin; do not drink to excess and you will not sin. And when you go on a journey, take counsel with your Creator and then proceed. What is meant by "take counsel with your Creator and then proceed"? Said R. Jacob in the name of R. Hisda, This refers to the prayer before setting out on a journey. And R. Jacob in the name

70

of R. Hisda said, Whoever is about to set out on a journey should offer the prayer for a journey. What is meant by "the prayer for a journey"? May it be your will, O Lord my God, to lead me forth in peace, and to direct my steps in peace, and to uphold me in peace, and save me from enemies and ambushes lurking on the way. And may You bless the work of my hands, and enable me to find grace, and kindness, and mercy in Your eyes, and in the eyes of all who see me. Be praised, O Lord, who listens to prayer.

29a–29b

On retiring for the night one recites the first paragraph of the Shema and then adds: Be praised, O Lord our God, King of the universe who closes my eyes in sleep, and my eyelids in slumber, and who enables the pupil of the eye to see the light. May it be Your will, O Lord my God, that I lie down in peace, and may it be my lot to pursue the study of your Torah. Enable me to form the habit to perform Your commandments, and guard me from the habit to perform acts of wrongdoing. Bring me not into sin, or transgression, or temptation, or disgrace. May a disposition for the good dominate me, and not the impulse to evil. Save me from evil mishaps, and from grievous disease, and may I not be disturbed by bad dreams or bad thoughts; and may my offspring be worthy in your sight. And enable me to rise again to the light of day, lest I sleep the sleep of death. Be praised, O Lord, who in His mercy gives light to the entire world.

60a–60b

■   MORAL MAXIMS   ■

A favorite saying often repeated by R. Meir was: Study with all your heart and soul that you may know God's ways and be attentive to His Torah. Guard His Torah in your heart and keep the fear of Him before your eyes. Guard your lips from every sin, and purify and sanctify yourself from fault and wrongdoing. And God will be with you everywhere.

A favorite saying often repeated by the sages of *Yabne* was: I am God's creation and my colleague is God's creation. My work is in the city, and his work is in the country. I rise early to my work and he rises early to his work. As he cannot excel in my work, I cannot excel in his work. And lest you say, I do much and he does little, we have learnt: It is all the same whether a person does much or little, as long as his heart is turned toward God.

A favorite saying often repeated by Abbaye was: Let a person always be prudent in the fear of God. "A soft answer turns away anger" (Prv 15:1). One should always foster peace among his brethren, and his relatives, and with all people, and even with a non-Jew he meets in the street, so that he may be beloved in the heavenly realm and well-liked in the earthly realm, and be acceptable among his fellow-creatures. It was said of Rabban Yohanan b. Zakkai that no one was ever first to greet him, not even a non-Jew he met on the street,

A favorite saying often repeated by Rava was: The goal of wisdom is penitence and good deeds, so that a person should not study Bible and Talmud and then be disrespectful to his father and mother and his teacher and to one greater than he in wisdom and status, as it is written: "The beginning of wisdom is the fear of the Lord, a good understanding have those who practice them [the fear of the Lord and wisdom, Ps 111:10]. It does not say, 'those who study them,' but 'those that practice them,' which refers to those who do it for its own sake and not for another motive. If one does it for an ulterior motive, it would have been better if he had not been created.

A favorite saying often repeated by Rav: [The world to come is not like this world]. In the world to come there will be no eating, or drinking, or procreation, or business, or jealousy or hatred or competition, but the righteous will sit with crowns on their heads feasting on the radiance of the divine presence. Thus it is written: "And they beheld God, and did eat and drink" [Ex 24:11, the divine presence was their food and drink].

17a

■   DEMOCRACY IN THE ACADEMY   ■

The rabbis taught: It once happened that a certain disciple came before R. Joshua and asked him whether the evening prayer is optional or obligatory. He told him that it was optional. He then came before Rabban Gamaliel and asked him whether the evening prayer was optional or obligatory, and he told him that it was obligatory. He then said to him: But R. Joshua told me that it was optional! He said to him: Wait till the masters enter the academy. When the masters entered, the student who raised the question rose and asked: Is the evening prayer optional or obligatory? Rabban Gamaliel replied that it was obligatory. Rabban Gamaliel then said to the sages: Is there anyone who disputes this? R. Joshua said to him: No. He said to him: But they quoted you to me as saying that it was optional! He continued: Joshua, stand on your feet and let them testify against you. R. Joshua stood up and said: If I were alive and he were dead, the living could contradict the dead, but now that I am alive and he is alive, how can the living contradict the living?

Rabban Gamaliel continued to sit and lecture, while R. Joshua remained standing, until all the people began to complain and they said to Huzpit the interpreter (who usually explained the lecturer's theme): Stop! and he stopped. They then said: How long will we allow his humiliation? Last Rosh Hashanah he humiliated him in the matter of the first-born. In the incident of R. Zadok he again humiliated him. Now, too, he insulted him. Come, let us depose him. But whom shall we appoint in his place? Shall we appoint R. Joshua, but he is personally involved in this case. Shall we appoint R. Akiba, but he may harass him because he does not have an illustrious family background.*

Let us appoint R. Eleazar b. Azariah, because he is wise and affluent and he is a tenth-generation descendant from Ezra. He is wise so that if anyone puts a question to him, he will be able to answer it; he is affluent so that if it should be necessary to participate in a celebration in honor of the Roman emperor, he will be able to go and participate; and he is a tenth generation descendant from Ezra, which gives him the merit of an illustrious ancestry and he will not be able to harass him. They came to R. Eleazar and asked him whether it would be agreeable to him to serve as head of the academy. He replied to them: I shall go and consult my family. He went and consulted his wife. She said to him: But they may soon remove you! He said to her: Let a person use a precious cup even if it is broken the next day. She said to him: But you have no white hair [you are but a youth]. He was then eighteen years old, and a miracle occurred and eighteen rows of his hair turned white. This was the meaning of R. Eleazar b. Azariah's statement: I am like a person seventy years old; he did not say, I am a person seventy years old.

*R. Akiba, a descendant of a family of converts to Judaism, had as his ancestor Sisera, the general of Jabin, king of Hazor, who waged war against the people of Israel (Ber. 27b, commentary Rav Nissim Gaon, and cf. A. M. Hyman, *Toldot Tannaim ve-Amoraim*, 3 vols. (Reprint. Jerusalem, 1964), vol. I. s.v. Rabbi Akiba ben Yoseph.

It was reported that on that day they removed the guard from the door of the academy, and all students were given permission to enter freely. Rabban Gamaliel had issued an order that no student was to enter the academy unless his outer manner as well as his inner character were of the highest excellence. Many seats had to be added that day in the academy. R. Yohanan reported a divergence of opinion on this point between Aba Joseph b. Dostai and the sages. One view was that they added four hundred seats, and one, that they added seven hundred seats.

Rabban Gamaliel was troubled by this, saying, Perhaps I kept the Torah away from the people of Israel! He was then shown in a dream white pitchers filled with ashes [implying that the additional students were of little worth]. But there was no significance to this dream, it was only to appease his own mind.

It was reported that on that day they formulated the tractate Eduyot, which means "testimonies" [clarifying the authorities who held various views in the law]; and whenever in the Talmud there is a reference to "that day," this is the day which is meant. There was not a law about which there had been any uncertainity in the academy which was not clarified that day.

Even Rabban Gamaliel did not stay away that day from the academy even a single hour. Thus we learnt: On that day Judah, a proselyte of Ammonite descent, came before them and asked: What is my status as far as entering [being permitted to marry] in the Jewish community? Rabban Gamaliel said to him, You are not permitted, while R. Joshua said to him, You are permitted. Said Rabban Gamaliel to him, But it is written, "An Ammonite or a Moahite shall not be allowed to enter the community of the Lord" (Dt 23:4)! R. Joshua said to him: But do the Ammonites and the Moahites still reside in their original territories? Sennacherib, king of Assyria, long ago came and mixed up all the nations, as it is written, "I [the king of Assyria is quoted as speaking] have removed the boundaries of peoples and plundered their treasures, and, as a mighty one, I brought down their inhabitants" (Is 10:13). And any individual who detaches himself from a group, it is assumed that he came from the preponderant elements in that group [which here would be of the other nations]. But Rabban Gamaliel said to him: But it is written, "Afterward I will restore the captives of the children of Ammon" (Jer 49:6), so that they have already returned! R. Joshua replied to him: But it is also written, "I shall restore the captives of My people Israel" (Am 9:14), and they have not yet returned. At once they voted to admit him to the Jewish community.

Rabban Gamaliel then said, This being the case, I shall go and apologize to R. Joshua. When he reached his house he noticed that the walls were black. He said to him, From the walls of your house it is apparent that you are a blacksmith. He replied to him, Woe to the generation, whose leader you are, because you know nothing of the troubled lives of the scholars, of their struggles to support themselves and earn a living. He said to him: I stand humbly before you, forgive me. But he paid no attention to him. He continued his plea: Do it out of respect for my father. He was then reconciled to him.

They said: Who will go and report this to the Sages? A certain launderer then said: I will go. R. Joshua then sent this message to the academy: Let the one who wore the robe wear the robe; and as to the one who did not wear the robe, let the one who wore the robe say to him, Take off your robe and I will put it on. Said R. Akiba to the sages: Let us lock the entrances so that the servants of Rabban Gamaliel shall not come and harass the Sages.

Said R. Joshua, It is better that I myself go to them. He came and knocked on the door, and said to them: Let the priest who is authorized to sprinkle the waters of purification and who is the son of one who sprinkled the water of purification, sprinkle the waters of purification. Shall one not authorized to sprinkle the waters of purification, whose father did not sprinkle the waters of purification, say to the one authorized to sprinkle the waters of purification whose father sprinkled the waters of purification, The waters you use are from a cave [not living water,] and the ashes from the stove [not from the burning of the red heifer].*

Said R. Akiba, R. Joshua, You have been reconciled. Was it not in defense of your honor that we acted? Tomorrow you and I will go early to see him [R. Eleazar b. Azaryah]. They wondered: How shall we do this? Shall we remove him? But we have studies. We may raise one to a higher stature of holiness, but we do not reduce him to a lower stature. Shall we arrange that the two lecture on alternate Sabbaths? This will create jealousy. Let Rabban Gamaliel lecture three Sabbaths a month

---

*[The requirements of living water and ashes from the red heifer for waters of the ritual purification is set forth in Nm 19:17].

and R. Eleazar b. Azariah one Sabbath. It was in the light of this arrangement that someone asked, Whose Sabbath was it? It was the Sabbath of R. Eleazar b. Azariah.

The disciple who raised the question whether the evening prayer was optional or obligatory was R. Simeon b. Yohai.

27b–28a

■   THE WAYS OF GOD'S PROVIDENCE   ■

R. Yohanan said: Three conditions are proclaimed by God Himself: a time of famine, a time of plenty, and a good leader. Famine, as is written: "The Lord called for a famine" (2 Kgs 8:1); plenty, as it is written: "I will call for the corn, and I will increase it" (Ez 36:29); a good leader, as it is written: "And the Lord said to Moses, See I have called by name Bezalel . . . and I have filled him with the spirit of God in wisdom, and in understanding, and in knowledge, and in all manner of workmanship" (Ex 31:1–4).

R. Isaac said: We do not appoint a leader over the community, unless we consult the community, as it is written: "See, the Lord called by name Bezalel the son of Uri" (Ex 35:30). The Holy One, praised be He, said to Moses: Moses, is Bezalel suitable to you? He replied: Sovereign of the universe, if he is suitable to you, he is surely suitable to me! He [God] replied: Nevertheless, go and consult them. He went and he said to the children of Israel: Is Bezalel suitable to you? They said to him: If he is suitable to the Holy One, praised be He, and to you, he is certainly suitable to us.

R. Samuel b. Nahmani said in the name of R. Jonathan: Bezalel was so called because of his wisdom. When the Holy One, praised be He, said to Moses, Go and tell Bezalel, Make for me a tabernacle, the ark and vessels, Moses reversed the order and he told him: Make an ark, vessels, and a tabernacle. Bezalel said to him, Master Moses, it is customary for a person to build a house first, and then he puts into it furnishings, but you tell me to build an ark, vessels, and then a tabernacle. Where will I put the vessels I shall make? Perhaps God's instructions were to build a tabernacle, and then an ark and vessels? Moses said to him: Perhaps you were in the shadow of God's presence and know [the name Bezalel means in Hebrew, literally, in the shadow of God]!

The rabbis taught: If one sees a statue of Hermes, he is to say:

76

THE TRACTATE BERAKHOT

Praised be He who is patient with those who act against His will. If he sees a place from which an idol has been uprooted, he is to say: Praised be He who has uprooted an idol from our land, and as it has been uprooted from this place, so may it be uprooted from all places in the land of Israel, and may You turn the hearts of those who serve them to serve You. But in the lands of the diaspora it is not necessary to say "and may You turn the hearts of those who serve them to serve You," because most of them are idolaters. R. Simeon b. Eleazar said: In the lands of the diaspora one is also to say this, because they will all become proselytes one day, as it is written: "I will then turn to the peoples a pure language that they may all call upon the name of the Lord" (Zep 3:9).

57b

The rabbis taught: One who sees a crowd of Israelites is to say: Praised be He who is Master of secrets for they do not resemble one another in their minds, nor in their faces. Ben Zoma once saw a crowd on one of the steps of the Temple Mount and he said: Praised be the Master of secrets, and praised be He who created all these to serve me. He used to say: How hard Adam had to work before he obtained bread to eat. He ploughed, he sowed, he reaped, he bound the sheaves, he threshed, he winnowed, he selected the ears, he ground them, he sifted the flour, he kneaded and he baked, and then he ate, while I get up and find that all these were done for me. And how hard did Adam work before he found a garment to wear! He sheared the wool, and washed it, and combed it, and spun it, and weaved it, and then he obtained a garment to wear, while I get up and find all these ready made for me. All kinds of craftsman come to my door, and I rise and find them all ready for me. He used to say: What does an appreciative guest say? What trouble my host took to please me! How much meat did he set before me! How much wine did he bring before me! How much cake he served me! All the trouble he took was to please me! But what does an ungrateful guest say? What did my host do for me? I ate only one piece of bread, I ate only one slice of meat, I drank only one cup of wine! All the trouble this host took was only for his wife and children! What does Scripture say of a good guest? "Remember to extol his work, of whom men have sung" (Jb 36:24). But of an ungrateful guest it is written: "Therefore men fear him, he has no regard for any who are wise of heart" (Jb 37:24).

58a

THE TRACTATE BERAKHOT

The rabbis taught: One who sees Sages of Israel is to recite: Praised be He who imparted of His wisdom to those who revere Him. If he sees Sages of other people he is to say: Praised be He who imparted of His wisdom to His creatures. On seeing kings of Israel one is to recite: Praised be He who imparted of His glory to those who revere Him. On seeing kings of other nations, he is to recite: Praised be He who imparted of His glory to His creatures.

Ulla and R. Hisda once walked along the road. When they passed the door of the house of R. Hana b. Hanilai, R. Hisda became faint and sighed. Said Ulla to him: Why are you sighing, did not Rav say that a sigh breaks half a person's body, as it is written: "Sigh therefore, son of man, with the breaking of your loins, and with bitterness shall you sigh before their eyes" (Ez 21:11); and R. Yohanan said that it breaks even the whole of a person's body, as it is written: "And if they say to you, Why do you sigh? You shall say, Because of the tidings which have come, and every heart shall melt, and all hands shall grow weak, and every spirit shall be despondent, and all knees shall be infirm as water (Ez 21:12). He said to him: How shall I not sigh? A house that had sixty bakers by day and sixty at night, and they baked for all the needy, and he [R. Hana] never removed his hand from his purse, because he said, Perhaps a worthy poor man might come, and while I reach for the purse he might be embarrassed. Moreover, his house had four doors to the four sides, and whoever entered hungry left full. During years of famine they use to put wheat and barley outside, so that whoever was ashamed to come and take in the daytime came and took at night. Now this house is in ruins! Shall I not sigh? He said to him: Thus R. Yohanan said: When the Temple was destroyed, a decree was issued against the houses of the righteous that they be destroyed, as it is written: "The Lord of hosts declared in my hearing: Surely many houses shall be desolate, large and beautiful houses without inhabitants" (Is 5:9). R. Yohanan further said: The Holy One, praised be He, is due to restore them, as it is written: "Those who trust in the Lord are as Mount Zion" (Ps 125:1). As the Holy One, praised be He, is destined to restore Mount Zion, so is He destined to restore the houses of the righteous. Nothing that he was still not satisfied, he said to him: Enough for the disciple to be like his master [it should suffice if R. Hana's house will be like the house of God].

58b

78

THE TRACTATE BERAKHOT

■   ON LOVING GOD   ■

A person is obligated to praise God for evil as well as for good. Thus it is written: "And you shall love the Lord your God with all you heart, and all your soul, and all your might" (Dt 6:5). *With all your heart* refers to both impulses, the good and the evil one; *with all your soul* means even if he takes your soul [your life]; *with all your might* means with all your possessions. Another explanation for *with all your might*: No matter what treatment He metes out to you.*

MISHNAH 9:5

What is meant by the statement that one "is obligated to praise God for evil as for good"? Can this mean that just as for good one recites the benediction praising God as "He who is good and bestows good," so is he to praise God for evil as "He who is good and bestows good"? But we have studied that for good tidings one is to praise God as "He who is good and bestows good" but for evil tidings one is to say: "Be praised, righteous Judge." Said Rava, What it really means is that one is to accept whatever happens cheerfully. Said R. Abba in the name of R. Levi: From what verse can one infer this? From the following: "I will sing of mercy and justice, to You, O Lord, will I sing" (Ps 101:1): Whether I am bestowed mercy I will sing, and whether I am bestowed judgment I will sing. R. Samuel b. Nahmani said, We infer it from the following: "In the Lord [YHWH] I will praise His word in God [Elohim] I will praise His word" (Ps 56:11). "In the Lord [YHWH] I will praise His word"—this refers to a good dispensation; "in God [Elohim] I will praise His word"—this refers to a dispensation of suffering.† R. Tanhum said, We infer it from the following: "I will raise the cup of salvation and call on the name of the Lord, I found trouble and sorrow, but I called on the name of the Lord" [a rearrangement of verses in Ps 116:13, 3,4]. The sages inferred it from the following: "The Lord has given, and the Lord has taken, may the name of the Lord be praised forever" (Jb 1:21).

---

*The Hebrew word here used for might, *meod*, suggests the Hebrew word for measure, *midah*.

†The name YHWH, usually translated as Lord, is regarded as referring to His attribute of mercy, while *Elohim* is regarded as referring to His attribute of justice. In the Biblical text the order is reversed: "In God [Elohim] I will praise His word, in the Lord [YHWH] I will praise His word."

79

Huna said in the name of Rav, citing R. Meir, and similarly it was taught in the name of R. Akiba: A person should always accustom himself to say: Whatever the All-Merciful does is for the best. Thus R. Akiba was once on a journey. He came to a certain town and he sought lodging but he was refused. He said: Whatever the All-Merciful does is for the best. He went and spent the night outdoors. He had with him a rooster, a donkey, and a lamp. A gust of wind came and blew out the lamp, a wild cat came and ate the rooster, and a lion came and ate the donkey. But he said: Whatever the All-Merciful does is for the best. The same night a band of robbers came and took captive the inhabitants of the town. He said to them [the Sages]: Did I not tell you, Whatever the Holy One, praised be He, does—it is all for the best.

60b–61a

And you shall love the Lord you God. It has been taught: Said R. Eliezer: If it says "with all your soul," why does it also say "with all your might," and if it says "with all your might," why should it also say "with all your soul"? In the case of a person who values his life more than his money, for him it says "with all your soul,"* and in the case of a person to which money is more important than his life, for him is written "with all your might." R. Akiba says: "with all your soul"—even if he takes away your soul.

The rabbis taught: The wicked government once issued a decree forbidding Jews to study the Torah. Pappus, the son of Judah, once met R. Akiba gathering public assemblies and engaging in the study of the Torah. He said to him: Akiba, are you not afraid of the government? He answered: I will explain it to you with a parable. A fox once walked along the side of a river, and he saw fishes swimming in swarms from one place to another. He said to them: Why are you running away? They said to him: Because of the nets which people have set against us. He said to them: Would you like to come up to the dry land, and we will live together as my ancestors lived with your ancestors? They said to him: Are you the one they call the cleverest among the animals? You are not clever—you are a fool! If we are afraid in the place which is out natural habitat, how much more so in the place where by nature we die! Similarly we—if we are in this state now when we sit and study Torah, where it is written, "For this is your life

---

*The Hebrew term here used for "soul," *nefesh*, really means one's vitality, or life force.

and the length of your days" (Dt 30:20)—how much more precarious would our existence be if we neglected it!

It was reported that shortly thereafter R. Akiba was caught and imprisoned and then they caught Pappus and arrested him, and put him next to him. He [R. Akiba] said to him: Pappus, who brought you here? He replied: How fortunate you are, R. Akiba, that you have been seized for pursuing the study of Torah! Alas for Pappus who has been seized for things trivial! When R. Akiba was taken out for execution, it was time to recite the Shema, and they flayed his skin with iron combs, while he took on himself the yokes of the kingdom of God [by reciting the Shema]. His disciples said to him, Master, even to this extent? He said to them: All my days I was troubled by this verse, "with all your soul," [which I interpret]: Even if He takes your soul. I said: When will I have the opportunity of fulfilling this? Now that I have the opportunity, shall I not fulfill it? He prolonged the word *ehad*, "one" [the Lord is one], and he expired reciting *ehad*. A heavenly voice came forth saying: How fortunate are you, R. Akiba, that your soul has departed with the word *ehad*. The ministering angels said before the Holy One, praised be He: Is this the Torah, and is this its reward? [He should have been] "of those who die by Your hand, O Lord" (Ps 17:14). A heavenly voice came forth saying: How fortunate are you R. Akiba, that you are destined for the life of the world to come.

61b

There are seven kinds of Pharisees: a "shoulder" Pharisee, a "wait-a-bit" Pharisee, a "calculating" Pharisee, an "economizing" Pharisee, a "show me my fault" Pharisee, a Pharisee out of fear, and a Pharisee out of love. The "shoulder" Pharisee carries his good deeds on his shoulder (an exhibitionist); the "wait-a-bit" Pharisee says: Wait for me while I perform a virtuous act [he is ostentatious]; the "calculating" Pharisee balances a wrong act with a virtuous act, crossing off one with the other; the "economizing" Pharisee speculates as to how he can economize and do a good deed with his savings; the "show me my fault" Pharisee asks to be shown any act of wrongdoing on his part that he may redress it by a virtuous act. The Pharisee of fear [of God] is like Job; the Pharisee of love [for God] is like Abraham. No one is as beloved as the Pharisee of love, like father Abraham. Father Abraham transmuted his evil impulse into good, as it is written: "You found his heart faithful to You" (Neh 9:8).

Yerushalmi 9:5 (14b)

81

THE TRACTATE BERAKHOT

The rabbis taught: When our Sages entered the vineyard [the academy] at Yavneh there were among them R. Judah, R. Jose, R. Nehemiah, and R. Eliezer, the son of R. Yose the Galilean. They all spoke in honor of those who extend hospitality, and they expounded texts. R. Judah, who was the first to speak on all occasions, began the discourse in honor of the Torah, and he expounded this verse: "And Moses took his tent and he placed it outside the camp" (Ex 33:7). The ark of the Lord was never more than twelve *mils* distant [from any part of the camp, so this was the maximum distance one had to go to reach the tent of Moses]. Yet the text says: "All *who sought the Lord* went out to the tent of meeting" [as the tent of Moses was called]. Scholars who go from city to city and from province to province to study Torah are surely to be called seekers of the Lord.

"And the Lord spoke to Moses face to face." Said R. Isaac: The Holy One, praised be He, said to Moses: Moses, you and I will clarify the Torah. Some say: The Holy One, praised be He, spoke thus to Moses: As I turned to you a cheerful face [I heeded your plea to forgive the offense of the golden calf] so you turn a cheerful face to the people of Israel and bring back your tent to its place.

"And he returned to the camp" (Ex 33:11). Said R. Abbahu: The Holy One, praised be He, said to Moses: Now people will say the Master [God] is angry and the disciple [Moses] is angry. What will happen to the people of Israel? If you return your tent to the camp, well and good, but if not, your disciple Joshua will serve in your place, and thus it is written: "He returned to the camp." Rava said: Nevertheless, God's word was not spoken in vain, as it is written: "And his servant Joshua did not depart from the tent" (Ex 33:11).

R. Judah continued to speak in honor of the Torah, expounding the verse: "Attend [*basket*] and hear, O Israel, this day you have become a people to the Lord your God" (Dt 27:9). Was it on that day that the Torah was given to the people of Israel? Was not that day the end of forty years since the Torah was given at Sinai? But this is meant to teach that the Torah is loved by those who study it each day as on the day it was given at Sinai. Said R. Tanhum the son of R. Hiya of the village of Acco: There is a proof for this in the fact that if a person who recites the Shema each morning and evening should not recite it one evening, it will seem to him as though he never recited it.

Said R. Eleazar in the name of R. Hanina: Scholars increase peace in the world. Thus it is written: "And all your children shall be taught of the Lord, and great shall be the peace of your children" (Is 54:13). *Bonayikh*, "your children," may be read *bonoyikh*, "your builders," thus asserting that those taught of the Lord build peace in the world. "A great peace will be the possession of those who love Your Torah, and nothing will make then stumble in life" (Ps 119:165). [Thus there will be] "peace within your walls, security within your palaces" (Ps 122:7). "For my brothers' and my companions' sake, I will now say, Peace be within you" (Ps 122:9). [Through the gift of the Torah] "the Lord will give strength to His people, the Lord will bless His people with peace" (Ps 29:11).

64a

II

The Tractate Shabbat

The tractate Shabbat is the first in the Order, or Division, of
Moed, which means "appointed seasons." This branch of the Talmud
deals with the feasts and fasts of the Jewish calendar. And since the
Sabbath is primary in the list of sacred occasions in Judaism, the first
tractate of the Talmud deals with the Sabbath.*

The duty to honor the Sabbath is part of the Ten Commandments
(Ex 20:8–12, Dt 5:12–16), but the call to honor the Sabbath is also
stressed in other parts of the Bible. It is mentioned in the following
passages: Genesis 2:2–3, Exodus 16:22–27, Amos 8:5, Nehemiah
10:32, 13:15–23. Essentially the Sabbath celebrates God's creation of
the world. There is a zone of imperfection—or incompletion—in the
world to make room for man's creative labor, and man is free to live in
the world and engage in whatever work he chooses, to develop it as his
initiative prompts him. Indeed there is a rabbinic interpretation that
work, which aims at the creative development of the world, is a divine
commandment, being included in the first part of the ordinance ordain-
ing the Sabbath: "Six days you shall labor and do all your work" (Ex
20:9). This is for six days of the week. The seventh day is the Sabbath,
a term that means "cessation." It is to be a cessation from work, a day
of rest, when man is to contemplate creation and feel the awe of God's
wondrous work, which pervades the world as it is and makes it a noble
home for human life.

---

*The sequence of tractates within an Order is also in accord with the number of chapters
within each tractate, in descending order.

84

THE TRACTATE SHABBAT

*It is not only man who is commanded to cease from his labors on
the Sabbath. The slave and even the animal are to rest as well. The
commandment is all-inclusive: "Neither you, nor your son, nor your
daughter, nor your man-servant, nor your maid-servant, nor your ox,
nor your ass, nor any of your cattle, nor the stranger that is within
your gates" may work that day. The boon of a universal day of rest
each week has its humanitarian dimension, and this links it with the
exodus from Egyptian bondage. The life of bondage was to remain in
the memory of the Israelite ex-slaves, and this was to make them
sensitive to suffering. This aspect of the Sabbath is stressed in the
Deuteronomic version of the Ten Commandments. While in the book
of Exodus the basis of the Sabbath is defined as a memorial to Creation
(Ex 20:11), in Deuteronomy the motive given is that "you shall remember that you were a slave in the land of Egypt" (Dt 20:15).*

*What is meant by work? If work is defined rigidly, life might have
to come to a standstill without some work being done on the Sabbath.
The general principles invoked for defining the nature of work are
based on Exodus 35:2–3. There the instruction to build the Tabernacle
is preceded by an admonition not to work on the Sabbath, which
appears superfluous. The rabbis inferred from this that whatever work
was involved in the building of the Tabernacle was not to be done on
the Sabbath. There are, of course, special circumstances affecting life
when refraining from work might imperil life and the rabbis recognized this and lifted the restriction in such instances.*

*The tractate Shabbat is the second largest in the Talmud. It com-
prises 176 folios, divided into twenty-four chapters. The Mishnah
discusses various aspects of the rules governing the observance of the
Sabbath. The Gemara elaborates on these, and in the course of its
expositions digresses into many interesting comments about underlying spiritual and moral values. One can always discern a thread linking
these comments, including those that appear as digressions from the
subject focused on in the Mishnah.*

■   PATIENCE AND THE FEAR OF GOD   ■

The rabbis taught: A person should always be patient like Hillel,
and not impatient like Shammai. It once happened that two men made
a wager, saying: "Whoever gets Hillel angry will receive four hundred
zuz." One said, I will get him angry. That day was Sabbath eve and

Hillel was washing his hair. This person went and placed himself at the door of his house, and called: Who here is Hillel? Who here is Hillel? Hillel put on his robe and went out to him, and asked: My son, what is it that you want? He said to him: I have a question to ask you. Ask, my son, he replied. He asked him: Why are the heads of the Babylonians round? He said to him: My son, you asked an important question. It is because they do not have skillful midwives. He left and after an hour's wait returned and called out: Who here is Hillel? Who here is Hillel? [Hillel] put his robe on and went out to him, and said to him: My son, what do you want? He replied: I have a question to ask. Ask, my son, he replied. He asked him: Why do the Palmyrians have weak eyes? He said to him: My son, you asked an important question. He said to him: It is because they live in a sandy area. He left and after waiting an hour returned and called out: Who here is Hillel? Who here is Hillel? [Hillel] robed himself and returned, and said to him: My son, what do you want? He replied: I have a question to ask. Why do the Africans have wide feet? He said to him: My son, you asked an important question. It is because they live in watery marches. He then said to him: I have many questions to ask, but I am afraid you will get angry. Dressed in his robe he sat before him and said: Ask whatever questions you have. He said to him: Are you the Hillel who is called the prince of Israel? He replied: Yes. The latter then said to him: If you are the one, may there not be others like you in Israel! He asked him: Why, my son? He said: On account of you I have lost four hundred *zuz*. Hillel said to him: Be careful not to become upset. It was worth your losing four hundred *zuz* and another four hundred *zuz* over Hillel, to learn through Hillel the virtue of patience.

The rabbis taught: A gentile once came before Shammai and asked him: How many Torahs do you have? He replied: Two, a Written Torah and an Oral Torah. The gentile said to him, I believe you with reference to the Written, but with reference to the Oral, I do not believe you. Make me a proselyte by teaching me the Written Torah. Angrily he scolded him and told him to leave. He then came before Hillel, who made him a proselyte. The first day he taught him *aleph, beth, gimmel*, the second day he reversed the names of the letters. He protested to him: But yesterday you did not teach them to me thus! Hillel replied to him: Did you not depend on me [with reference to the names of the letters of the alphabet]? Then depend on me also with reference to the Oral Torah.

Again it happened that a gentile came before Shammai and said to him: Teach me the whole Torah while I stand on one foot. He pushed him away with the builder's yardstick which he had in his hand. He then came before Hillel, who made him a proselyte. He taught him: That which is hateful to you, do not do to others, the rest is commentary; go now and study.

There was another case in which a gentile passed a school and he heard a scribe recite: "And these are the garments they shall make: a breastplate and an *ephod*" (Ex 28:4). He asked: For whom are these? They told him: They are for the High Priest. That gentile said to himself: I shall go and become a proselyte so that they can make me a High Priest. He went before Shammai and said to him: Make me a proselyte with the understanding that you will appoint me High Priest. He pushed him away with the builder's yardstick in his hand. He then came before Hillel, who made him a proselyte. He [Hillel] then said to him: Is anyone appointed king unless he is familiar with the strategies of kingship? Go now and study the strategies of kingship. He went and read in Scripture: "And the stranger [a non-Levite] who comes to attend to the work [of tabernacle] shall die (Nm 1:51). He asked: To whom does this verse refer? They said to him: Even to David, King of Israel. He [the gentile] then reasoned within himself: If concerning the people of Israel, who are called children of God, and out of love for them He called them "Israel my first-born son" (Ex 4:22), the verse declares "And the stranger who comes near shall die"— how much more so would this apply to a simple proselyte who comes only with his staff and travelling bag! He then went before Shammai and said to him: But am I eligible to be a High Priest? Is it not written: "And the stranger who comes near shall die"? He then went before Hillel, and said to him: Kind Hillel, may blessings rest on your head for bringing me under the wings of God's presence. In time the three proselytes met in one place; and they said: The impatience of Shammai tried to drive us away from the world, but the patience of Hillel brought us under the wings of the divine presence. . . .

Said Rava: When a person is brought before the heavenly tribunal for judgment he is asked: Did you conduct your business with integrity? Did you set aside time for the study of the Torah? Did you raise a family? Did you persist in the hope for redemption? Did you search after wisdom? Were you able to infer one truth from another? Nevertheless, if "the fear of the Lord is his treasure" (Is 33:6), all will be well, but if not, not. This may be compared to the person who instructs his agent: "Take up for me a *kor* of wheat to the loft," and thus he did.

Then he asked him: Did you mix with the wheat a *kab* of *humtin* [a substance used as a preservative for wheat]? He replied: No. In that case, he said, it would have been better if you had not taken it up. . . .

Said Raba bar Huna: A person who possesses Torah but does not have the fear of God is like a treasurer who has been entrusted with the key to the inner chamber but has not been entrusted with the key to the outer gate. How is he to enter? R. Yannai proclaimed: Alas for the person who has no courtyard but makes a gate for it [learning is only a gate to the fear of God]! R. Judah said: The Holy One, praised be He, created His world only that people should revere Him, as it is written: "God made it so that they should be in awe of Him" (Eccl 3:14).

R. Simon and R. Eleazar were sitting when R. Jacob b. Aha passed by. Said one to his companion: Let us rise before him because he is a sin-fearing man. Said the other: Let us rise before him because he is a person of learning. The first one retorted: I tell you to rise because he is a sin-fearing man, and you tell me to rise because he is a person of learning!

We may infer that it was R. Eleazar who said that he was a sin-fearing man, because R. Yohanan said in the name of R. Eleazar: Nothing in this world is so cherished by the Holy One, praised be He, as the fear of God, as it is written: "And now, O Israel, what does the Lord your God ask of you but to fear the Lord your God' (Dt 10:12); and it is also written: "Behold [*hen*], the fear of the Lord, that is wisdom" (Jb 28:28).

30b–31b

■   EVIL MUST BE PROTESTED   ■

Rav and R. Hanina, R. Yohanan and R. Hanina taught: Whoever has the opportunity to protest the misdeeds of his household and fails to do so shares in the misdeeds of his household; whoever has the opportunity to protest the misdeeds of his city and does not do so shares in the misdeeds of his city; and whoever has the opportunity to protest the misdeeds of the world and does not do so shares in the misdeeds of the world. Said R. Papa: And the household of the Exilarch [the chief of the Jewish community in Babylonia] shares in the misdeeds of the whole world. Thus R. Hanina said: Why is it written: "The Lord will enter into judgment with the elders of the people, and the princes thereof" (Is 3:14). If the princes sinned, how does this involve the elders? We must interpret this to mean that the elders were at fault because they did not reprimand the princes.

Judah sat before Samuel, when a woman came and cried before him, but he paid no attention to her. He said to him: Does not the master agree with the statement: "Whoever shuts his ear to the cry of the poor, he, too, shall cry and shall not be heard" (Prv 21:13)? He replied: Keen scholar, I am your chief who will go unscathed, but the chief of your chief will pay the penalty. There sits Mar Ukva, the head of the court, to whom apply the words: "House of David, thus has the Lord spoken: 'Execute justice in the morning, and deliver the one who has been robbed from the hand of his oppressor, lest My anger go forth like fire and burn with none to quench it, because of their evil deeds' " (Jer 21:12).

Said R. Zera to R. Simon: The master should reprimand the household of the Exilarch. They will not listen to me, he replied. Even though they will not listen, the master should reprimand them, he continued.

54b–55a

■　　WEAPONS AND THE SABBATH　　■

A person should not go out on the Sabbath wearing a sword, a bow, a shield, a lance, or a spear, and if he does he should bring a sin-offering. R. Eliezer said: They are ornaments for him [and are permitted], but the sages hold that they are a disgrace to the one wearing them, for the verse states: "And they shall beat their swords into plowshares, and their spears into pruning hooks; nation shall not lift sword against nation, neither will they learn war any more" (Is 2:4).

MISHNAH 6:4

It was taught: They said to R. Eliezer: If they are merely ornaments, why will they become obsolete in the Messianic age? He replied: Because they will be unnecessary, as it is stated: "Nation will not lift sword against nation." But let them remain only as ornaments? Abbaye stated: It would be as meaningless as holding a candle at noontime. And this stands in contradiction with Samuel, for Samuel stated: The only difference between this age and the messianic age will be the termination of the servitude of exile [of the people of Israel]. Thus it is written: "For the poor will never cease out of the land" (Dt

15:11, implying that arms may still be needed even in the Messianic age]. But these views [about the obsolescence of arms in the Messianic age] support the view of R. Hiyya b. Abba, for R. Hiyya b. Abba stated: All the prophets prophesied concerning the messianic age, but as to the world to come—"no eye has seen it—only you God alone" (Is 64:3). Some said: His colleagues asked R. Eliezer: Since these weapons are ornaments why will they be in disuse in the messianic age? He answered them: Even in the messianic age weapons will not be discontinued. This would agree with the view of Samuel, and it disagrees with R. Hiyya b. Abba.

Abbaye asked R. Dimi and others say R. Avya, but according to another tradition R. Joseph asked R. Dimi and others say R. Abbaye but according to another tradition Abbaye asked R. Joseph: Why does R. Eliezer hold that they are ornaments? Because the verse states: "Gird your sword on your thigh, O mighty one, it is your glory and your majesty" (Ps 45:4). Said R. Kahane to Mar the Son of R. Huna: That verse is to be applied to the mental clashes of scholars in the study of Torah. He replied to him: But a verse cannot be detached from its explicit meaning. Said R. Kahane: By the time I was eighteen years of age I had studied all the six divisions of the Talmud, but I did not know until now that a verse cannot be detached from its plain meaning. What does this convey to us? That a person should continue to study, even though full understanding will not come until later on.

■   PATTERNS OF STUDY   ■

Said R. Jeremiah in the name of R. Eleazar: When two scholars sharpen each other's minds in the study of the law—the Holy One, praised be He, will prosper them as it is written: "And in your majesty prosper" (Ps 45:5)—the word for "majesty," *vahadarkha*, may be read as *va-hiddedkha*,* which means "your sharpening." Moreover, they will rise to greatness, as it says [in the conclusion of the previously quoted phrase]: "prosper, ride forth." But one might assume that this is so even if their studies are not sincerely motivated. Therefore the previously quoted verse continues: "for the sake of truth." One might assume that this is so even if they became conceited

---

*The Hebrew letters for *r* and *d* are almost the same and are often interchanged.

[because of their knowledge]. Therefore does the verse finally add, "and meekness and righteousness. . . ."

Said R. Jeremiah in the name of R. Simon b. Lakish: When two scholars are humble toward each other in the study of the law, the Holy One, praised be He, listens to them, as it is written: "Those who revered the Lord, spoke one with another [nidberu], and the Lord heeded and heard them" (Mal 3:16). The Hebrew word dibbur [from which nidberu derives] suggests lowliness, as is implied in the verse: "He subdued nations under us" [yadber, Ps 47:3]. What is meant by "and for those who thought on His name" [the conclusion in the verse from Malachi: "And it was recorded in a book of remembrance before Him, for those who feared the Lord and thought on His name"]. Said R. Ami: If a person contemplated to carry out a commandment and was prevented from doing so, Scripture ascribes it to him as though he did it. . . .

Said R. Aba in the name of R. Simon b. Lakish: When two scholars form a team (madgilim) [in the absence of a teacher to study the Torah], the Holy One, praised be He, loves them. Thus it is written: "And his banner [diglo, related to madgilim "to form a team"] over me is love" (Sg 2:4). Said Rava, But this applies only when they are familiar with the basics of the subject under study and only when there is no sage in the town from whom they can learn.

Said R. Aba in the name of R. Simeon b. Lakish: The person who extends a loan to the needy is greater than the one who gives charity, and one who associates a poor person with him in business enabling him to earn for himself is greater than all others.

63a

■ GOD OUR FATHER, OUR REDEEMER ■

Rava expounded: Why does the verse begin with "Go now, and let us reason together, says the Lord" (Is 1:18)? It should have been written "Come now' instead of "Go now" [the usual translation is "Come now," but the Hebrew term used, lekhu na, means literally "go now"]. In the hereafter the Holy One, praised be He, will say to the children of Israel: Go to your ancestors, and let them reprove you. And they will say to Him: Sovereign of the universe, to whom shall we go? Shall we go to Abraham, who, after you told him that his children would be afflicted strangers in an alien land for four hundred years (Gn 15:13) did not pray for mercy on our behalf? Shall we go to Isaac, who blessed Esau with dominion (Gn 27:40), and did not pray for us? Shall we go to Jacob, who, after you told him that you will go down with him to Egypt (Gn 46:4), also failed to pray for us? To whom shall we go? The Lord will then say: Since you placed your faith only in me, "if your sins be as scarlet, they shall be white as snow."

Said Samuel b. Nahmani in the name of R. Jonathan: What is the significance of the verse: "For you are our Father, for Abraham does not know us, and Israel [Jacob] does not acknowledge us, you, O Lord are our Father, our Redeemer, from everlasting to everlasting in your name" (Is 63:16)? In the hereafter God will say to Abraham: Your children have sinned against me, and he will answer: Sovereign of the universe, let them be wiped out for the sake of your holy name. He will then say: Let me tell it to Jacob, who suffered raising his own children; perhaps he will pray for mercy on their behalf. He said to him: Your children have sinned. He answered Him: Sovereign of the universe, let them be wiped out for the sake of your holy name. He will then say: There is no sense in the old, nor counsel in the young. He then said the Isaac: Your children have sinned. He replied: Sovereign of the universe, are they my children and not your children? When they said that they will obey even before they said that they will listen you called them "Israel my first-born son" (Ex 4:22).* Now they are my children, not your children! Moreover, how long have they sinned? How long is the lifetime of a person? Seventy years. Subtract twenty for which you do not punish.† There remain only fifty. Subtract twenty-five which comprise the nights that are spent in sleep. Now there remain only twenty-five. Subtract twelve and a half that are spent in prayer, eating, and going to the lavatory. And now there remain only twelve and a half. If you wish to assume responsibility for all, well and good; if not, half be on you and half on me. And if you wish that all be on me, I already offered myself to you as a sacrifice. Then they all began to chant: You are our father. But Isaac will say to

---

*The incident in Exodus 4:22 happened while the Israelites were still in Egypt, while the promise to obey even before they heard the commandments took place at Sinai. Rashi notes this and suggests that God foresaw their response at Sinai and therefore He called them His first-born.

†Rashi notes that according to Numbers 14:29, God did not punish those below the age of twenty.

them: Rather than praising me, praise the Holy One, praised be He, and Isaac will tell them to direct their eyes toward the Holy One, praised be He. At once they will raise their eyes on high and exclaim: "You, O Lord, are our Father, our Redeemer, from everlasting to everlasting is Your name."

89b

■　　THE DESTRUCTION OF JERUSALEM　　■

Abbaye said: Jerusalem was destroyed only because the Sabbath was desecrated there. Thus it is written: "They have disregarded My Sabbath, so that I am profaned among them" (Ez.22:26).

R. Abbahu said: Jerusalem was destroyed because the recitation of the Shema morning and evening was neglected there. Thus it is written: "Woe to them who rise up early in the morning that they may run after strong drink" (Is 5:11); and it is further written: "They have lyre and harp, timbrel and flute and wine at their feasts, but they do not consider the deeds of the Lord" (Is 5:12); and then it is written: "Therefore are My people gone into exile for lack of knowledge" (Is 5:13).

R. Hamenuna said: Jerusalem was destroyed because the education of school children was neglected there. Thus it is written: "Pour out [God's wrath] because of the children in the street" (Jer 6:11). Why pour it out? Because the children are in the street [instead of in school].

Ulla said: Jerusalem was destroyed because her people were not ashamed of one another. Thus it is written: "Were they ashamed when they committed abominations? No, they were not ashamed" [Jer 6:15, and the verse continues with a prediction of their downfall].

R. Isaac said: Jerusalem was destroyed because they failed to distinguish between the great and the ordinary (lit. "and the small"). Thus it is written: "And the people were like priest," and the verse which follows states: "The earth shall be utterly laid waste" (Is 24:2, 3).

R. Amram the son of R. Simeon b. Abba said in the name of R. Simeon b. Abba who said in the name of R. Hanina: Jerusalem was destroyed because her people did not reprimand one another. Thus it is written: "Her princes have become like the deer that find no pasture" (Lam 1:6). Just as with the deer, the head of one is at the tail of the other, so the Israelites of that generation hid their faces in the ground, and did not reprimand one another.

R. Judah said: Jerusalem was destroyed because scholars were despised there: "But they mocked the messengers of God, and despised His word, and scoffed at His prophets, until the wrath of the Lord rose against His people, till there was no remedy" (2 Chr 36:16). What does the phrase "till there was no remedy" suggest? Said R. Judah in the name of Rav: There is no remedy for the affliction of one who despises a scholar. R. Judah in the name of Rav said: What is the meaning of the verse: "Touch not My anointed, do not harm My prophets" (Ps 105:15)? "My anointed" refers to schoolchildren, "prophets" refers to scholars.

Rava said: Jerusalem was destroyed because people of integrity ceased there. Thus it is written: "Run to and fro in the streets of Jerusalem, and look in her public squares; if you can find a man, a person who does justice, and seeks faithfulness, I will pardon her" (Jer 5:1).

118b

■   THE BASIC VIRTUES   ■

R. Yohanan said: Extending hospitality to strangers is as great as attending the academy, for the Mishnah likens making room for guests to removing an impediment in the academy. R. Dima of Nehardea said: It is greater than attending the academy, since the Mishnah mentions making room for guests before referring to the problem of the academy.

R. Judah in the name of Rav said: Extending hospitality to strangers is more important than communion with God [lit. "receiving the *shekinah*"], for it is written: "And he [Abraham] said: My Lord, if I have found favor in your sight do not pass away from your servant" (Gn 18:3).* Said R. Eleazar: Come and see how different the conduct of the Holy One, praised be He, is from that of mortals. In the case of mortals the lesser one will not say to the greater one: Wait for me until I will come, but in the case of the Holy One, praised be He, it is written: "O Lord, if I have found favor in your sight, do not pass away from your servant."

---

*The usual interpretation is that Abraham was addressing the three strangers whom he saw at a distance, but the text here takes it that he was addressing God, who had revealed Himself to him, urging Him to wait while he ran to invite the three strangers to his home.

THE TRACTATE SHABBAT

R. Judah b. Shela said in the name of R. Ashi who said in the name of R. Yohanan: There are six things, the fruit of which a person enjoys in this world, and the principal remains for him in the world to come: Extending hospitality, visiting the sick, devotion in prayer, early attendance at the academy, raising one's children to study the Torah, and judging one's neighbor charitably. But is this really so? Did we not study: These are virtues [lit., "fruits"] a person will enjoy in this world while their principal will remain for him in the world to come: honoring parents, deeds of lovingkindness, promoting peace between a person and his neighbor, but the study of the Torah is the equivalent of them all [since the Torah teaches all virtues]. The implication is only these but not the others. These are also included in the others.

The rabbis taught: He who judges others charitably will himself be judged charitably. It once happened that a man from upper Galilee was employed by a person in the south for three years. On the eve of the Day of Atonement he said to him: Pay me my wages that I might go home and support my wife and children. He replied: I have no money. Then he said to him: Give me produce. He replied: I have none. So the dialogue continued: Then give me land—I have none; then give me cattle—I have none; then give me pillows and bedding—I have none. He put his pack on his back and left for home in a sorrowful disposition.

After the festival the employer took the wages together with three donkeys, one laden with food, another with drink, and one with all sorts of delicacies, and set out for the workman's house. After they ate and drank he paid him his wages. Then he said to him: When you asked me for your wages and I told you that I had no money, what did you suspect me of? He answered: I thought that you might have come across inexpensive merchandise and spent your money on it. And when you asked me to pay you in cattle and I said I had none—what did you suspect me of? He answered: I thought that they might have been hired out to others. And when you asked me to pay you in land and I told you I had none—what did you suspect me of? He replied: I thought it might have been leased to others. And when I told you I had no produce—what did you suspect me of? He answered: I thought that perhaps the tithe had not been contributed from it [and thus it could not as yet be used]. And when I told you that I had no pillows and bedding—what did you suspect me of? He answered: I thought that you might have dedicated all your possessions to the Temple. I swear to you, he exclaimed: This is what happened—I made a vow giving away all my property because my son Hyrcanus would not study the Torah. Afterward when I met my friends in the south, they absolved me of my vow. And as for you—because you judged me charitably, may God also judge you charitably.

127a–127b

■   WORK ON THE SABBATH   ■

One may not hire laborers on the Sabbath or ask his neighbor to hire laborers for him (Mishnah 23:3). But is an action consisting of mere speech forbidden on the Sabbath? R. Hisda and R. Hamenuna both said that one may figure the accounts involving Temple funds on the Sabbath. And R. Eleazar said: One may fix grants for charity on the Sabbath; and R. Jacob b. Idi said in the name of R. Yohanan: One may attend to matters involving the saving of life or the public welfare on the Sabbath and one may go to the synagogue to attend to communal affairs on the Sabbath; and R. Samuel b. Nahmani said in the name of R. Yohanan: One may go to the theater, the circus, or the basilicus [where one met with Roman officials] to attend to communal affairs on the Sabbath; and the school of Menashe taught: One may make arrangements for a child's betrothal on the Sabbath, or for a child's education or to teach him a trade. [The answer is]: The verse specifies that on the Sabbath you are not "to pursue your own business or speak ordinary speech" (Is 58:13)—one's own business may not be transacted on the Sabbath, but one may transact heavenly affairs [one is under a religious commitment to attend to all matters listed above and they are therefore permissible on the Sabbath].

150a

It was taught: Rabban Simeon b. Gamaliel said: For a one-day-old infant [to save its life] one may desecrate the Sabbath, but for David, King of Israel, when dead, one may not desecrate the Sabbath. For a one-day-old infant one may desecrate the Sabbath—the Torah reasoned: Desecrate on his behalf one Sabbath so that he may live to observe many Sabbaths; in the case of David, King of Israel, when dead, one is not to desecrate the Sabbath, because once a person is dead, his opportunity to perform divine commandments has come to an end. This is in accordance with the statement of R. Yohanan: It is written: "Free among the dead" (Ps 88:6)—once a person is dead, he is free of all commandments.

96

THE TRACTATE SHABBAT

■   ON CONFRONTING DEATH   ■

The rabbis taught: "And the spirit will return to God who gave it" (Eccl 12:7)—give it back to Him as He gave it to you, in a state of purity. This may be compared to the case of an earthly king who distributed royal robes to his servants. The wise ones among them folded them up and put them away in a chest, while the fools among them worked in them. After some time the King wanted his robes. The wise ones returned them clean, while the fools returned them soiled. The king was pleased with the wise ones, but he was angry with the fools. Concerning the wise ones he said: Let the robes be returned to the storehouse, and they return to their homes in peace. Concerning the fools he said: Let the robes be given to the laundry, while they be confined in jail. The action of the Holy One, praised be He, is similar. As to the bodies of the righteous He says: "Let them come in peace, let them repose in peace" (Is 57:2), and concerning their souls it says: "The soul of my lord will be bound up in the bond of life with the Lord my God" (1 Sm 25:29). As to the bodies of the wicked He says: "There is no peace for the wicked, says the Lord" (Is 48:22), and as to their souls it says: "And the souls of your enemies He will hurl away, as out of a sling" [a continuation of the verse 1 Sm 25:29].

We learnt elsewhere: R. Eliezer said: Repent one day before you die. His disciples asked R. Eliezer: But does a person know when he will die? He answered them: Then certainly he should repent this day for he may die tomorrow, and thus he will always be in a state of penance. King Solomon, in his wisdom, also advised this: "At all times let your garments be white, and let no oil be wanting on your head" (Eccl 9:8). Said Rabban Yohanan b. Zakkai: This may be compared to the case of a king who invited his servants to a banquet but did not specify the time. The wise ones dressed themselves and sat waiting at the entrance to the palace, saying: In a king's palace nothing is ever missing [we might be called any time], while the fools continued with their work, saying: Can there be a banquet without preparation [giving us plenty of time to prepare]? Suddenly the king invited his servants to come in. The wise ones came before the king properly dressed, while the fools entered with their clothes soiled. The king was happy with the wise ones, but he was angry with the fools. He declared: Let those who are properly dressed for the banquet sit down and eat and drink, while those who are not properly dressed are to stand and look on.

151b–153a

III

The Tractate Yoma

The tractate *Yoma* deals with the Day of Atonement, the title being the Aramaic term for "the Day." In the Tosefta this treatise is actually called Yom ha-Kippurim, *The Day of Atonement*. It consists of eight chapters, the first seven of which discuss the Temple ritual on that day, over which the High Priest presided. The last chapter discusses the personal observance of the Day of Atonement on the part of the individual.

Two dimensions of the observance of the Day of Atonement are dealt with in this tractate: the cultic and the personal. The principal statement about the Day of Atonement in the Bible is in Leviticus 16, and here it is conceived largely as an annual purification of the Temple, the altar, and the people themselves from everyday sins and impurities. The rites of purification were largely cultic, consisting of elaborate ceremonies involving the offering of sacrifices and making confession in the Temple, with the High Priest as the presiding officer. The tractate *Yoma*, in its earlier mishnaic section, discusses the High Priest's role in great detail, the preparatory steps he took to orient himself for the service of the day, the particular vestments he wore in the course of the service, and the precise details of the sacrifices offered.

The last chapter focuses on the personal. In addition to abstaining from work, according to the passage in Leviticus, one was to afflict oneself, which is defined in the Mishnah as abstention from "eating, drinking, washing, anointing, putting on sandals, and marital intercourse" (Mishnah 8:1). The Mishnah goes on to define each, and tells how and to what extent this abstention is to take place. Minors, for example, are excluded from the duty to abstain from food, and so is a person in ill health, because whenever life might be imperiled all laws inhibiting normal behavior, whether it be on the Sabbath or the Day of Atonement, are superseded.

The last theme in the Mishnah focuses on penitence and reconciliation, which are not mentioned in the passage in Leviticus. For sins committed in man's relationship with God penitence is a prerequisite if there is to be full atonement. For sins committed against one's fellowman one must make amends by apologizing or redressing the wrong done, so as to achieve full reconciliation.

As usual, the Gemara elaborates on the detailed provisions of the Mishnah but it is clearly discernible, from the illustrative selections here included, that for the teachers quoted in the Gemara the moral dimension was primary. They stress repeatedly that God is not placated by ritual, and that only righteousness can bring one to His favor. They call for integrity in the service of God, and portray early masters as refusing to repeat traditional praises of God, when they found them contradicted by experience. They advocate the importance of studying Torah, but caution against following this to divert us from the quest for moral perfection. They affirm the sanctity of life, and when life is imperiled they call for ignoring all ritualistic prohibitions such as eating on the Day of Atonement, or working on the Sabbath. Straying from the optimum goal is inevitable from time to time, given the human condition, but this can be redressed through penitence.

The Talmud also touches on some of the historic conditions that tended to reflect adversely on the status of the High Priest during this period. This was the time after the destruction of the Temple, when there had developed a tradition of an individual-centered piety, based on the synagogue, personal prayer, the study of Torah, and the performance of the commandments, in which the vicarious atoning of the Temple rites played no part. The Talmud notes, moreover, that the High Priests, during the Second Temple Period, had declined in moral stature. They were often suspected of sympathizing with the aristocratic Sadducean party. In many cases they had become puppets of the Hasmonean kings and the later Roman occupying power, who made and unmade High Priests at will as it suited their imperial interests, or on the basis of a bribe offered (9b–10a, 18a–19b).

The final Mishnah closes with this statement: Said R. Akiba: How fortunate you are, O children of Israel, before whom is it that you purify yourselves, and who is it who purifies you? It is your Heavenly Father, as it is written: "I will sprinkle clean waters on you,

*and you shall be clean" (Ez 36:25). Again it says: "O Lord, the hope
[mikveh, which also means "a pool of water"] of Israel" (Jer 17:13). As
the mikveh cleanses the unclean, so does the Holy One, praised be He,
cleanse Israel. It is not the mediating efficacy of the Temple rites
presided over by the High Priest that gains cleansing for the individual. He gains it by the moral and spiritual renewal of his life, and he
gains directly through the grace of God.*

■   THE PRIORITY OF RIGHTEOUSNESS   ■

Rabbah b. Bar Hana said in the name of R. Yohanan: What is the
meaning of the verse: "The fear of the Lord prolongs life, but the years
of the wicked will be shortened" (Prv 10:17)? "The fear of the Lord
prolongs life" is illustrated by the first Temple, which survived for four
hundred and ten years, and in which only eighteen High Priests offici-
ated. "But the years of the wicked will be shortened" is illustrated by
the second Temple, which existed for four hundred and twenty years,
and in which more than three hundred High Priests served. Subtract
forty years when Simon the Just served as High Priest and eighty years
when the High Priest Yohanan served, and ten years when Ishmael b.
Phabi served, and some add eleven years when Eleazar b. Harsom
served. Calculate and you will find that of the others, not one of them
served a full year.

Why was the first Temple destroyed? Because of three offenses
which were committed then: idolatry, immorality, and bloodshed. But
why was the second Temple destroyed, considering that they studied
the Torah and kept the commandments and performed acts of lovingkindness? Because groundless hatred was prevalent among the people. This teaches us that the offense of groundless hatred is the equivalent of the three offenses of idolatry, immorality, and bloodshed.

And was there no groundless hatred at the time of the first Temple?
Is it not written: "They are thrust down to the sword with My people,
smite therefore upon your thigh" (Ez 21:17), and R. Eliezer said: This
applies to people who eat and drink together, and then stab each other
with the daggers of their tongue! But that passage speaks only of the
princes of Israel, as is written in the same verse: "Cry and wail, son of
man, for it is upon my people, it is upon all the princes of Israel." We
have also learnt: "Cry and wail, son of man." One might have assumed

that this is directed at all the people. The text therefore specifies: "It is upon all the princes of Israel."

9b–10a

They assigned to him [the High Priest] elders from among the elders of the Beth Din, and they read to him from the rites of the day. They said to him: Sir High Priest, read yourself for you may have forgotten or you may never have studied.

MISHNAH 1:3

It is conceivable that he might have forgotten. But is it conceivable that he might never have studied? Were such persons appointed? Did we not study: "And the priest that is highest among his brothers" (Lv 21:10)—this means he was to excel over his fellow-priests in vigor, in personality, in wisdom, and in financial independence. Others say: If he was devoid of means, his fellow-priests endowed him. This was based on the verse "And the priest that is highest among his brothers," which may be interpreted to mean: Make him excel through his fellow-priests [the Hebrew permits this rendering]. Said R. Joseph: This is no difficulty. The one condition prevailed during the first Temple, the other during the second Temple. Thus R. Ari stated: Martha, the daughter of Boethus, gave King Yannai a *tarkabful* of *denors* [*tarkab* is a measure and *denor* is a coin] to appoint Joshua b. Gamala [her husband] among the High Priests.

18a

They said to him: Sir High Priest, we are representatives of the Beth Din and you are our representative and the representative of the Beth Din. We put you under oath in the name of the One who caused His name to be associated with this House that you will not change anything from the instructions we have given you. He turned aside and wept and they turned aside and wept.

MISHNAH 1:5

He turned aside and wept that they suspected him, and they turned aside and wept that there was occasion to suspect him.

Yerushalmi 1:5 (39a)

Said R. Hiyya b. Ba: The sons of Aaron died on the first of the month Nisan. Why then is their death mentioned on the Day of Atonement? It is to each us that just as the Day of Atonement effects forgiveness for the children of Israel, so does the death of the righteous effect forgiveness for the children of Israel.*

R. Judah b. R. Shalom said: Why does the text mention the death of Aaron in the account of the breaking of the tablets of the law (Dt 10:1–6)? It is to teach us that the death of the righteous is as tragic an event before God as the breaking of the tablets.

Yerushalmi 1:1 (38b)

■   THE ATTRIBUTES OF GOD   ■

R. Joshua b. Levi said: Why were they called the men of the Great Assembly? Because they restored the traditional acclaim of God's majesty. Moses had come and proclaimed: "God, great, mighty and awesome" (Dt 10:17). But Jeremiah came and said: Aliens revel mockingly in His Temple, so where is His awesomeness? He therefore omitted in his acclaim of God the term "awesome" (Jer 32:18). Daniel came and said: Aliens are enslaving His children, so where is His might? He therefore omitted in his acclaim of God the term "mighty" (Dn 9:4). They [the men of the Great Assembly] came and said: On the contrary, this is His might, that He contains His anger and is long-suffering with the wicked. And these are His awesome acts, that were it not for the Holy One, praised be He, how could one single nation [Israel] survive among the nations? But how could the earlier teachers of [Jeremiah and Daniel] undo what had been ordained by Moses? Because they knew that He is a God of truth, they refused to apply to Him attributes that were not truthful [in the liturgy arranged by the men of the Great Assembly God is spoken of as "great, mighty, and awesome"].

■   TORAH AND CHARACTER   ■

The rabbis taught: This is the order of interrogation when the poor, the rich, or a wrongdoer appears before the divine tribunal for

---

*The righteous suffer most when evil is rampant, and their suffering and death stirs people to bethink their way, and to move toward penitence by resisting evil in themselves and in the world.

judgment. The poor person is asked: Why did you not pursue the study of the Torah? If he should say: I was poor, and was preoccupied with earning a livelihood, he is asked: Were you poorer than Hillel? It was told of Hillel the elder that each day he worked and earned a *tropaik* [half a denar]; one half he gave to the guard at the academy, and the other half he spent for his own sustenance and that of his family. One day he did not earn anything, and the guard refused to admit him. He climbed up and sat over an opening in the roof, in order to listen to the words of the living God expounded by Shemaya and Avtalyon. It was reported that this happened on a Friday, during the season of *tevet* [winter], and snow fell on him and covered him. After dawn broke, Shammai said to Avtalyon: Brother, every day this place is light, and now it is dark. Is it perhaps a cloudy day? They looked up and saw the form of a person above the window. They climbed up and found him covered with a layer of snow three cubits thick. They brought him down, bathed and anointed him, and placed him opposite the open fire, and they said: It is proper to violate the Sabbath for the sake of such a person.

When a rich man is asked, Why did you not study the Torah, if he should answer that he was a rich man and busy with his business affairs, they ask him: Were you then more wealthy than R. Eleazar b. Harsom? It was told of R. Eleazar b. Harsom that his father left him an estate of one thousand towns and one thousand ships at sea. But he himself used to put his pack on his back and go from city to city, and from province to province to study the Torah. Once his own servant found him and [not recognizing him] seized him for forced labor. He said to them: Please, leave me alone so that I may go to study the Torah. Their reply was: We swear to you by the life of R. Eleazar b. Harsom that we will not let you go. He paid them a large sum of money that they should free him. He had never seen them before, but he spent day and night studying the Torah.

When a wrongdoer is asked, Why did you not study the Torah, if he should reply that he was of handsome appearance and distracted by his sensual passions, he is asked: Were you more distracted by your sensual passions than the righteous Joseph? It was reported that each day the wife of Potiphar tried to seduce the righteous Joseph with words. The clothes she wore for him in the morning she did not wear in the evening, and what she wore in the evening she did not wear in the morning. She said to him: Yield to me, but his answer was: No. She said to him: I will have you put in jail. He replied: "The Lord releases the imprisoned" (Ps 146:7). She said to him: I will put down your haughtiness. He replied: "The Lord raises up those who are bowed down" (Ps 146:8). She said: I will blind your eyes. He replied: "The Lord opens the eyes of the blind" (Ps 146:8). She offered him a thousand talents of silver to yield to her, to lie with her, to be with her, but he refused to yield to her, to lie with her in this world, to be with her in the world to come.

It thus turns out that Hillel condemns the poor, R. Eleazar b. Harsom the rich, and Joseph the wrongdoers.

35b

"Within and without shall you overlay it" [the ark with gold, Ex 25:11]. Said Rava: A scholar who is not in his inner character as he is in his outer appearance [lit. "in his inside as on his outside"] is not a scholar. Abbaye or, according to some, Rabbah b. Ulla said: Such a person is abominable, for it is written: "Surely one is to be called abominable and corrupt who pursues wickedness as he drinks water" (Jb 15:16).* R. Samuel b. Nahmani said in the name of R. Jonathan: What is the significance of the verse: "Of what use is money in the hand of a fool with which to buy wisdom when he has no sense?" (Prv 17:16). Woe to the enemies of [true] scholars who engage in the study of the Torah but who lack the fear of God (Ex 25:11). R. Yannai proclaimed: Alas for one who has no courtyard but who makes a gate for the courtyard [the Torah is only preparatory to the fear of God].

72b

What type of situation constitutes a "profanation of God's name"? Isaac of the school of Yannai said: If one's reputation causes embarrassment to his colleagues. R. Nahman said: When people are moved to say: May the Lord forgive so and so. Abbaye said: It is explained in the following which we have studied: "And you shall love the Lord your God" (Dt 6:5)—that you inspire love for the name of God. Thus when a person studies Scripture, and Mishnah, and ministers to scholars, and is honest in his business dealings, and speaks gently to people—what do people say of him? How fortunate is his father who taught him Torah, how fortunate is his teacher who taught him Torah. Alas for those who have not studied Torah. So and so studies Torah, and see how noble his ways are, how goodly his actions. Of such a person the

---

*Water is identified with Torah. A person who imbibes Torah and yet is wicked is truly abominable.

verse says:"And He said to me, you are my servant, Israel, through whom I am glorified" (Is 49:3). But when a person studies Scripture, and Mishnah, and ministers to scholars, but is dishonest in business, and does not speak gently with people—what do people say of him? Alas for so and so who studied Torah, alas for his father who taught him Torah, alas for his teacher who taught him Torah. So and so studied Torah, yet see how corrupt his behavior is, and how ugly are his ways. Of such a person the verse says: "These are the people of the Lord, yet they have gone out of His land" (Ez 36:20).

85a

■ THE HIGHEST GOOD IS TO SAVE LIFE ■

If a pregnant woman smelt food on the Day of Atonement [and felt a craving for it], she is to be given food until she feels relieved. A sick person is given food on the advice of experts, and if no experts are present, he is to be fed according to his own wish, until he says, Enough!
MISHNAH 8:5

The rabbis taught: If a pregnant woman smelt the meat of a Temple sacrifice, or of pork [and felt a craving for it], one is to put for her a reed into the broth and place it to her mouth [so that she can suck it]. If she feels relieved, well and good, but if not, she is to be fed the broth itself. If she feels relieved, well and good, but if not, she is to be given the fat meat itself, for nothing must stand in the way of saving a life, except idolatry, incest, and murder.

R. Yannai said: If the sick person says, I need food, and the physician says that he does not need it, we listen to the sick person. What is the reason for this? "The heart knows its own bitterness" (Prv 14:10). But is not this obvious? One might have assumed that the physician is better informed. Hence the lesson. If the physician says, He needs it, but the sick person says that he does not, we listen to the physician. What is the reason for this? Because it is possible that he [the sick person] has been seized by stupor [and does not feel the need of food].

Mar, the son of R. Ashi said: When a sick person says: I need it, even if there should be a hundred experts who say that he does not need it, we listen to him, because it is written: "The heart knows its own bitterness." But we learnt in the Mishnah that if no experts are present

105

he is to be fed according to his own wish. This would argue that it is only when no experts are present that he is fed according to his own wish, but not when experts are present. The statement in the Mishnah is to be understood thus: When do we go according to the experts? When the sick person himself says I do not need it. But if he should say he needs it, we ignore the experts and feed him according to his own wish, because it is written: "The heart knows its own bitterness."

82a–83b

■   THE SABBATH IS MADE FOR MAN   ■

This, too, was stated by R. Mattiah b. Heresh: for one who has a pain in his throat it is permissible to put medicine in his throat on the Sabbath, for there is a possibility that it may endanger life, and whenever there is a possible danger to life, the laws of the Sabbath are superseded.

MISHNAH 8:6

Why was it necessary to add: "And whenever there is a possible danger to life, the laws of the Sabbath are superseded"? R. Judah said in the name of R.: They meant that where there is a danger to life, we suspend the laws of the Sabbath not only on the one Sabbath, but also on another Sabbath. In what kind of situation is this applicable? If it has been estimated that he would need medication for eight days, and the first day is on the Sabbath, it might have been assumed that one ought to wait till the evening so as to avoid violating two Sabbaths; this is therefore added.

We have learnt similarly: One is to warm water for a sick person on the Sabbath, whether to give him a drink or to wash him, and they said: This is not only for the one Sabbath but also for an additional Sabbath. Nor may we say: Let us wait, perhaps he will feel better, but we warm the water for him immediately, because wherever there is a possible peril to human life, we suspend the laws of the Sabbath, and where such a possibility exists we suspend the laws not only on the one Sabbath but also on another Sabbath. And this work is not to be done through gentiles or minors, but by adult Jews.

The rabbis taught: One must attend to the saving of life on the Sabbath, and the more zealous one is in doing so, the more praiseworthy he is; and there is no need to ask the permission of a Beth Din [a juridical body] to do this. What type of situation is meant by this? If one saw a child fall into the sea he is to spread a net and rescue it, and the faster the better, and he need not ask for permission from a Beth Din, even if he is thereby bringing up fish. If he saw a child fall into a pit, he is to dig out a segment of the wall and bring it out even if he is thereby making a step [into the pit]. If he saw the door closing on a child, he is to break it, to get the child out, and the faster the better, even though he thereby makes chips of wood. One is to put out a fire on the Sabbath, and prevent it from spreading, and the faster the better; and there is no need to ask for the permission of a Beth Din, even though he produces coals.

84b

R. Jonathan b. Joseph said: "For it [the Sabbath] is holy to you" (Ex 31:14)—it [the Sabbath] has been entrusted to you, not you to it. R. Simeon b. Menasye said: "And children of Israel shall keep the Sabbath" (Ex 31:16). The Torah said: Disregard for his sake one Sabbath that he may keep many Sabbaths. R. Judah said in the name of Samuel: If I had been there I would have stated something preferable to what they said. "He shall live by them" [the commandments, Lv 18:5]—not that he shall die through them. Said Rava: All others can be refuted except that of Samuel, which is beyond refutation.

85b

■   THE WAYS OF PENITENCE   ■

Said R. Hama b. Hanina: Great is penitence for it brings healing to the world, as it is written: "I will heal their waywardness, I will love them freely" (Hos 14:5). Said R. Levi: Great is penitence for it reaches up to the throne of the divine Presence, as it is written: "Return, O Israel, unto the Lord your God" (Hos 14:2). Said R. Yohanan: Great is penitence for it suspends a negative commandment of the Torah, as it is written: "If a man should divorce his wife, and she leaves him and marries another, shall he return to her again? Will not such a land be greatly polluted? But [God yet says to Israel] though you have played the harlot with many lovers, return to Me, says the Lord" (Jer 3:1). Said R. Yohanan: Great is penitence for it brings closer the redemption, as it is written: "A redeemer will come to Zion, and to those who

107

turn away from transgression in Jacob" (Is 59:20) Why will a redeemer come to Zion? Because of those who turn away from transgression in Jacob.

Said Resh Lakish: Great is penitence for it makes willful wrongs innocent errors, as it is written: "Return, O Israel, unto the Lord your God, because you have stumbled over your wrongdoing [*avonekha*] (Hos 14:2). "Wrongdoing" [*avonekha*] designates a deliberate act, yet the text refers to it as a "stumbling"! But is this correct? Did not Resh Lakish say: Great is penitence because it turns willful wrongs into virtues, as it is written: "And when the wicked turns away from his wickedness, and does what is lawful and right, he shall live through it" (Ez 33:19) [the former wrongs now nourish life]. This is no difficulty. The one statement refers to one who repents out of love, and the other to one who repents out of fear.

R. Samuel b. Nahmani said in the name of R. Jonathan: Great is penitence because it prolongs a person's life, as it is written: "And when the wicked turns from his wickedness . . . he shall live through it" (Ez 33:19).

It has been taught: R. Meir used to say: Great is penitence, because even if one person repents the whole world is forgiven, as it is written: "I shall heal their waywardness, I shall love them freely, for my anger is turned away from him' (Hos 14:5)—it does not say "from them," but "from him."

What do we mean by a penitent? Said R. Judah: If the opportunity to sin presents itself once and then a second time, and he does not yield to it. R. Judah indicated: It means if the opportunity to sin involved the same woman [with whom he had sinned earlier], at the same time and in the same place.

Why does the Mishnah repeat twice: I will sin and repent, I will sin and repent? It is in accordance with the statement of R. Huna in the name of Rav, for R. Huna said in the name of Rav: If a person has committed a transgression once and then repeated it, it has become permissible to him. It has become permissible? But this is unthinkable! What it means is that it has become as though it were permissible.

R. Isaac said: When one has offended another person, even it if is only with words, he must make amends to him, as it is written: "My son, if you have become surety for your neighbor, if you have pledged yourself for another person, if you have been snared by your lips, if you have been trapped by the words of your mouth, do this, my son, and free yourself, for you have come into your neighbor's power—

humble yourself and plead with your neighbor" (Prv 6:1–2). If he has a claim on you of money, open your hand and restore it to him, and if not, send many friends to placate him.

R. Abba had a grievance against R. Jeremiah, who went and sat on the doorstep of R. Abba. The servant came out to empty water, and some drops fell on his head. He said: They have made me like dung, and he applied this verse to himself: "He raises the poor from the dust' (Ps 113:7). R. Abba heard of this and came out to him and said: Now I must placate you, as it is written: "Go, humble yourself, and plead with your neighbor."

85–87a

The Tractate Taanit

The tractate Taanit is part of the Order, or Division, of Moed, which deals with feasts and fasts of the Jewish calendar. The term taanit means a fast and the tractate discusses the special fasts that were proclaimed in a time of drought. The failure of rain to fall in its season was looked on as a divine retribution because of some act or acts or wrongdoing on the part of the people. The fasts, with other tokens of contrition and remorse, together with special prayers, were an effort to win God's favor and to be renewed in his grace.

The people were advised explicitly that the acts of contrition were not efficacious in themselves. To be fully efficacious they had to be followed by penitence, or a change in their way of life. Thus the elders addressed the people as the fast was assumed with these words: Our brethren, Scripture does not say of the people of Nineveh: "And God saw their sackcloth and their fasting," but: "And God saw their works, that they turned from their evil way" (Jon 3:10). In the prophets it is said: "And rend your hearts and not your garments" (Jl 2:13).

While the basic theme of this tractate is the crisis of drought and the penitential response to invoke God's invervention to redress it, many other aspects of the religious life are dealt with as well.

Water, especially in the dry Middle East, is idealized as the most precious element, indispensable to sustain life. It eventually became a metaphor for the Word of God. It is so used in the Bible. In pondering this analogy, the rabbis noted that water tends to leave the heights and settle in the lowlands. This suggested to them an extension of the analogy, that the Word of God, too, the Torah, leaves the haughty mind, and will prosper only in a person of humble disposition. This stimulated a discussion on the larger theme of humility.

The fact that fasts were proclaimed in special crisis situations, such as drought, encouraged some people to assume voluntary fasts to invoke God's favor as in times of personal trouble, or to expiate some wrong for which a person felt guilty, or as an act of general piety. This brought up the general subject of asceticism and its place in religious life. Some rabbis approved it, but the consensus seems to have been opposed to it. The rejection of worldly pleasures, within the limits in which their enjoyment was deemed legitimate, was regarded by many rabbis as an affront to God, who created them for man's benefit.

The drought was a crisis in the community, and this led the rabbis to discuss the general subject of the individual's relationship to the community. Man, they expounded, was not meant to be a loner. He was to see himself as part of his community, to feel identified with it in its troubles, and to contribute to its well-being. The rabbis believed that the world is sustained through the merits of good people, and that disasters came upon it because of wrongdoing prevalent in its midst. This led them to discuss the virtuous life, and this tractate is rich in many episodes telling of the virtuous lives of good people who lived at the time.

The Talmud generally prefers to end its themes on a happy note. Having discussed the sad occasions when the people of Israel were troubled by drought and other mishaps, it finally cites two happy events, the most joyous in the Jewish calendar, when the people celebrated the end of acrimony among the tribes, and when young men and women came out to meet for the purpose of finding a mate, so as to fulfill the divine imperative to marry and contribute to the continuity of life.

■   THE WAY OF HUMILITY   ■

What are we to infer from the verse: "Iron sharpens iron" (Prv 27:17)? It is to teach us that just as iron is sharpened by other iron, so do two scholars sharpen each other's minds when they study the law together.

Rabba b. Bar-Hana said: Why has the Torah been compared to fire, as it is written: "Is not my word like fire, says the Lord?" (Jer

23:29). It is to teach us that just as fire is not kindled of itself, so the words of the Torah do not abide with one who studies alone. This is in accordance with the teaching of R. Yose b. Hanina: What is the meaning of the verse: "A sword upon the loners [*badim*, usually translated as "boasters" but the Hebrew *bad* also means "alone"] and they shall become fools" (Jer 50:36)? It means that scholars who engage in study by themselves destroy themselves. Moreover, they stultify themselves, as the verse says: "And they will become fools." Indeed, they became sinners. Thus the term for "they shall become fools" in the above verse is *noalu* and elsewhere the same term is associated with sinning: "For we have done foolishly [*noalun*] and we have sinned" (Nm 12:11).

R. Nahman b. Isaac said: Why have the teachings of the Torah been likened to a tree [*etz* which also means "wood"]? Thus it is written: "It is a tree of life to those who hold fast to it" (Prv 3:19). It teaches us that just as a small piece of wood can set fire to a big one, so can a lesser scholar sharpen the mind of a great one. The same meaning was conveyed by the statement of R. Hanina: I have learned much from my teachers, and more from my colleagues than from my teachers, but from my disciples I have learned more than from all others.

R. Hanina b. Idi said: Why have the words of the Torah been compared to water? Thus it is written: "Let all who are thirsty go toward the water" (Is 55:1). It teaches us that just as water leaves the heights and descends toward a low place so the Torah will not be retained by a person unless he is of a humble spirit.

R. Oshaya said: Why have the words of the Torah been compared to these three liquids: water, wine, and milk? For it is written: "Let all who are thirsty go toward the water" (Is 55:1), and "Go and buy and eat, go and buy without money and without charge wine and milk" (Is 55:1). It is to teach us that just as these liquids can be kept only in lowly vessels, so the Torah can be retained only by a person who is of a humble spirit.

This was illustrated when the daughter of the emperor said to R. Joshua b. Hananiah: Beautiful wisdom in an ugly vessel! He replied to her: Does not your father keep wine in an earthen vessel? In what other kind of vessel should he keep it? she asked. He said to her: You who are of the elite should keep it in vessels of gold and silver. She went and told her father and he put the wine in vessels of gold and silver, but it became sour. When they reported this to him, he asked his daughter: Who advised you to do this? She said: R. Joshua b. Hananiah. They called him, and [the emperor] asked him: Why did you tell her this? He replied: I spoke to her according to the way she spoke to me. But there are people who are of attractive appearance who are learned! The answer is that if they had been of less attractive appearance there is the likelihood that they would be more learned.

Another interpretation: Just as these three liquids will be rendered unfit for use if they are not watched over, so will the teachings of the Torah be forgotten if neglected.

7a–7b

"And the Lord will smite Israel as a reed is shaken in the water" (1 Kgs 14:15). R. Judah said in the name of Rev: This verse implies a blessing. For R. Samuel b. Nahmani said in the name of R. Jonathan: What is meant by the verse: "Faithful are the wounds of a friend, but the kisses of an enemy are deceitful" (Prv 27:6). The dire forebodings pronounced by [the prophet] Ahijah the Shilonite against Israel were better than the blessing pronounced on them by the wicked Balaam. Ahijah the Shilonite cursed them by comparing them to a reed. He said to the children of Israel: "And the Lord will smite Israel as the reed is shaken in the water"—just as the reed grows by the water, and its stock grows new shoots, and it is sustained by many roots, and even if all the winds come and blow against it, they will not move it from its place, for it sways with the wind, and when the wind subsides the reed resumes its position. Balaam blessed them by comparing them to a cedar, as it is written: "like cedar trees" (Nm 24:6)*—as the cedar does not grow by the water, its stock does not grow new shoots, it does not have many roots, all the winds blowing on it will not move it from its place, but if, however, a south wind should blow at it, it will uproot it and turn it upside down. Moreover, the reed was deemed worthy to be used as a pen with which to write the scroll of the Torah, the Prophets, and the other writings.

The rabbis taught: A person should always be soft like a reed and not unbending like a cedar. Once R. Eleazar b. R. Simeon was coming from his teacher in Migdal Gedar, and he was riding leisurely on his donkey by the riverside, and he was happy and proud of himself because he had studied much Torah. He came upon a man who was

---

*In the Bible the full statement of Balaam is "like cedar trees beside the water," but the phrase "beside the water" is ignored in the homily. Cf. Rashi and Tosefot ad locum and Yalkut Shimeoni on Numbers 24:6. The manuscript edition of the Talmud omits the reference to the Bible and states simply that Balaam compared Israel to a cedar.

particularly homely looking, who extended to him greetings: Peace be upon you, master. He did not return the greeting, but he said: How homely this poor fellow is. Are all the people of your city as homely as you are? He replied: This I do not know, but go and tell the craftsman who made me how homely is the vessel he made. At once he [R. Eleazar] realized that he had sinned. He dismounted from the donkey and prostrated himself before that man and said to him: I humble myself before you, forgive me. He replied: I will not forgive you until you go to the craftsman who made me and tell him how homely is this vessel which he made. He [R. Eleazar] walked behind him until they reached his native city. The people of the city came out to meet him [R. Eleazar], greeting him with the words: Peace on you, our master, our master, our teacher, our teacher. The man said to them: Whom are you calling master, master? They said: The one who is walking behind you. If that one is a master, he exclaimed, then may there not be many like him in Israel. Why, they asked him. He replied: He did thus and so to me. Nevertheless, they pleaded with him, Forgive him, because he is a great man in his knowledge of Torah. For your sake, he said, I will forgive him, provided he will not be in the habit of acting this way again. At once R. Eleazar b. R. Simeon went forth and expounded: A person should always be soft like a reed, and not unbending like a cedar. And this is the reason that the reed was deemed worthy to be used as a pen with which to write a scroll of the Torah, phylacteries, and the Shema that is placed on the doorpost.

20a–20b

■ ON ASCETICISM ■

Samuel said: Whoever takes on himself a fast is a sinner. This is in agreement with the master quoted in the following: R. Eleazar Ha-Kappor Beribbi said: Why does the verse state [of the nazirite]: "And he shall make atonement for him, for he sinned because of the soul" (Nm 6:11). Against what soul did this person sin? It refers to the fast that he afflicted himself by abstaining from wine. If one who afflicts himself by abstaining from wine is called a sinner, how much more so is a person a sinner if he abstains from everything [by fasting]. R. Eleazar said: He [a nazirite] is called holy, for it says: "He shall be holy, he shall let the locks of the hair of his head grow long" (Nm 6:5). If one [a nazirite] who abstains only from wine is called holy, how much more so shall one who abstains from everything [by fasting] be called holy.

But did R. Eleazar say this [that fasting makes a person holy]? Did not R. Eleazar say: A person should always consider that there is a holy component to his physical self. That [the statement calling him holy] refers to one who can bear self-affliction, the other to one who cannot.

Resh Lakish said: One who avoids fasts is called pious, as it is written: "One who does good to himself is a merciful man but one who afflicts his own flesh is cruel" (Prv 11:17). Said R. Sheshet: A young scholar who takes on himself a fast let a dog eat his meal. R. Simeon b. Lakish said: A scholar is not allowed to take on himself a fast because he thereby weakens himself in his heavenly labors.

11a–11b

The rabbis taught: When a city is surrounded by gentiles, or threatened with inundation by a river, or when a ship is tossed about at sea, or when an individual is being pursued by gentiles or robbers, or is overcome by an evil spirit, an individual may, in all such cases, afflict himself by fasting. R. Yose said: An individual may not afflict himself by fasting because he may thereby come to need the help of other people, and they may not act mercifully toward him. Said R. Judah: What is R. Yose's reason? It is based on the verse: "And man became a living being" (Gn 2:7). God says: Keep alive the soul I have given you.

22b

■   THE INDIVIDUAL AND THE COMMUNITY   ■

R. Tanhum b. Hanilai said: Rain does not descend unless the sins of Israel have been forgiven.

R. Hisda said: Rain is withheld because of those who fail to give the tithe and other contributions from their produce.

R. Simeon b. Pazi said: Rain is withheld because of those who slander other people.

R. Sela in the name of R. Hamenuna said: Rain is withheld because of those who are guilty of insolence.

R. Ketina said: Rain is withheld because of those who neglect the study of Torah.

R. Ami said: Rain is withheld because robbery is rampant in the land.

R. Ami also said: Rain descends because of those who persevere in their faith.

R. Yohanan said: Rain is withheld because of those who pledge charity but do not pay.

R. Yohanan further said: Rain may fall for the merit of even one individual.

7b–9a

The rabbis taught: At a time when the people of Israel are in trouble and an individual separates himself from them, the two ministering angels who accompany a person come and place their hands on his head and say: This person who separated himself from the community shall not witness the deliverance of the community.

Elsewhere we learnt: When the community is in trouble, a person should not say: I will go to my home, and eat and drink, and enjoy myself. If he does so, then to him will apply the verse: "And behold joy and gladness, killing oxen and slaying sheep, eating meat and drinking wine, [saying]: Let us eat and drink for tomorrow we die" (Is 22:13). And what does it say after this? "And the Lord of hosts revealed Himself to my ears: 'Surely this iniquity will not be forgiven you till you die' " (Is 22:14).

But a person should identify with the sufferings of the community. Thus we find that Moses our master identified with the suffering of the community, as it is written: "And the hands of Moses were heavy, and they took a stone and placed it under him, and he sat on it" (Ex 17:12). Did not Moses have one pillow or cushion to sit on? But this is what Moses said: Since the people of Israel are suffering I will share their suffering with them.

Whoever identifies himself with the suffering of the community will be deemed worthy to witness the deliverance of the community. And if a person should say: Who will testify against me? The stones in his house, and the beams in his house will testify against him. Thus it is written: "For the stone will cry out from the wall, and the beams from the woodwork will answer to it" (Hb 2:11). In the school of R. Shela it was said: The two ministering angels who accompany a person will testify against him, as it is written: "For He will give His angels charge over you" (Ps 91:11). R. Hidka says: A person's own soul testifies against him, as it is written: "Guard the door of your mouth from her who lies in your bosom" (Mi 7:4) [here interpreted to refer to one's soul]. Some say: The organs of a person's body testify against him, as it is written: "You are my witness, says the Lord" (Is 43:10).

They said: When a person departs to his eternal home, all his actions are unraveled before him, and he is told: You did thus and so, in such and such a place and in such and such a time, and he replies, Yes. He is told to sign and he signs, as it is written: "It will be signed by the hand of every man" (Jb 37:7). Moreover, he will acknowledge the fairness of the judgment, telling them: You have tried me equitably, as it is written: [I will confess my sins] "that you may be justified in Your decree, and be considered right in Your judgment" (Ps 51:6).

11a

On the twenty-eighth day of the month [Adar] the good news reached the Jews that they would no longer be kept from adhering to the Torah. For once a decree had been issued against the Jews, forbidding them to pursue the study of the Torah, or to circumcise their children, and ordering them to desecrate the Sabbath. What did Judah b. Shammah and his colleagues do? They went to take counsel with a Roman matron, whose home was frequented by the leading personalities of Rome. She advised them to stage a demonstration at night. They demonstrated at night, and they cried out: O heavens, are we not all the children of one father, are we not the children of one mother? Why have we been singled out from all nations and tongues that You decree evil decrees against us? Thereupon the decrees were rescinded, and that day was declared a holiday.

18a

R. Yohanan said: All his life that righteous man [Honi] used to be troubled by the verse: "A song of ascent. When the Lord brought back the captives of Zion, we were like in a dream" (Ps 126:1). He wondered: Is it possible for a person to be as though dreaming for seventy years [the duration of the Babylonian exile]? One day he was on a journey and he noticed a man planting a carob tree. He asked him: How long will it take for this tree to bear fruit? Seventy years, the man replied. He then asked him: Are you sure you will be alive in seventy years? The man replied: I found the world ready with previously planted carob trees. As my forefathers planted them for me, I will plant them for my children.

Honi sat down to eat, and he fell asleep. A grotto formed around him and concealed him, and he slept for seventy years. When he awoke he saw a man gathering the fruit of the carob tree. He asked him: Are you the person who planted the carob tree? He replied: I am his grandson. He said to himself: This means that I slept for seventy years! He noted that his donkey had given birth to several generations of mules. He went to his home and asked: Is the son of Honi Ha-Maagol alive? They told him: The son is not, but his grandson is. He then announced: I am Honi Ha-Maagol, but they did not believe him. He went to the academy and he heard the scholars say: The tradition is as clear as it would have been in the days of Honi Ha-Maagol, for when he entered the academy he would resolve for the scholars any difficulty that confronted them. He said to them: I am he, but they did not believe him, and they did not show him the proper deference due him. He became depressed and he prayed that he might die, and he died. Said Rava: This illustrates the popular saying: Either fellowship or death.

23a

■   THE VIRTUOUS LIFE   ■

Rava said to Rafram b. Papa: Tell us of some of the good deeds R. Huna was accustomed to do. He replied to him: Of his childhood I have no recollection, but of his old age I do. On a cloudy day [when winds were blowing] they used to take him out in a gilded carriage and he inspected the whole town, and wherever there was an unsafe wall he would demolish it. If the owner had the means he would rebuild it, but if not, then he would rebuild it with his own funds. On the day prior to the Sabbath he used to send his emissary to the market, who purchased any vegetables the farmers had left unsold, and he threw them into the river. But why did he not give them to the poor? He did not, because he was afraid that they might at times depend on him and not purchase any for themselves. But he could have given it as fodder for the animals. He did not, because he held that what is used as food for a person is not given as fodder for animals. But why did he purchase them at all? He was afraid that this would discourage the farmers from bringing their vegetables to the market in the future. Whenever he came upon some [new] medicine, he would fill a container with it and put it outside his house, saying: Let all who need it come and take of it. Some say that he was knowledgeable of the disease which afflicts people with unclean hands, and he would put out a pitcher of water and announce: Whoever needs it let him come [and wash his hands] so that he not endanger his life. When he ate he would open the door and announce: Whoever is in need let him come and eat. Rava said: All other acts I could emulate except the last, because there are too many needy people in Mehoza.

20b–21a

A message of peace was proclaimed in the heavenly academy for Abba the physician each day, for Abbaye each Sabbath eve, and for Rava on the eve of every Day of Atonement. Abbaye was disturbed because of the preference shown Abba the physician. People said to him: You cannot do what he does. And what was the special merit of Abba the physician? Whenever he examined patients he separated men from women, and he had a special cloak which he put on a woman so that he could insert the instrument without looking at her body. He also had a place hidden from public view in which patients deposited the fees that he charged. Those who could afford it deposited their fees there, and those who could not were not embarrassed. When a young scholar came to him he would not accept a fee. If he encountered a needy person he would give him some money and say to him: Go and regain your strength.

The sages sent an emissary [to R. Adda b. Ahavah] and they asked him: What virtuous practices do you pursue? He replied: No one ever preceded me to the synagogue, and I never left while anyone was still there. I never paced four cubits without meditating on some subject of Torah, but I never contemplated a subject of Torah when I found myself in a dirty alley. I did not have regular hours for sleep [giving priority to the claims of various responsibilities], and I did not disturb my colleagues by walking among them during a session in the academy [when they were usually seated on the floor], and I did not inconvenience my colleagues by entering or leaving a session in the academy. I never used a nickname in referring to a colleague, and I did not rejoice in a mishap which occurred to a colleague. I never went to bed still bearing ill-will toward a colleague. I never came near a person who was indebted to me in the marketplace [not to embarrass him], and I never became impatient with any member of my household.

Yerushalmi 3:11 (67a)

R. Beroka Hazaah used to frequent the market of Be Lapat, where Elijah often appeared to him. Once he asked him: Is there any one in this market who is worthy of a share in the world to come? He [Elijah] replied: No. While they were talking, two men passed by and he said: These two are due for a share in the world to come. He [R. Beroka] approached them and asked: What is your occupation? They replied: We are merrymakers. When people are sad we cheer them up, and when we see two people who have quarreled we try to make peace between them.

22a

R. Hiyya b. Luliana expounded: What is the significance of the verse: "The righteous shall flourish like a palm tree, he shall grow tall like a cedar in Lebanon" (Ps 92:13)? Since it mentions a palm tree, why does it add "a cedar," and if it compared him to a cedar why does it add "a palm tree"? But if it only mentions a palm tree without mentioning a cedar I might have thought that just as the trunk of the palm tree does not grow new shoots once it is cut down, so the righteous, God forbid, will have no continuity when his life is terminated. It is for this reason that it mentions a cedar. Had it mentioned a cedar and not a palm tree I might have thought that just as a cedar does not bear fruit, so the righteous do not bear fruit [keeping their righteousness to themselves]. It is for this reason that it also mentions a palm tree.

25a–25b

■   DAYS OF CELEBRATION   ■

Said Rabban Simeon b. Gamaliel: There were no happier days in Israel than the fifteenth of Av and the Day of Atonement. On those days the daughters of Israel came out dressed in white, all in borrowed robes in order not to embarrass those who did not possess any. All those robes were cleansed by immersion in water. And the daughters of Israel danced in the vineyards. And this is what they called out: Young man, consider when you choose for yourself. Don't set your eyes on beauty, set your eyes on a good family. "Charm is deceitful and beauty is vain, a woman who fears the Lord—she is to be praised" (Prv 31:30); and it is further written: "Give her of the fruit of her hands, and let her work praise her in the gates" (Prv 31:31).

MISHNAH 4:7

We understand why the Day of Atonement was a happy day. It was a day of atonement and forgiveness, and on that day were the second tablets with the Ten Commandments given to the children of Israel. But what made the fifteenth of Adar a happy day? Said R. Judah in the name of Samuel: On that day were the tribes of Israel allowed to intermarry.* How was this permission justified? An inference was drawn from the verse: "This is what God commanded concerning the daughters of Zelaphhad" (Nm 36:6)—this rule shall prevail only in that generation.

Rabbah b. Bar-Hanna said: On that day the members of the tribe of Benjamin were allowed to intermarry with members of the others tribes. The ban against intermarriage with the tribe of Benjamin [after a brief civil war between that tribe and the rest of Israel] is recorded in the verse: "And the men of Israel took an oath in Mizpah, saying: None of us shall give his daughter in marriage [to the men of] Benjamin" (Jgs 21:1). How was this permission justified? An inference was drawn from the verse: "None of us"—but not our children.

R. Idi b. Avin said in the name of R. Joseph: This was the day when the last of the generations that perished in the wilderness died. Ulla said: This was the day when King Hoshea ben Ellah abolished the guards stationed by Jeremboam ben Nevat to prevent the Israelites from going on a pilgrimage to Jerusalem, proclaiming that whoever wished to go was free to do so.

R. Matthna said: On that day those who died in the battle of Bethan [against the Romans] were permitted to be buried.

On those days the daughters of Israel came out and danced in the vineyards.

It was taught: Whoever was without a wife went there.

The rabbis taught: The beautiful ones among them called out: Set your eyes on beauty, for the precious attribute in a woman is beauty. Those who came from a distinguished family called out: Set your eyes on a good family, for the noblest attribute of a woman is to raise a family. The homely ones said: Make your selection to serve God and enhance us with adornments.

30b–31a

---

*When a man died leaving only daughters they inherited his property, but in order not to alienate it from his tribe they were to marry only men from their own tribe, for the property of the wife normally became the property of the husband. The ruling was made after the daughters of Zelaphhad, who had no brothers, were allowed to inherit their fathers' property. The case is discussed in Numbers 36.

V

The Tractate Hagigah

The tractate Hagigah belongs to the Order of Moed, which deals with the fasts and feasts in the Jewish calendar year. The term Hagigah means "festive offerings." It refers to the peace-offerings brought to the Temple by the pilgrims during the three pilgrimage festivals: Pesah, Shavuot, and Sukkot. The place of this tractate in the Order of Moed varies with the different editions of the Talmud. It comes last in the standard edition, from which our selections are drawn.

The primary theme of this tractate is to define the regulations to be observed by the pilgrims as they go on the pilgrimage to Jerusalem on the three festivals, but it diverges to consider some more general problems involved in man's quest for nearness to God.

The selections from this tractate included here reflect the more general subject of the quest for nearness to God. The first category, A Report from the Academy, is a discussion that took place during a visit by two scholars to their teacher during a festival, and the subject they reported on was initiated by a homily based on a verse dealing with a pilgrimage festival. The second category, The Costs of Wrongdoing, takes as its point of departure the love God showed Israel by desiring their presence at the Temple on the pilgrimage festivals, which is contrasted with the various expressions of His displeasure in them because of their wrongdoing. The last category, The Fate of an Apostate, tells of efforts to seek closeness to God through various forms of esoteric speculation, and the perils to which those "seekers" have often been exposed. Various episodes are recorded in the Talmud about the tragic fate of one such seeker, Elisha b. Avuyah. He had been one of the foremost rabbinic Sages and later became an apostate. Thereafter *he was no longer called by his real name, but came to be known as "Aher," "another."*

The tractate devotes the last chapter to a technical discussion of various aspects of ritual purity that applied primarily to those who came into the precincts of the Temple area.

■　　A REPORT FROM THE ACADEMY　　■

The rabbis taught: It once happened that R. Yohanan b. Beroka and R. Eleazar b. Hisma went to visit R. Joshua in Pekiin. He said to them: What new teaching was expounded in the academy today? They answered him: We are your disciples and from your water we drink [we go by the teachings which you impart to us]. Said he to them: "Nevertheless, it cannot be that a session of the academy should be devoid of some new teaching. Whose Sabbath was it?" "It was the Sabbath of R. Eleazar b. Azariah." "What was the subject of the discourse today?" They replied: It was the chapter which calls for a public reading of the Torah at the end of the sabbatical year, before the festival of Sukkot (Dt 31:10–12). And what point did he make? He expounded: "Assemble the people, the men, the women, and the children." If men came to learn, the women came to listen, but why did the children come? It was to bestow a reward to those who brought them. He said to them: You possessed a precious jewel, and you wanted to deprive me of it.* This, too, he expounded: "You have this day acknowledged the Lord, and the Lord acknowledged you this day" (Dt 26:17–18). The Holy One, praised be He, said to Israel: You have made me the unique object of your love, and I will make you the unique object of my love. You made me the unique object of your love, as it is written: "Hear, O Israel, the Lord is our God, the Lord is one" (Dt 6:4). And I will make you the unique object of my love, as it is written: "And who is like your people Israel, a unique nation on the earth" (1 Chr 17:21).

He further expounded: "The words of Sages are like goads, and like nails firmly planted are [the teachings of] the masters of assem-

---

*The implication here is that women were not to study Torah. The same passage is quoted in the Palestinian Talmud but here there is the additional note that this view disagrees with that of Ben Azzai, who ruled that a woman is also under the obligation to study Torah (1:1, 75d).

blies, all were given by one shepherd" (Eccl 12:11). Why are the words of Torah compared to goads? It is to teach us that just as the goad directs the cow [which ploughs] along the furrow, thereby to grow the produce that sustains life, so words of Torah direct those who study it from the paths that lead to death to the paths that lead to life. It might be assumed that just as the goad is without a fixed position so the words of Torah are without a fixed position; the text therefore uses another metaphor—"like nails." But lest it be assumed that just as a nail effects a reduction [it makes a hole in the surface] rather than an increase, so do words of Torah limit rather than enhance, the text therefore uses the term planted." As a plant bears fruit and multiplies, so do words of Torah bear fruit and multiply. The "masters of assemblies" are the scholars who meet in many assemblies and pursue Torah. Some pronounce unclean, and some clean, some forbid and some permit, some invalidate and some validate. But lest a person complain, In this case how can I study the Torah, the text therefore adds: "All were given by one shepherd." One God gave them, one master conveyed them from the Lord of all creation, praised be He, as it is written: "And God spoke all these words" (Ex 20:1). You, too, make your ear like a hopper, and cultivate an understanding heart, to comprehend the views of those who declare unclean and those who declare clean, of those who forbid and those who permit, of those who invalidate and those who validate.

He [R. Joshua] reacted with these words: It is not an orphaned generation which has R. Eleazar b. Azariah in its midst.

3a–3b

■   THE COSTS OF WRONGDOING   ■

When R. Huna came to this verse he wept: "Three times a year shall all your males be seen before the Lord your God" (Ex 23:17). A servant whose master looks forward to see him should become alienated from him? Thus it is written: "When you come to appear before Me, who asked this of you, to trample my court?" (Is 1:12).

When R. Huna came to this verse he cried: "And you shall sacrifice peace offerings and eat there" (Dt 27:7). A servant whose master looks forward to eating at his table* should become alienated from

---

*This is of course a metaphor for the acceptance of the offerings presented on the altar.

him? Thus it is written: "To what purpose are the many sacrifices you bring to me, says the Lord" (Is 1:11).

When R. Eleazar came to this verse he cried: "And his [Joseph's] brothers could not answer him because they were in panic before him" (Gn 45:3). If the reproof of a mortal can have such effect, how much more so the reproof of the Holy One, praised be He. . . .

When R. Ami came to this verse he cried: "Seek righteousness, seek humility, perhaps you will be spared in the day of the Lord's anger" (Zep 2:3). So much, and only "perhaps"?

When R. Ashi came to this verse he cried: "Hate evil and love good and establish justice in the city [lit. in the gate], perhaps the Lord, the God of hosts, will show mercy to the remnant of Joseph" (Am 5:15). So much, and only "perhaps"? . . .

When R. Yohanan came to this verse he cried: "And I will draw near you in judgment, I will be a swift witness against the sorcerers, and adulterers and against those who swear falsely, and those who oppress the hireling in his wages" (Mal 3:5). A servant whose master draws near to judge him, and hastens to testify against him—what redress is there for him? . . .

Said Resh Lakish: Whoever subverts the cause of a proselyte, it is as if he subverted the cause of heaven. Thus the above verse continues to specify: "and those who turn aside the stranger" [ger, which in talmudic usage means a proselyte]. The word for "who turn aside," the Hebrew mate, may be read mati, which means "who turn Me aside."

Said R. Hanina b. Papa: Whoever commits an act of wrongdoing and regrets it, he is at once forgiven, as it is written [in the conclusion of the verse from Malachi]: "And they do not fear Me." This suggests that if they did fear God they would be forgiven at once. . . .

What is the meaning of the phrase "whether good or evil" [in Eccl 12:1: "For God will bring every action to judgment . . . whether good or evil]? The scholars of the school of R. Yannai said: This is illustrated by one who gives charity to a poor person but does so in public view. Thus R. Yannai once saw someone give a zuz to a poor person in public and said to him: It would have been better if you had not given him than giving him in a way which put him to shame. Scholars of the school of R. Shela said: This is illustrated by one who gives charity to a woman in secrecy because he brings her under suspicion . . . .

The rabbis taught: These three the Holy One, praised be He, weeps over every day: One who can study the Torah, but does not; one who cannot study the Torah, yet he does; and a leader who acts haughtily toward the community.

4b–5b

■   THE FATE OF AN APOSTATE   ■

The story of Creation should not be expounded before two persons, nor the chapter on the chariot* before one person, unless he is a Sage, and has an independent understanding of the subject. Whoever ponders on four themes, it would have been better for him if he had not come into the world; what is beyond [the heavenly realm], and what is beyond [the earthly], what was before [Creation], and what will come after [it is ended].

MISHNAH 2:1

Four Sages entered the garden (*pardes*) [of esoteric speculation]. One peeked and died, one gazed and was afflicted [mentally], one gazed and cut the shoots,† one entered in peace and left in peace. Ben Azzai gazed and was afflicted. Concerning him it is written: "If you have found honey, eat only what is enough for you" (Prv 25:16). Ben Zoma gazed and died. Concerning him it is written: "Grievous in the sight of the Lord is the death of His faithful" (Ps 116:15). Aher cut down the plants. Who was Aher? It was Elisha b. Avuyah, who used to kill the zeal of young scholars in the study of the Torah. It was said of him that whenever he was shown a student who excelled in the study of the Torah, he used to kill it in him. When he came into the academy and saw students sitting before a teacher, he would say: What are they doing here? This one should be a mason, this one should be a carpenter, this one should be a fisherman, this one should be a tailor. When they heard this they left their studies and departed. Concerning him the verse says: "Let not your mouth lead you to sin" (Eccl 5:5), because he destroyed his own handiwork.

---

*The "chariot" refers to Ezekiel 1, which depicts God as sitting on a celestial chariot, which is borne by angels in all directions.

†To "cut the shoots" as used here means either that he rejected the teachings of religion or that he dissuaded young students from studying the Torah. Another tradition is that Elisha lost his faith because he witnessed the suffering of the innocent and the martyrdom of the Sages during the Roman war against Judea.

After some time Elisha took sick. They came and told R. Meir: Your teacher is sick. He came to visit him, and found him in a state of illness. He said to him: Aren't you going to repent? He replied: In this state will a penitent be accepted? He [R. Meir] replied: Is it not written: "You turn man back to dust, and say: Return, you children of man" (Ps 90:3)? Until the soul is brought to its lowest point, it is welcomed back. At that point Elisha cried, and he died. R. Meir was happy at heart, saying: It appears that my master died in a state of penitence.

R. Levi said: It is written: "It is the glory of God to conceal things, and the glory of kings to search things out" (Prv 25:2). "It is the glory of God to conceal things"—this refers to what was before Creation; "it is the glory of kings to search things out"—this refers to things as they are since creation.

Yerushalmi 2:1 (77b–77c)

After he became an apostate, Aher asked R. Meir: What is the meaning of the verse: "Gold and glass cannot equal it, nor can it be exchanged for jewels of fine gold" (Jb 28:17)? He answered him: This refers to the teachings of the Torah, which are difficult to acquire, like vessels of gold, and like jewels of fine gold, but which may perish as a vessel of glass. He [Aher] said to him: But your teacher R. Akiba did not interpret it as you did, but thus: Just as vessels of gold and glass can be repaired even if they are broken, so may a scholar who has lapsed into wrongdoing change his ways. He [R. Meir] said to him: Then you, too, come back. He replied: I have heard from the other side of the Curtain:* Return you wayward children—except Aher.

The rabbis taught: It once happened that Aher rode horseback on a Sabbath, and R. Meir followed him, to learn Torah from his lips. He [Aher] said to him: Meir, go back, I have assessed from the pace of the horse's movement that we have reached the limit of the zone permissible for walking on the Sabbath. R. Meir said to him: You, too, come back. He replied: Have I not already told you that I heard from the other side of the Curtain: Come back you wayward children—except Aher.

R. Meir persisted and he brought him to a schoolhouse. Aher said to a child: Recite for me the verse you studied. The child recited for him: "There is no peace, says the Lord, for the wicked" (Is 48:22). He

---

*An esoteric term to differentiate the earthly from the heavenly realm.

brought him to another schoolhouse, and he again said to a child: Recite for me the verse you studied. He recited for him: "If you wash yourself with nitre, and use much soap—your sin is marked before me, says the Lord God" (Jer 2:22). He took him to yet another schoolhouse and he said to a child: Recite for me the verse you studied, and the child recited: "And you, O desolate one, what do you accomplish by dressing in scarlet that you adorn yourself with ornaments of gold, that you put paint on your eyes? In vain you beautify yourself" (Jer 4:30). He took him to another schoolhouse, until he had taken him to thirteen schoolhouses, and in all of them the verses quoted were similar. When he asked the last one to recite his verse, he said: And to the wicked [lerasha] God said: "What business have you to declare my statutes!" (Ps 50:16). That child was a stutterer, and it sounded as though he said: "And to Elisha God said . . ." Some say that he [Elisha] had a knife with him, and he cut him (the child) up and sent the pieces to each of the thirteen schools, but others say that he [Elisha] declared: If I had a knife with me I would cut him to pieces!

When Aher died, they said [in the heavenly chambers], Let us not bring him to judgment, nor let him have a share in the world to come. Let us not bring him to judgment because he studied the Torah, but let him not have a share in the world to come because he sinned. Said R. Meir: It would be better if he were brought to judgment so that he might in the end come to possess a share in the world to come. When I die [I shall intercede to have him judged and] smoke will rise from his grave. When R. Meir died, smoke did rise from Aher's grave. Said R. Yohanan: Some accomplishment, to have his master subjected to burning! There was one among us who went astray, and we could not save him! If I had taken him in hand, who would have snatched him from me? When I die, I will extinguish the fire from his grave. When R. Yohanan died the smoke from Aher's grave came to an end. The one who eulogized him [R. Yohanan] said: Even the keeper of hell's gate could not prevail against you, master!

The daughter of Aher came to Rabbi [Judah the Prince], and said to him: Master, support me. He said to her: Whose daughter are you? She answered him: I am Aher's daughter. He said to her: Are there still of his seed in the world? Does not the verse say: [The wicked will have] "neither son, nor grandson among his people, nor any survivor where he once resided" (Jb 18:19)? She said to him: Remember his Torah; do not remember his actions. At once a fire descended and it surrounded Rabbi's [Rabbi Judah's] bench. Rabbi [R. Judah] wept and said: If it be so with those who disgrace themselves through it [the Torah], how much more so with those who honor themselves through it.

But how could R. Meir study Torah from Aher? Did not Rabba b. Bar Hana say in the name of R. Yohanan: What is meant by the verse: "For the lips of the priest shall preserve knowledge, and they shall seek instruction [Torah] from his mouth, for he is a messenger of the Lord of hosts" (Mal 2:7)? If the teacher is like a messenger of the Lord of hosts, they should seek instruction from his mouth, but if he is not, they should not seek instruction from his mouth. Said Resh Lakish, R. Meir found his justification by expounding a verse: "Incline your ear, and listen to the words of the wise, and apply your heart to my teaching" (Prv 22:17). It does not say "to their teaching," but "to my teaching." R. Hanina said: He inferred his justification from this verse: "Listen, O daughter, and see, incline your ear, forget your people and your father's house" (Ps 45:11) [listen and learn, but ignore the actions of the one who teaches you]. But the verses contradict each other [the verse from Malachi bans studying from an unworthy teacher]. There is no contradiction. The verse forbidding studying from an unworthy teacher refers to a child, the verse which permits it applies to an adult. R. Dimi reported that in Palestine they explained it thus: R. Meir found a date, he ate the inside and threw away the peel.

Rava expounded: What are we to infer from the verse: "I went down to the nut garden, to look at the blossoms of the valley" (Sg 6:11)? Why have scholars been compared to a nut? It is to teach us: As the nut may be soiled with mud and filth, yet the kernel on the inside does not become spoiled, so a scholar, even if he goes astray, the Torah he has acquired has not become spoiled. Rabbah b. Shela encountered the prophet Elijah and he asked him: What is the Holy One, praised be He, doing? He answered him: He is quoting the teachings of all the Sages, but not those of R. Meir. He said to him: But why not? He answered: It is because he studied under Aher. He protested: But R. Meir found a pomegranate, he ate the inside and discarded the shell. He [Elijah] replied: Just now he is quoting: My son Meir says: When a person suffers, what does the Holy One, praised be He, say? "I feel a heaviness in my head, in my arm" [an idiom for "I grieve"]. If God is so troubled when the blood of the wicked has been shed, how much so is He troubled when the blood of the innocent has been shed.

15a–15b

VI

The Tractate Yebamot

The tractate Yebamot is the first in the Order of Nashim, which means "women," and which deals with laws relating to marriage and the family. Yebamot is derived from the Hebrew word yabam, which means a man who is under obligation to marry his deceased brother's wife if he died childless. Such a marriage is known as a levirate marriage (Dt 25:5–9). The legal material covered in this tractate deals with various rules and regulations governing levirate marriage, as well as with the option open to the surviving brother if he does not want to go through with such a marriage. A ceremony known as "halizah" is specified in the Bible to liberate the surviving brother-in-law from the duty of marrying his brother's widow.

In addition to the laws pertaining to levirate marriage, this tractate also discusses the status of a minor girl who was given in marriage by members of her family without her consent, and her right to reject such a marriage. The last two chapters discuss the revision in the customary law requiring two witnesses to establish a legal fact in the case of a woman whose husband has disappeared. The presumption of his death may be established through the testimony of one witness—or of the woman herself. There are altogether sixteen chapters in this tractate, comprising 122 folio pages.

The selections deal, for the most part, with some general statements about marriage and the family, but some other passages that were introduced incidentally in some of the talmudic discussions are included. One of the most significant statements in this tractate is the discussion between R. Meir and his colleagues on the use of birth control during marital intercourse.

130

THE TRACTATE YEBAMOT

A person should not abstain from carrying out the obligation to "be fruitful and multiply" (Gn 1:28) unless he already has two children. The Beit Shammai ruled: This means two sons, and the Beit Hillel ruled: A son and a daughter, because it is written: "Male and female He created them" (Gn 5:2). The duty of procreation applies to a man, but not to a woman. R. Yohanan b. Beroka said: Concerning both it is written: "And God blessed them and said to them: Be fruitful and multiply" (Gn 1:28).

MISHNAH 6:6

This means that if he has children he may abstain from the duty of procreation but he may not abstain from the duty of living with a wife. This supports the view of R. Nahman who reported a ruling in the name of Samuel, that even though a person has many children, he may not remain without a wife, as it is written: "It is not good for a man to be alone" (Gn 2:18). Others held the view that if he had children, he may abstain from the duty of procreation and he may also abstain from the duty of living with a wife. Shall we say that this contradicts what was reported by R. Nahman in the name of Samuel? No. If he has no children, he is to marry a woman capable of having a child, but if he already has children, he may marry a woman who is incapable of having children.

Elsewhere it was taught: R. Nathan said: According to the Beit Shammai, a person satisfies the obligation to "be fruitful and multiply" if he has a son and a daughter, and according to the Beit Hillel if he has a son or a daughter. Said Rava: What is the reason for the view of the Beit Hillel? It is written: "He created it not to be a waste, He formed it to be inhabited" (Is 45:18), and [by having a son or a daughter] he has already contributed to making it a place of habitation.

It was stated: If a person had children while he was an idolator, and was later converted [to Judaism], R. Yohanan said that he has already fulfilled the duty of procreation but Resh Lakish said that he has not fulfilled it, because when a person is converted he is like a born-again child.

The Mishnah does not agree with the view of R. Joshua, for it was taught that R. Joshua stated: If a person married in his youth he is also to marry in his old age; if he had children in his youth, he is also to have children in his old age, for it is written: "Sow your seed in the

131

morning and do not withdraw your hand in the evening, for you do not know which will prosper, this or that, or whether both alike will be good" (Eccl 11:6).

Said R. Tanhum in the name of R. Hanilai: A person who is without a wife is without joy, without blessing, without good. Without joy—as it is written: "You shall rejoice, you and your household" (Dt 14:26); without blessing—as it is written: "That a blessing may rest on your house" (Ez 44:30) ["house" in such a context has generally been interpreted to mean one's wife]; without good—as it is written: "It is not good for a man to be alone" (Gn 2:18). In Palestine they said: He is without Torah, and without protection [from the ravages of life]. Without Torah—as it is written: "In truth, I have no one to help me [a wife], and sound wisdom [Torah] is driven from me" (Jb 6:13); without protection—as it is written: "A woman protects a man" (Jer 31:22). R. b. Ila said: He is without peace—as it is written: "And you shall know that your tent [when presided over by one's wife] is at peace, and you will visit your habitation and you will not sin" (Jb 5:24).

Said R. Joshua b. Levi: A person who knows his wife to be a God-fearing woman and he does not have marital relations with her is a sinner, as it is written: "And you shall visit your habitation [a euphemism for having relations with one's wife] and you will not sin."

The rabbis taught: When one loves his wife as himself, and honors her more than himself, and trains his sons and daughters in the right path and arranges for their marriage at a young age—concerning such a person does the verse say: "And you shall know that your tent is at peace."

Said R. Eleazar: A man without a wife is not a complete man, as it is written: "Male and female created He them, and He called their name *adam*, 'man' " (Gn 5:2).

Turn away your eyes from the charms of another man's wife, lest you be trapped in her net. Do not join in fellowship with her husband, to drink with him wine and strong drink, for through the appearance of a beautiful woman have many been destroyed, and a mighty host are all her slain.

Do not be aggrieved about tomorrow's troubles for you do not know what a day will bring forth. Tomorrow may come, and you may be no more. You will thus have worried about a world that is not yours.

Keep away multitudes from your house, do not bring everyone to your house.

Many are your well-wishers, but disclose your secret only to one in a thousand.

It was taught: R. Eliezer said: A person who does not share in propagating the race is as though he were guilty of bloodshed, for it is written: "Whoever sheds the blood of a person, by man shall his blood be shed" (Gn 9:6), and following this is the verse "and you be fruitful and multiply" (Gn 9:7). R. Jacob said: It is as though he diminished the divine image, for it is written: "For in the image of God He made man" (Gn 9:7). Ben Azzai said: It is as though he shed blood, and diminished the divine image, for after both the reference to bloodshed and the divine we have the admonition: "And you be fruitful and multiply." They said to Ben Azzai [who was unmarried]: Some preach well and practice well, some act well but do not preach well, but you preach well but do not act well. Ben Azzai answered them: What can I do, I am addicted to the study of the Torah. The continuity of the world can be assured through others.

Other Sages say: He causes the divine presence to depart from Israel. Thus it is written: "[I will keep my covenant] to be God to you and to your descendants after you" (Gn 17:7). When there are descendants after you, the divine presence will be with them, but when there are no descendants after you, with whom will the divine presence be? With sticks and stones?

61b–64a

On what does the Mishnah base the exemption of a woman from the duty of procreation? Said R. Ilai in the name of R. Eleazar b. Simeon: On the verse: "Fill the earth and subdue it" (Gn 1:28). It is customary for the man to subdue, and it is not customary for a woman to subdue. On the contrary, the word for "subdue" is written in the plural form. Said R. Nahman b. Isaac: The word for "subdue" is customarily pronounced *vekivshua*, which is plural, but it is written *vekivsha*, which is singular. R. Joseph said: It is based on this verse: "I am God Almighty, be you faithful and multiply." Here it is written *pre ureve*, in the singular, and not in the plural, *pru urevu*.

R. Ilai in the name of R. Eleazar b. Simeon also said: As it is proper for a person to admonish someone who is likely to give heed, it is also proper not to admonish someone who is likely not to give heed. R. Abba said: One is under obligation not to admonish such a person, as it is written: "Do not reprove a scorner, lest he hate you; reprove a wise man and he will love you" (Prv 9:8).

R. Ilai in the name of R. Eleazar b. Simeon also said: It is permissible for a person to deviate from the truth for the sake of peace. Thus it is written: "Your father commanded . . . so shall you say to Joseph, Forgive, I beg you . . ." (Gn 50:16–17).* R. Nathan said: We are commanded to do so. Thus it is written: "And Samuel said: How can I go [to anoint David as king]? If Saul hears of it, he will kill me [and God, in response, told him to say, if questioned, that he came to offer a sacrifice, 1 Sm 16:2].

In the school of R. Ishmael it was taught: Great is peace, because for its sake God Himself misquoted a statement. Initially [when Sarah disbelieved the angel's promise that she would bear a child] the verse quoted her as saying: "And my husband is old" (Gn 18:12), but in the end [when God quoted her statement to Abraham] it is written: "and I am old" (Gn 18:13).†

Judith, the wife of R. Hiyya suffered a great pain at childbirth. She changed her clothes and came before R. Hiyya and asked: Is a woman subject to the duty of procreation? He replied: No. She then went and drank a sterilizing potion. In the end, her action became known. He said: Would that you have borne me one more fruit of the womb.

But is a woman not subject to the duty of procreation? But R. Abba b. R. Ketina reported the case of a woman who was half-slave and half-free, and the rabbis ordered her master to free her.‡ R. Nahman B. Isaac replied: People had been taking liberties with her.

65b–66a

■   FLEXIBILITY IN THE LAW   ■

Abbaye said: The caution against splintering into deviant groups applies only in the case of two courts of law, such as one deciding

---

*There is no record that Jacob left such instructions, but we must assume that Joseph's brothers made this up for the sake of establishing peace in the family.

†In other words, God misquoted so that Abraham might not be offended that his wife thought him too old to father her child.

‡A half-slave and half-free woman could marry neither a slave nor a free person. Her anomalous status developed because she had been owned by two masters, one of whom had liberated her from his share in her servitude. She was to be freed so that she could marry and raise a family.

according to the views of the Beit Shammai and one according to the views of the Beit Hillel, but two courts of law in separate cities would not be subject to this limitation. Rava challenged this. But were not the Shammaites and the Hillelites like two courts of law [and they differed freely from each other in the same locale]? Said Rava: The caution applies in a case of one court in the same city, with half the judges deciding according to the Beit Shammai and the other half according to the Beit Hillel. But in the case of two courts of law in the same city there is no objection.

14a

It was taught: Whoever wants to take upon himself restrictive rules, to follow the restrictive decisions of the Beit Shammai as well as the restrictive decisions of the Beit Hillel—concerning such a person it is written: "The fool walks in darkness" (Eccl 2:14). Whoever follows the lenient decisions of the one school as well as the other is called a wicked person. But one is to follow either the decisions of the Beit Shammai, both those that are lenient and those that are restrictive, or one is to follow the decisions of the Beit Hillel, both those that are lenient and those that are restrictive. This was the position taken before the proclamation of the consensus [*bat kol**] that while both positions are the words of the living God, the law is always to follow the view of the Beit Hillel. Where was this consensus proclaimed? Said R. Bivi in the name of R. Yohanan: The consensus was proclaimed in Yavneh.

Yerushalmi 1:6 (3h)

Said R. Akiba: When I went to Nehandea to ordain a leap year I met Nehemiah of Bett-Deli who said to me: I heard that in Eretz Yisrael the only one who allows a woman to remarry on the testimony of one witness [as to her husband's death] is R. Judah b. Baba. I told him that this was so. He then said to me: Tell them in my name that, because, as they know, the country is in confusion as a result of ravaging troops [and it is difficult to obtain in every case two reliable witnesses], I have the tradition from Rabban Gamaliel the Elder that a woman may be free

---

Bat kol means literally an echo, or a reverberating sound. Sometimes it designates a divine voice, when it was said to replace prophecy after it had lapsed. It is also used to designate a popularly circulated report (see Saul Lieberman, *Hellenism in Jewish Palestine* [New York: The Jewish Theological Seminary of America, 1950], pp. 194–99).

to remarry on the testimony of one witness. When I reported this to Rabban Gamaliel [of Yavneh, his grandson] he rejoiced and said: We have found a supporting colleague for R. Judah b. Baba. This stimulated Rabban Gamaliel's memory and he recalled that some men had been killed in Tel-Arza and Rabban Gamaliel [the Elder] had permitted their wives to remarry on the testimony of one witness. And the law was established permitting a woman to remarry on the testimony of one witness, even if he only quotes a report from another witness, and even if the other witness is a slave, or if it is a woman, or even a bondwoman.

MISHNAH 16:7

    R. Bivi taught in the presence of R. Nahman: Three categories of woman* are to practice birth control by inserting an absorbent during marital intercourse: a minor, a pregnant woman, and a nursing mother. A minor, lest she become pregnant and die; a pregnant woman, lest she cause the fetus to become a *sandal*,† and a nursing mother lest she wean her child prematurely, and this cause his death. And what is a minor? From the age of eleven years and a day to the age of twelve years and a day. One who is over or under this age carries on her marital intercourse in the usual manner. This is the view of R. Meir. But the Sages say: The one as well as the other carries on her marital intercourse in the usual manner, and may heavenly mercy protect them, for the verse states: "The Lord watches over the simple" (Ps 116:6).‡

12b–100b

    It was taught: I might have assumed that the respect due to father and mother supersedes the observance of the Sabbath. The verse therefore states explicitly: "Let every man revere his mother and his father, and you shall keep my Sabbaths" (Lv 19:3). You are all under the obligation of honoring Me."

    It was taught: I might have assumed that if one's father said to him [if he was a priest], Submit to ritual impurity, or, Do not return a lost

---

*According to some interpretations, the types of women listed are obligated to practice birth control; according to others they are allowed to do so.

†This is a technical term for a degeneration of the fetus into a fish-shaped abortion due to superfetation.

‡Those who interpret R. Meir's position as obligatory regard the differing view of the Sages as only directed at the obligation, but they would rule that contraception in such cases is permissible, and some commentators even extend the permissive position as applying to all women, regardless of circumstances.

object to its owner, he is under obligation to listen to him. The verse therefore states explicitly: "Let every man revere his mother and his father, and you shall keep my sabbaths"—you are all under the obligation to honor Me.

5b–6a

■ THE REJECTION OF THE GIBEONITES ■

R. Hana b. Adda said: King David decreed against the admitting of the Nethinim [the Gibeonites]* as members of the Jewish people. Thus it is written: "And the king called the Gibeonites and spoke to them—now the Gibeonites were not of the children of Israel" (2 Sm 21:2). Why did he issue this decree against them? It is written: "There was a famine in the time of David for three consecutive years." The first year he said to the people: Perhaps there are idolators among you, and it is written: "And you will serve other gods and bow down to them and He will restrain the heavens and there will not be any rain" (Dt 11:16–17). They investigated and did not find any. The second year he said: Perhaps there are transgressors among you, and it is written: "The showers have been withheld and there has been no latter rain, you have a harlot's brow and will not blush for shame" (Jer 3:3). They investigated and did not find any. The third year he said: Perhaps there are among you people who pledged to charity but do not redeem their pledges, and it is written: "Like clouds and wind without rain, so is he who boasts of gifts that are not given" (Prv 25:14). They investigated and did not find any. David then said: The matter depends only on me. Immediately he sought the presence of the Lord. What does this mean? Resh Lakish explained: He consulted the Urim and Thumim.[†] How did he know this? He derived it by the analogical use of the word *pene*, "the presence of." Here the verse states: "And David sought the presence (*pene*) of the Lord" (2 Sm 21:1), and a consultation

---

*The term *Nethinim* used in the Talmud corresponds to the Gibeonites mentioned in the Bible. By pretending to come from a distant area, Joshua entered a pact with them, but when it was discovered that they lived in Canaan, in a city near Jerusalem, they were spared, but served as "hewers of wood and drawers of water" in the Temple service. King Saul was harsh with them. They sought absorption into the Jewish people, but, according to the Talmud, their display of vindictiveness finally moved King David to exclude them.

†These were sacred lots worn by the High Priest in his breastplate, and were consulted by him for divine guidance (Ex 28:30).

of the Urim and Thumim is described similarly: "He shall inquire through the Urim and Thumim in the presence of [*lifne*, a derivation from *pene*] the Lord" (Nm 27:21). "And the Lord said: It is because of Saul and his bloody house, because he put to death the Gibeonites" (2 Sm 21:1). "Because of Saul"—because he was not properly mourned for: "and his bloody house—because he put to death the Gibeonites." But where do we find that Saul put to death the Gibeonites? It was because he killed the inhabitants of Nov, the city of the priests who supplied them with food and water; it was regarded as though he had killed them. Justice was demanded *for* Saul because he had not been properly mourned for, and justice was demanded *against* Saul because he killed the Gibeonites! Yes, indeed, for Resh Lakish stated: What is meant by the verse: Seek the Lord, all you humble of the earth, who carried out His judgment" (Zep 2:3). Wherever judgment is carried out against a man, there one is also to mention his virtuous deeds.

David said: As to Saul: It is past twelve months since his death, and it would not be in accordance with custom to mourn for him now. As to the Nethinim [the Gibeonites], let us call them and conciliate them. At once "the king called the Gibeonites and said to them: What shall I do for you, and how can I make amends that you may bless the inheritance of the Lord [the people of Israel]? And the Gibeonites said to him: It is not a matter of silver or gold between us and Saul or his house, neither is it for us to put to death any other man [in Israel] . . . but let seven of his (Saul's) sons be handed over to us, and we will hang them before the Lord" (2 Sm 21:2–4, 6).

He tried to placate them but they would not be placated. He then said: There are three characteristics which distinguish this people (Israel). They are merciful, bashful, and charitable. Merciful—as it is written: "And He will endow you with mercy, and He will be merciful toward you and multiply you" (Dt 13:18); bashful—as it is written: "That the fear of Him may always be before you" (Ex 20:20); charitable—as it is written: [God loved Abraham because] "He would command his children and his household [to practice charity and justice]" (Gn 18:19). Only those who share in these characteristics are worthy of joining this people.*

78b–79a

---

*According to the Bible (2 Sm 21:7), King David readily agreed to the request of the Gibeonites. The Talmud, however, in reinterpreting the story, told of his revulsion at their vindictiveness.

THE TRACTATE YEBAMOT

R. Eleazar went and expounded the law but did not do so in the name of R. Yohanan. R. Yohanan heard about it and was annoyed. R. Ammi and R. Assi said to him: Did it not happen in the synagogue of Tiberias that R. Eleazar and R. Yose became so excited in their argumentation about a door bolt which had a knob at one end that in their anger they tore a scroll of the Torah? Is it conceivable that they tore it? Rather say that it became torn. R. Yose b. Kisma was there at the time and he said: I will be surprised if this synagogue does not become a place of idolatry, and so it was. R. Yohanan was even more annoyed. You compare my annoyance over my disciple to an argument between two colleagues! R. Jacob b. Idi then came in and said: The verse states: "As the Lord commanded Moses His servant, so did Moses command Joshua, and so did Joshua; he left nothing undone of what the Lord commanded Moses" (Jos 11:15). Did Joshua specify after every word that this had been taught him by Moses? But Joshua sat and delivered his discourse without quoting its source, and everyone knew that it was the Torah of Moses. Similarly your disciple R. Eleazar sits and expounds, without mentioning its source, and everyone knows that it is yours. R. Yohanan then said to R. Ammi and R. Assi: Why could you not conciliate like our colleague the son of Idi?

But why was R. Yohanan so annoyed? He acted in the light of a statement by R. Judah in the name of Rav: What is the meaning of the verse: "I shall dwell in your house forever" (Ps 61:5)? The word for "forever," *olamin*, also means "worlds." Is it possible for a person to live in two worlds? But David said before the Holy One, praised be He: Sovereign of the universe, may it be your will that teachings be quoted in my name in this world, for R. Yohanan said in the name of R. Simeon b. Yohai: When a teaching is quoted in the name of a scholar in this world, his lips stir in his grave [he enjoys immortality].

96b–97a

VII

The Tractate Ketubot

Ketubot also belongs to the Order of Nashim or Women, and it contains the discussion of marriage and the various obligations it involves for husband and wife. The term derives from ketav, *which means a written statement, and* ketubah *(plural* ketubot*) refers to the marriage contract a groom gives to his bride at the time of marriage. This sets forth the obligations assumed by the husband for his wife's proper maintenance during the time of their marriage, and it also provides a settlement of a specified sum he is to make to her if he divorces her. The same settlement is to be made to her from his estate if he dies before her.*

There is no explicit provision in the Bible for such a document, but, according to the Talmud, it was instituted by the rabbis to discourage divorce. It was assumed that the sum to be paid as the divorce settlement, a considerable sum at that time, would inhibit the husband from a hasty divorce action. The sum of this settlement was fixed at two hundred zuz *for a virgin, and one hundred for a nonvirgin, but this was only a minimum. Larger sums could be specified, depending on the status of the families involved.*

As is the case in talmudic discussions generally, the rabbis roam freely from theme to theme, but the starting point is always some aspect of marriage and the family. The selections in this section focus on this general theme of the tractate, but they also touch on a number of other subjects—a collection of various ethical admonitions, a number of comments illustrating the true meaning of lovingkindness, and an extended exposition of what is meant by impartiality in the adminis-

THE TRACTATE KETUBOT

tration of justice. The prayers to be recited at a rite of bethrothal and a rite of marriage appear early in the tractate. In ancient times these were separate events, but they have now been joined into the one marriage service. These prayers have become standard at a Jewish marriage.

There are one hundred twelve folio pages in this tractate, divided into thirteen chapters.

■   PRAYERS AT A BETROTHAL AND A MARRIAGE   ■

What prayers are offered at a rite of betrothal? Ravin b. R. Adda and Rabbah b. R. Adda both stated in the name of R. Judah: Be praised, O Lord our God, King of the universe, who have hallowed us with your commandments and have instructed us concerning illicit marriages, and have forbidden us those betrothed to us, but have permitted us those married to us under the wedding canopy by the sacred rite of matrimony. R. Aha the son of Rava concluded this, in the name of R. Judah, with the following: Be praised, O Lord our God, who have hallowed your people Israel with the wedding canopy and the rite of matrimony.

What prayers are offered at a rite of marriage? Said R. Judah: Be praised, O Lord our God, King of the universe, who have created all things for your glory, and who have created man, and who have created man in your own image, after your own likeness, and who have established through him an enduring edifice of life. Be praised, O Lord, Creator of man.

May Zion who has been made barren of her children soon rejoice as her children return joyfully to her. Be praised, O Lord who causes Zion to rejoice at the return of her children.

Bestow abundant joy to this beloved couple as you bestowed joy to the first man and wife in the Garden of Eden. Be praised, O Lord, who bestows joy on the groom and bride.

Be praised, O Lord our God, King of the universe, who have created joy and gladness, a groom and his bride, mirth and exultation, dancing and jubilation, love and harmony, peace and companionship. O Lord our God, may there soon be heard again in the cities of Judah and the streets of Jerusalem, glad and joyous voices, the voices of groom and bride, the jubilant voices of those joined in marriage under the wedding canopy, the voices of young people feasting and singing.

141

Be praised, O Lord our God, who causes the groom to rejoice with his bride.

7b–8a

■   CONSOLING THE MOURNERS   ■

R. Hiyya b. Abba was the Bible teacher of Resh Lakish's child and some say he was his Mishnah teacher. When his [R. Hiyya's] child died, Resh Lakish did not go to see him the first day. The next day he took with him his interpreter, Judah b. Nahmani, and went to console him. He said to him [Judah b. Nahmani]: Rise and say something in honor of the Holy One, praised be He. He commenced and said: God's greatness is spelled out in the multitude of His great work, His might is revealed in His many awesome acts. He calls the departed to continued life. His wonders are beyond comprehension, His miracles are numberless. Be praised, O Lord, who calls the departed to life eternal.

Then he said to him: Rise and say something to comfort the mourners. He commenced and said: Our brethren who are wearied and crushed by this bereavement, set your hearts to consider this: This is the way of life from its very inception. It is the law which has prevailed since the dawn of creation. Many have drunk [from this cup], many will yet drink from it. As the former generations drank from it, so will the latter generations drink from it. Brethren, may He from whom all comfort flows bestow His comfort on you. Praised be He who comforts the mourners.

Then he said to him: Say something in honor of those who came to console the mourners. He commenced and said: Brethren, you practice lovingkindness, you are the children of those who practiced lovingkindness; you keep the covenant of our father Abraham [who practiced lovingkindness], may the Lord who rewards noble deeds reward you according to your kindness. Praised be He who rewards acts of lovingkindness.

Then he said to him: Rise and say something concerning all Israel. He commenced and said: Sovereign of all worlds, redeem and rescue, deliver and help your people Israel from pestilence, from the sword, from plunder, from the blast and from mildew, and from calamities that erupt and descend on our world. May you answer us even before we call. Be praised, O Lord, who wards off the epidemic [the untimely death of the son of Resh Lakish was regarded as an instance of an epidemic].

■   ETHICAL ADMONITIONS   ■

Bar Kapara taught: What inference can we draw from the verse: "You shall have a peg among your implements" (Dt 23:14)? The word for "your implements," *azenekha*, may be read as *aznekha** which means "your ear." This suggests that if a person hears anything unseemly, he should put his finger in his ear. The rabbis taught: One must not expose one's ears to idle talk, for they are the first among the bodily organs to be burnt by it.

5b–6a

The rabbis taught: What does one chant when dancing in honor of a bride? The Beit Shammai say: It depends on what the bride is like; the Beit Hillel say: [One salutes her with the words:] Beautiful and gracious bride. Said the Beit Shammai to the Beit Hillel: If she were lame or blind, are we to chant to her: Beautiful and gracious bride? The Torah admonished us: "Keep away from a false statement" (Ex 23:7)! The Beit Hillel replied to the Beit Shammai: According to your opinion, what if a person made a bad purchase in the market, shall one commend it or disparage it? Certainly one is to commend it. The rabbis inferred from this that a person should always act agreeably toward people.

R. Samuel b. Nahmani said in the name of R. Jonathan: It is permissible to stare at a bride all the seven days after the wedding, so as to arouse her husband's love for her, but the law is not in accordance with this view.

16b–17a

R. Kahane said: One may not keep in one's home a note certifying a loan that it was assumed would be consummated later on, because it is written: "Do not keep in your home what is inequitable" (Jb 11:14).

---

*In a Hebrew text only the consonants are given; the vowels are supplied by the reader as he understands the word.

R. Joshua b. Levi said: One may not keep in one's home a note that has already been paid, because it is written: "Do not keep in your home what is inequitable."

19a–19b

The rabbis taught: A person may write down his testimony on a document, and on the basis of it, give evidence after many years. Said R. Huna: This is so provided he recalls some of the testimony [without the document]. R. Yohanan said: Even if he does not recall any of it by himself. Said Rabbah: One may infer from the position of R. Yohanan that if two people knew evidence and one of them had forgotten it, the other may remind him of it.

The question was raised: What about the litigant—may he remind the witness of the evidence? R. Habiba said: Even the litigant himself may do it. Mar, the son of R. Ashi, said: The litigant himself may not do it. And the law is that the litigant himself may not do it, unless the witness is an educated person. Thus R. Ashi knew evidence in behalf of R. Kahane. The latter asked him: Do you recall this evidence? He answered that he did not. But were not the facts thus and so? he said to him, but he replied that he did not know. In the end R. Ashi recalled it, and he testified on his behalf. He noticed that R. Kahane was surprised and he said to him: Do you think I depended on you? I put my own mind to it, and it came back to me.

20a–20b

Said R. Nahman in the name of Rabbah b. Avuah: The verse states: "You shall love your neighbor as yourself" (Lv 19:18)—this means that [if a criminal is to be executed] you are to choose for him an easy death.

37b

The school of Hezekiah taught: "An eye for an eye" (Ex 21:24)—but not an eye and a life for an eye [if carried out literally, the blinding of the culprit's eye might cause his death, and, hence, only monetary compensation is to be exacted].

38a

R. Nathan said: How do we know that one must not breed a dangerous dog in one's home or that one is not to put up a damaged ladder in one's home? From the verse: "You shall not bring blood guilt on your house" (Dt 22:8).

41b

Said R. Ilai: It was ordained in Usha that if a person wishes to distribute gifts to charity, he is not to distribute more than a fifth [of his possessions]. We have learnt similarly: If one wants to distribute gifts to charity, he is not to distribute more than a fifth [of his possessions], lest he will himself become dependent on the gifts of others. It once happened that a certain person sought to give away more than a fifth to charity and his colleague did not allow him to do it. Who was this? The friend who did not allow him was R. Yeshavev. Others say that the person who wanted to give away more than a fifth was R. Yeshavev, and the friend who did not allow him was R. Akiba.

"Happy are those who keep justice, who act charitably at all times" (Ps 106:3). How is it possible to act charitably at all times? This, our teachers in Yavneh and others say, R. Eliezer explained, is illustrated by a person who maintains his sons and daughters when they are young. R. Samuel b. Nahmani said: This is illustrated by a person who brings up an orphan boy or girl in his home, and arranges for their marriage.

"Wealth and riches is in his home, and his charity endures for all time" (Ps 112:3). R. Huna and R. Hisda offered different interpretations of this text. One said: This is illustrated by one who studied Torah and teaches it to others. The other said: This is illustrated by one who arranges for the writing of the Pentateuch, the Prophets and the other Writings, and lends out the text to others.*

50a

■   BETWEEN HUSBANDS AND WIVES   ■

Why did the rabbis institute that the husband give his wife at the time of their marriage a *ketubah*?† It was done so that it might not be an easy matter for him to divorce her.

39b

---

*Before the advent of printing, books were written in manuscript form and were rare. To lend them to others was the bestowal of a great favor.

†A marriage contract specifying that in the event of a divorce or widowhood, a virgin would receive a settlement from her husband or his estate of two hundred *zuz* and a nonvirgin one hundred *zuz*.

If the husband did not write a *ketubah* for his wife, she has the right to collect two hundred *zuz,* if she was a virgin at the time of the wedding, and one hundred *zuz,* if she was a widow at the time of the wedding, because the rights granted her under the *ketubah* is a condition laid down by the Beth Din.

If he assigned to her a field worth a hundred *zuz* instead of two hundred and did not write that his possessions are surety for her *ketubah,* he is nevertheless liable for the full amount, since this is a condition laid down by the Beth Din. Though they said that one who was married as a virgin is guaranteed under the *ketubah* two hundred *zuz,* and one who was married as a widow one hundred *zuz,* if the husband should wish to add to this sum, even another hundred *zuz,* he may do so.

MISHNAH 4:7, 5:1

Samuel said to R. Judah: Fine scholar that you are, have nothing to do with transfers of inheritance, even from a bad son to a good son, for one never knows what his children will be like.

53a

Is it not obvious that one should be able to increase the sum specified in the *ketubah?* One might have assumed that the rabbis laid down a fixed sum, in order not to embarrass one who cannot afford to do so. It is for this reason that the Mishnah mentions this.

54b

R. Huna b. Hinena tested us with this question: If she wishes to nurse the child, and he tells her not to, we follow her wish, because the pain of not doing so is hers [through the accumulation of milk in her breast]. If he asks her to nurse the child and she does not wish to do so, what is the law? Whenever this is not customary in her family, we go by her wish. But what if it is customary in her family, but not in his? Do we follow the custom in his family or in hers? We resolved it by this consideration: Her marriage is meant to raise her status, not to lower it. Said R. Huna: From what verse may we infer this? From the verse: "And she is married [*beulat,* which may also be read to mean 'she is ascendent'] to her husband" (Gn 20:3), she shares in the higher status of her husband, not in his lower status. R. Eleazar said: We infer it from this verse: "Because she [Eve] was the mother of all living" (Gn 3:20)—she was given to her husband to enjoy life, not to suffer pain.

61a

THE TRACTATE KETUBOT

If a person took a vow not to have marital intercourse with his wife, the Beit Shammai say that he may persevere in this for only two weeks, and the Beit Hillel say only one week.

Students may leave their home for the study of Torah without their wives' permission for only thirty days, but laborers for only one week.

MISHNAH 5:6

R. Akiba was a shepherd in the employ of Kalba Savua. His daughter, who was impressed with his modesty and his noble qualities, said to him: If I married you, would you go to study in the academy? He replied: Yes. They were married secretly, and she sent him to the academy. Her father heard of it, and banished her from his house, and he took a vow that she would not enjoy any benefit from his possessions. He [Akiba] spent twelve years in the academy. When he returned he brought with him twelve thousand disciples. He overheard an old man say to her: How long will you live like a widow? To which she replied: If he listened to me he would spend twelve years more in the academy. He said to himself: I am acting then with her consent. He went and spent twelve more years in the academy. When he returned he brought with him twenty-four thousand disciples. His wife heard of his return and came out to meet him. Her neighbors said to her: Borrow some nice clothes and put them on. But she said: A good man knows the inner essence of a person.* On approaching him, she prostrated herself and kissed his feet. His aides were about to push her aside but he said to them: Leave her alone, what is mine and what is yours are really hers.

Her father heard that a distinguished scholar had come to town, and he said to himself: I will go to him, perhaps he will annul my vow. When he came to him, he [Akiba] said to him: Would you have made your vow if he (the man your daughter married) were a scholar? He replied: If he had known one chapter [of the holy writings], even one law, I would not have taken on myself that vow. He then said to him: I am that man. He prostrated himself and kissed his feet, and gave him half of his possessions.

62b–63a

---

*She quoted Proverbs 12:10: "A righteous man knows the soul of his beast."

THE TRACTATE KETUBOT

The rabbis taught: If an orphan boy and an orphan girl applied for support, the orphan girl is to be granted support first, and then the orphan boy, because it is customary for a man to go begging but not for a woman. If an orphan boy and an orphan girl applied for a marriage grant, the orphan girl is to be given the grant first, and then the orphan boy, because a woman's embarrassment is greater than that of a man.

The rabbis taught: If an orphan applied for assistance to marry, a house is to be rented for him, a bed and all household objects are to be secured for him, and then the marriage is to be arranged for him, for it is written: [You are to give the needy person] "sufficient for his needs, whatever he may need" (Dt 15:8)—"sufficient for his needs" means a house; "whatever" he may need refers to a bed and table, "he may need" refers to a wife. Thus the verse says: [And God said] "I will make for him a helpmate" (Gn 2:18).

The rabbis taught: If a person is without means but refuses to accept charity, he is to be extended help as a loan, but later it is to be given him as a gift. This is the view of R. Meir. But the Sages say: It is to be extended to him as a gift, but later it is to be given him as a loan. As a gift? But he refuses to accept it! Said Rava: The initial approach is to offer it to him as a gift. If he has the means but does not want to maintain himself [and lives like a pauper], he is to be offered help as a gift, but it will later be collected from him. It will be collected from him? But will he then refuse to accept help? Said R. Papa: It will be collected from his estate after his death. R. Simeon says: If he has the means but does not want to maintain himself we have no obligation to help him. If he is without means and does not wish to accept charity, we are to ask him to bring a pledge and accept a loan, so as thereby to lift his spirit.

There was a poor man in the neighborhood of Mar Ukba for whom he was accustomed to deposit four *zuz* each day in the slot underneath his door. One day the poor man said: I will go and see who does me this kindness. That day Mar Ukba was delayed in the academy, and his wife met him and walked home with him. As the poor man noticed them stooping at his door he came out to meet them. They fled, and he stepped into a fireplace from which the fire had just been cleared away. He burnt his feet and his wife said to him: Lift up your feet and put them on mine. He was upset and his wife said to him: I am usually at home, and my beneficence is direct [I give them food they can enjoy immediately and my act is thus of greater merit]. What was the reason for his [Mar Ukba's] behavior? He acted in the light of a statement by Mar Zutra b. Tuvia in the name of Rav, and some say R. Huna b. Bizna in the name of R. Simeon Hasida, and some say R. Yohanan in the name of R. Simeon b. Yahai: Better that a person throw himself into a fiery furnace than put another person to shame in public.

There was a poor man in the neighborhood of Mar Ukba to whom he was accustomed to send four hundred *zuz* on the evening of every Day of Atonement. Once he sent it through his son who came back and said to him: He does not need it. What makes you say this? his father asked. I have seen, he replied, that he is served old wine. Mar Ukba said: He is a person of such delicate taste! He doubled the amount and sent it to him.

When he felt himself nearing death, he asked to be shown the record of his charitable contributions, and he found that the total he had given was seven thousand Sijan *denars*. He exclaimed: My provision for the journey [to meet my Maker] is scanty, and the journey is a distant one, and at once he distributed half his wealth to charity.

But how could he do this? R. Ilai reported that it was ordained in Usha that a person is not to give more than a fifth of his possessions to charity, lest he become dependent on other people! This applies only during a person's lifetime, but at the time of death there is no limit.

67a–67b

R. Yohanan issued a warning: Beware of flies that swarm about a person afflicted with the skin disease *raathan*.* R. Zera refused to sit in the same draft with a person afflicted with this disease. R. Eleazar did not enter into the same tent with such a person. R. Ami and R. Assi would not eat eggs laid in the same alley where such a person walked. But R. Joshua b. Levi mingled with such persons when he studied the Torah, saying: The student of Torah is "a lovely bird and a graceful doe" (Prv 5:19). If it bestows gracefulness on those who study it, it surely will protect them [against the disease]. When he drew near

---

*Raathan has been identified as gonorrhea. It is defined by Jastrow in his *Dictionary of the Talmud* as "a skin disease attended with extreme weakness." The Talmud (77b) lists these as its symptoms: the eyes tear, the nostrils run, spittle flows from the mouth, and flies swarm about the person.

death, the angel of death was told to go and fulfill his every wish. When he came and revealed himself to him, he [R. Joshua b. Levi] said to him: Show me the place to which I am destined to go in the hereafter. He said: Very well. Then he said to him: Give me your sword [he sought to disarm the angel of death], for otherwise you may frighten me on the way. He gave it to him. When they came there the angel lifted him up and showed him the place. The latter jumped and threw himself on the other side of the partition. He [the angel] grabbed his cloak, but R. Joshua swore that he would not go back. Said the Holy One, praised be He, if in his lifetime he had an oath annulled and did not keep it, then he must go back, but if not, he need not return.* The angel then demanded: Return to me my sword, but he refused to return it. A heavenly voice then called out to him: Return it, for it is needed in the world of mortals. The prophet Elijah then welcomed him, proclaiming: Make room for the son of Levi, make room for the son of Levi.

77b

Said R. Jacob b. Aha in the name of R. Lazar: "Do not hide yourself from your own flesh" (Is 58:7). This is applicable to the duty one owes to his divorced wife. R. Yose Ha-Galili's wife used to subject him to much suffering. R. Lazar b. Azariah came to him and said: Master, divorce her, she does not accord you the respect due you. He replied: The settlement on her *ketubah* would be too much for me. I will give you the money for the settlement, and divorce her, he continued. He gave him the money, and he divorced her. She then went and married a police officer. The latter lost his possessions and became blind. She led him begging through all sections of the city. Once she led him through the whole city but no one gave them anything. He asked her: Is there no other alley in the city where we can go? She replied: There is another alley where we did not go but my first husband lives there and I don't have the temerity to go there. He beat her to go there. R. Yose Ha-Galili then passed, and he heard their voices abusing themselves in public. He gave them a house and provided them with food all their life. He did so in consideration of the admonition in the verse: "Do not hide yourself from your own flesh," which he interpreted to apply to one's divorced wife. Nevertheless,

---

*R. Joshua had apparently never failed to keep an oath and so did not have to return.

one might overhear her saying: Was it not better to suffer the pain of my external condition than the pain in my inner self [in being supported by my ex-husband]?

Yerushalmi 11:3 (34b)

For thirteen of the seventeen years that Rabbi [Judah Hanasi] lived in Sephoris he suffered pain in his teeth. During all those years there was no case of a woman dying during childbirth or suffering a miscarriage in all of Eretz Yisroel. What misdeed might have brought on him the pain in his teeth? Once he passed and saw a calf led to the slaughter. It bowed and said to him: Master, save me. But he replied: This is what you were created for. In the end what merit caused his relief? Once he passed and saw some people about to kill a nest of mice, and he said to them: Leave them alone, "His mercies are over all His works" (Ps 145:9).

Yerushalmi 12:3 (35a)

■   IMPARTIAL JUSTICE   ■

R. Judah reported in the name of R. Assi: The judges who try civil cases in Jerusalem used to collect their salaries to the sum of ninety-nine *maneh* from the Temple treasury. If they were not willing, they would receive an increase. If they were not willing—are we dealing with evil [greedy] people? What it means is, if this sum was insufficient to meet their needs, an increase was given them, even if they were disinclined to accept it.

The judge Karna used to accept one *istra* from the man who was due to win the case, and one *istra* from the one due to lose it, and then he would render the decision. But how could he do this? Is it not written: "And you shall not accept a gift" (Ex 23:8)? And even if you say that this refers only where he accepts payment from one litigant, lest he become biased, but since Karna accepted from both he would not be biased, is this permissible? Did we not learn: "And you shall not accept a gift"—What is the point of this verse? If it is to teach us that one is not to acquit the guilty and convict the innocent—this has already been stated: "You shall not pervert justice" (Dt 16:19). But what the Torah teaches us is that one is not to accept a gift even when the intention is to acquit the innocent and convict the guilty. The answer is that the prohibition is meant to cover a case where the gift is given as a bribe, but Karna accepted it as a fee for his professional services.

And is it permissible to accept a fee for one's professional services? Did we not learn: One who accepts a fee for acting as judge, his decisions are invalid. This applies only where he accepts a fee for rendering a decision. Karna accepted a fee for loss of time from his own work. But is a judge permitted to accept a fee for loss of time from his own work? Was it not taught: Contemptible is the judge who accepts a fee for rendering judgment, but his decision remains valid. What kind of fee is referred to here? Is it a fee for acting as judge? In that case how can his decision remain valid? Were we not taught that one who accepts a fee for acting as judge, his decisions are invalid? It must therefore mean a fee for the loss of time from his own work, and yet we are told that such a judge is contemptible! This declaration refers only to where the loss of time from his own work is not obvious. Karna's loss, however, was obvious. He was employed to test wine for its durability by means of smell, and for this he received a fee. This is similar to the case of R. Huna, who, when a case came before him, used to say: Provide me with a man to irrigate my land, and I will try your case.*

Said R. Abbahu: Consider how blinded are the eyes of those who accept graft. When a person has a pain in his eyes, he pays a fee to a physician, and he may be cured, and he may not be cured; and those men accept a bribe, even if it is only a *perutah*, and blind their eyes, as it is written: "A gift blinds the eyes of those who have sight" (Ex 23:8)

The rabbis taught: "A gift blinds the eyes of the wise" (Dt 16:19)—this is certainly the case with fools; "and it perverts the words of the righteous" (ibid.)—this is certainly the case with the wicked. But do fools and the wicked serve as judges? But this is what the verse means: "A gift blinds the eyes of the wise"—even a great Sage who accepts a gift will not depart from this world without succumbing to blindness of the heart; "and it perverts the words of the righteous"— even a person who is righteous in every respect if he accepts a gift will not depart from this world without suffering confusion in judgment.

When R. Dimi came [from Palestine to Babylonia] he reported that R. Nahman b. Kohen had expounded: What is the meaning of the verse: "By justice a king establishes the land but he destroys it by

---

*The office of rabbi as well as judge in those days was not professionalized. As volunteers these men therefore had to cope with the problems mentioned.

accepting gifts" (Prv 29:4)? If a judge is like a king who is not in need of favors from other people, he will establish the land, but if he is like a priest who moves among the threshing floors to collect the priestly offerings—he destroys it.

Said Rava: What is the objection to accepting a gift? Once one has accepted a gift, one is drawn to the giver, and he feels that he is part of him, and no one can see himself as being in the wrong. What is the etymology of the word *shohad*, which means a bribe? *Shehu* [for he is] *had* [one], he becomes one [with the giver].

Said R. Papa: A person should not serve as judge for one whom he loves or for one whom he hates. One cannot see the guilt of one he loves or the merit of one he hates.

Said Abbaye: If a rabbinic scholar is beloved by the people of his city, it is not because of his superiority, but because he does not reprove them concerning their responsibilities toward God.

The rabbis taught: "You shall not accept a gift" (Ex 23:18). There was no need to admonish us against accepting a gift of money. But any other type of gift is also forbidden, since the verse does not specify not to accept a gift of money. What is meant by any other type of favor? This is illustrated by the case of Samuel, who once crossed a river on a ferry, when a man came over and gave his hand to assist him. Samuel asked him: What brings you here? He replied: I have a lawsuit to bring before you. Samuel then said to him: I am disqualified from hearing your case.

R. Ishmael b. Yose used to receive from his tenant farmer a basket of fruit every Friday, but once he brought it to him on Thursday. He [R. Yose] asked him: Why the change? He replied: I have a trial scheduled to come before you and I said that I would, at the same time, bring this to the master. He refused to accept it, and said to him: I am disqualified to act as judge in your case. He appointed two other rabbis to try his case. While attending to this he kept on thinking: He [his tenant farmer] might argue thus or he might argue thus. Then he said: A plague on those who accept gifts! If I who did not accept the gift, and if I had accepted it, I would only have accepted what is my own, feel biased, how much more so would those who really accept gifts feel it [biased].

A man once brought a dish of small fish from the river Gilli to R. Anan. He [R. Anan] asked him: What made you do this? He replied: I have a case to bring before you. He refused to accept it, saying: I am disqualified to act as judge in your case. He then said to him: I do not press you to act as judge in my case, but let the master accept my present, in order not to thwart me from bringing a firstfruit offering. For it was taught: "And there came a man from Baal-shalishah, and brought the man of God [Elisha] the bread of the firstfruits, twenty loaves of barley, and fresh ears of corn in his sack" (2 Kgs 4:42). Was Elisha [who was not a priest] entitled to eat firstfruits [which is only eaten by the priests]? But it is meant to teach us that whoever gives a present to a scholar it is as though he has brought an offering of firstfruits [to the Temple]. He then said to him: I did not wish to accept it but since you gave me such a good reason I shall accept it. He sent him to R. Nahman with this message: Would the master please try the case for this man, because I, Anan, am disqualified to act as judge in his case. The latter said to himself: Since he sent me such a message, this man must be his relative. There was then pending before him the case of orphans, and he said: To attend to the other case is a positive commandment, and to attend to this case is a positive commandment. However the commandment to show respect for the Torah must be given precedence. He put aside the case of the orphans and he attended to the case of that man. When the other litigant saw the respect shown him, he became speechless, and he could not speak in his own behalf. The prophet Elijah used to reveal himself to R. Anan and he would study the Seder Eliyahu with him. After this incident Elijah no longer came to him.

105a–106a

VIII

The Tractate Sotah

The tractate Sotah, a unit in the Order of Nashim, has as its primary theme a wife's infidelity to her marital vows. The term sotoh means to go astray, and the term sotah means a woman who has gone astray. The biblical treatment of this theme is Numbers 5:12–31, which provides that if a husband suspects his wife of infidelity, she is to be subjected to an ordeal of drinking "bitter water." If she is guilty, this would effect a swelling of her stomach, and she would then be disgraced. If she is innocent the ordeal would leave her unaffected.

It is interesting that in the code of Hammurabi a woman suspected of infidelity would have to take an oath that she is innocent. If, however, her behavior had caused scandal, even if there was no proof of her guilt, she was thrown into the river, and if she sank it was taken as proof of her guilt.

The Talmud discusses the various aspects of the law of the suspected woman, limiting to some extent its applicability. It is stipulated that the law was to be applied only if the husband had previously warned his wife, in the presence of witnesses, not to associate with the man who aroused his jealousy, and there had to be witnesses that she had disregarded the warning. If she confessed her guilt she was to be divorced and she forfeited the monetary allowance provided for in the ketubah.

The primary subject of this treatise is marital infidelity, and this stimulated the rabbis to discuss many other problems in the moral life. There is an extended discussion of the evils of pride and the importance of cultivating humility and selflessness, plus an interesting exposition of the difference between serving God out of fear and serving him out of love. The ceremony associated with the ordeal of the suspected woman included the reading of a scriptural passage, and the Talmud states that this may be done in any language. An excursus from this statement lists other rites that may be done in any language, including the recitation of the Shema, the recitation of the Amidah, and the Grace after meals.

The discussion of the moral life includes illustrative references to several biblical characters, climaxed with an extended description of the ministry of Moses. He is pictured as having fulfilled in his life the ideal of the suffering servant, as defined later on by the prophet Isaiah. R. Simlai cited Isaiah 53:12, and showed how the selflessness of Moses may well be analyzed in terms of the categories in this verse of Isaiah. Another Sage, R. Eliezer the Great, expounded the thought that Moses did not die but was transformed into a wholly spiritual essence, and as such abides with God and continues to serve, presumably as an atoning advocate of his people before the throne of God's judgment. Another extremely interesting pronouncement in this tractate is a condemnation of judges who decide cases "by the book," considering only the authority of precedent without considering the underlying reasons of the law, and the unique particularities of the cases before them.

The selections from this tractate presented here cover all these subjects. Sotah is one of the shorter tractates of the Talmud. It consists of forty-nine folio pages, which are divided into nine chapters.

■　　THE DRIFT TO SIN　　■

It has been taught: Rabbi [Judah Ha-Nasi] said: Why does the Torah place the discussion of the nazirite [who vowed certain ascetic practices, principally absention from wine] before the discussion about the *sotah* [the woman suspected of unfaithfulness to her marital vows]? It is to suggest that whoever sees the suspected woman as she is subjected to the ordeal of proving her innocence should resolve to abstain from drinking wine.

Resh Lakish said: A person does not commit a transgression unless a spirit of folly has entered into him. Thus the phrase "if a woman go astray" [*tisteh*] may be read to mean "if a woman becomes foolish" [*tishteh*] (Nm 5:12).

Said R. Samuel b. Nahmani in the name of R. Jonathan: Whoever performs one commandment in this world, it goes before him in the world to come, as it is written: "Your righteousness will go before you" (Is 58:8), and whoever commits one transgression in this world, it clings to him and goes before him on the Day of Judgment, as it is written: "The paths of their way are turned aside, they go up into waste and perish" (Jb 6:18). R. Eleazar said: It becomes attached to him like a dog, as it is written: "He [Joseph] did not listen to her, to lie with her, to be with her" (Gn 39:10)—to lie with her in this world, to be with her in the world to come.

Rava said: Whoever has intercourse with a harlot will in the end be reduced to begging for bread. R. Hiyya b. Abba said: A person imbued with a haughty spirit will in the end stumble over a married woman, as it is written: "And the adulteress hunts for the precious life" (Prv 6:26) ["precious" is here taken as haughty].

Rava said: Whoever has intercourse with a married woman, even if he had studied Torah, which is described as "more precious than rubies" (Prv 3:15), and the latter has been interpreted to mean that it makes him higher than the High Priest who enters the innermost chamber of the Sanctuary—she will hunt him down to the judgment of hell.

R. Yohanan in the name of R. Simeon b. Yohai said: A person who is imbued with a haughty spirit is as though he worshiped idols. In the case of haughtiness it is written: "Everyone who is proud of heart is an abomination to the Lord" (Prv 16:5), and concerning an idol the same term is used: "You shall not bring an abomination to your house" (Dt 7:26). And in his own name R. Yohanan said: Such a person is as though he denied God, as it is written: "And your heart will be lifted up, and you will forget the Lord your God" (Dt 8:14).

R. Hama b. Hanina said: It is as though he had incestuous relations with all the near-relations that are forbidden to him. Thus of haughtiness the verse says: "Everyone who is proud of heart is an abomination to the Lord" and the same term [abomination] is used in alluding to incestuous relations, as it is written: "For whosoever will practice these abominations will be cut off from the midst of their people" (Lv 18:27).

Where in the Torah is there an admonition against having a haughty spirit? Said Rava in the name of Zeiri, It is to be found in this verse: "Hear, and give heed, be not proud" (Jer 13:15). R. Nahman said: We find it in this verse: "And your heart will be lifted up and you will forget the Lord your God" (Dt 8:14), and this is introduced by the admonition: "Beware lest you forget the Lord your God" (Dt 8:11).

2a–5a

Said R. Jeremiah b. Abba: Four categories of people are not admitted to God's presence: Those who scoff, those who flatter, those who lie, those who slander. Those who scoff, as it is written: "He stretched out His hand against scoffers" (Hos 7:5). Those who flatter, as it is written: "For a flatterer shall not come before Him" (Jb 13:16). Those who lie, as it is written: "He who speaks falsehood will not be established before mine eyes" (Ps 101:7). Those who slander, as it is written: "For you are a God who has no pleasure in wickedness, evil will not abide with you" (Ps 5:5).

42a

■   A SELFLESS LIFE   ■

R. Joseph said: A person should learn to emulate the mind of his Creator. The Holy One, praised be He, ignored all the mountains and heights and caused His presence to abide on Mt. Sinai and He ignored all the goodly trees and caused His presence to be revealed in a [burning] bush.*

R. Joshua b. Levi said: Come and see how highly esteemed the lowly of spirit are before the Holy One, praised be He. When the Temple was in existence, when a person sacrificed a burnt offering, he was rewarded for a burnt offering. If he sacrificed a meal offering he was rewarded for a meal offering. However, one who was of a humble disposition was regarded as though he had brought all the sacrifices, as it is written: "The sacrifices of God are a broken spirit" (Ps 51:19). Moreover, his prayers will not be disparaged, as the verse continues: "A broken and contrite heart God will not despise."

5b

"And he [Abraham] planted a tamarisk tree [eshel] in Beer-Sheba" (Gn 21:33). Said Resh Lakish: This means that he established an orchard and planted there all kinds of choice fruit-bearing trees. R. Judah and R. Nehemiah differ in interpreting this. One said that he planted there an orchard and the other said that he established there a hospice. It is appropriate, according to the one that refers to it as an orchard, that the verse uses the term "and he planted," but if one interprets this

---

*Mt. Sinai was regarded as one of the lowly mountains. The reference to the burning bush is omitted in some texts.

as referring to a hospice, why does the verse use the term "and he planted"? But we do find this term used in the sense of establishing, as in the verse: "And he will plant the tent of his palace between the seas and the glorious holy mountains" (Dn 11:45).

"And he [Abraham] called on the name of the Lord, the eternal God" (Gn 12:33). Said Resh Lakish: Do not read the word *vayikra*, which means "and he called," but as though written *varyakri*, which means "and he caused to call." This suggests that Abraham caused all passers-by to call on the name of the Lord. How did he do this? After they ate and drank they rose to praise him, but he would say to them: Did you eat what belonged to me? You eat of what belongs to the God of the universe. Thank and praise Him who by His word created the universe.

10a–10b

R. Huna the son of R. Hanina also said: What is meant by the verse: "You shall walk after the Lord your God" (Dt 13:5)? Is it possible for a mortal to walk after the divine presence (*shekinah*)? We have been told: "The Lord your God is a devouring fire" (Dt 4:24)! What it means is that you are to imitate His attributes. He clothes the naked, as it is written: "And the Lord God made for Adam and his wife garments of skin, and He clothed them" (Gn 3:21); you too are to clothe the naked. The Holy One, praised be He, visits the sick, as it is written: "And the Lord appeared to him [Abraham, after his circumcision] by the oak of Mamre" (Gn 18:1); you too are to visit the sick. The Holy One, praised be He, comforts mourners, as it is written: "And after the death of Abraham, God blessed his son Isaac" (Gn 25:11); you too are to comfort mourners. The Holy One, praised be He, buried the dead, as it is written: "And He buried him [Moses] in the valley" (Dt 24:6); you too are to bury the dead.

14a

R. Yose the son of R. Hanina said: The Torah abides only with one who strips from himself worldly concerns, as it is said: "I, wisdom, have made my dwelling place with those who are stripped of everything" [*arma*, lit. "naked," but the term also means "cunning," and it is so generally translated; Prv 8:12]. R. Yohanan said: The Torah abides only with one who has annihilated his ego, as it is written: "And wisdom will be found from nothing" [*meayin*, which also means "from where?" and it is so generally translated; Jb 28:12].

He [R. Joshua] used to say: A fool of a pietist, and a cunning rogue destroy the world. What is a fool of a pietist like? Thus, if a woman is drowning in a river, and he says, It would be wrong for me to look at her [naked body] and rescue her. What is a cunning rogue like? R. Yohanan said: It is illustrated by one who presents his case before a judge before the other party to the lawsuit enters. R. Zerika said: It is illustrated by one who is permissive with himself, but exacting with others.

21b–22A

R. Joshua b. Levi said: We must not invite a stingy person to lead in the recitation of grace after a meal.* Thus it is written: "A gracious person is to be blessed [yevorah], for he has given of his bread to the poor" (Prv 22:9). Do not read the word *yevorah* but *yevareh*,† which means: "He shall pronounce the blessing."

R. Joshua b. Levi also said: How do we know that even the birds recognize a stingy person? Because it is written: [For a greedy person] "the net is spread out in vain in the eyes of any bird" (Prv 1:17).

R. Joshua b. Levi also said: Whoever accepts the hospitality of a stingy person violates a prohibition. Thus it is written: "Do not eat the bread of a stingy person . . . eat and drink, he tells you, but his heart is not with you" (Prv 23:6, 7).

R. Joshua b. Levi also said: The atonement offering of a heifer by the elders of a city in whose outskirts a dead body was found (Dt 21:1–9) was instituted only because of people with a callous spirit. Thus it is written: [The elders are to say]: "Our hands did not shed this blood." But could it occur to us that the elders of the Bet-Din were guilty of bloodshed? Their statement meant: This man [found slain] did not come to us for help and we sent him away, we did not see him and abandoned him; he did not come to our attention and we allowed him to leave without food, we did not see him and allowed him to leave without escort.

38b

R. Abbahu also said: At first I thought that I was humble, but after I saw how R. Abba of Acco explained a text in one way, and his interpreter ignored it and offered an explanation of his own, and R. Abba was not offended, I said to myself: I am not humble.

---

*The text has: We do not give an ungracious person the cup of blessing. The leader of grace did so with a cup of wine in hand, over which he recited a special blessing.

†The Hebrew spelling is without vowels, and the word can be read either way.

And how did R. Abbahu show his humility? The wife of his interpreter once said to his [R. Abbahu's] wife: My husband is not dependent on your husband, but the reason he takes instruction from him is merely out of respect. His wife reported this to R. Abbahu, but his reply was: What difference does it make? Through me and through him is God's praise enhanced.

He also showed it in the following incident: The Sages resolved to appoint R. Abbahu as head of the academy. When he realized that R. Abba of Acco was heavily in debt, he declined, saying: There is a more worthy scholar available for the office.*

R. Abbahu and R. Hiyya b. Abba once came to the same town. R. Abbahu expounded aggada [a nonlegal subject] while R. Hiyya b. Abba expounded halakhah [a theme focusing on law]. All the people ignored R. Hiyya b. Abba and came to hear R. Abbahu. The former was disturbed, and R. Abbahu said to him: I will tell you a parable: This may be compared to two people, one of whom sells precious stones and the other was a huckster selling petty merchandise. To whom will all the people hurry? Surely to the seller of petty merchandise. Everyday R. Hiyya b. Abba used to accompany R. Abbahu to the inn, because he was highly esteemed by the government authorities, but that day R. Abbahu accompanied R. Hiyya b. Abba to the inn. Nevertheless this did not set his mind at ease.

40a

■   THE MINISTRY OF MOSES   ■

It has been taught: Rabbi Eliezer the Great said: Over an area twelve *mil* square, corresponding to the encampment of the Israelites, a heavenly voice called out: "And Moses died there" (Dt 34:5), the great scribe of Israel. But others say that Moses did not die. Here the verse says: "And he [Moses] died *there*," but elsewhere we are told: "And he [Moses] was *there* with the Lord" (Ex 34:28). As in the latter case the word *there* means that he stood and served, so here also the term *there* means that he stood and served.[†]

---

*The appointment would enable R. Abba to secure funds to repay his debts.

†Cf. Sifre on Numbers 25:13, where it is stated that "to the present time," Phineas "did not cease but stands and makes atonement, and will do so until the dead are restored to life."

THE TRACTATE SOTAH

"And He buried him [Moses] in the valley, in the land of Moab, opposite Beth-Peor" (Dt 34:6). Said R. Beraukhya: It is a sign within a sign. Despite [the above details], the verse concludes with "and no man knew the place of his burial." The wicked government [an allusion to Rome] once sent to the governor of Beth-Peor this inquiry: Show us where Moses is buried. When they stood on the hills [the grave] seemed to be in the valley, and when they stood in the valley, it seemed to be on the hill. They then divided into two groups; to those who stood on the hill it seemed to be in the valley, and to those who stood in the valley it seemed to be on the hill. This confirmed the statement in the verse: "And no man [ish] knew the place of his burial." Said R. Hama the son of R. Hanina: Even Moses did not know where he was buried. Thus the verse here says: "And no *man* [ish] knew the place of his burial," and elsewhere it says: "And this is the blessing with which Moses the *man* [ish] of God blessed the children of Israel" (Dt 33:1).*

R. Hama the son of R. Hanina also said: Why was Moses buried at Beth-Peor? It was to effect atonement for the sin committed by the Israelites at Beth-Peor (Nm 25:1–9).

R. Simlai expounded: Why was Moses so eager to enter Eretz Yisrael? Was it necessary for him to eat of its fruit, to sate himself with its beauty? But this is what Moses said: The children of Israel were given many commandments which could only be carried out in Eretz Yisrael. Let me enter the land so that they may be fulfilled through me. The Holy One, praised be He, said to him: Since you are only interested in fulfilling the divine commandments[†] I shall deem it as though you fulfilled them. Thus it is written: "Therefore will I grant him a portion with the great, and he will divide the spoil with the mighty, because he poured out his soul to death, and was numbered with the transgressors, yet he bore the sins of many, and made intercession for the transgressors" (Is 53:12). "Therefore will I grant him a

---

*Moses was also called *ish*, man, and thus was also included among those who did know the place of his burial. R. Samuel Eliezer Ha-Levi Adels (Mharsha) in his Talmud commentary (ad locum), explains that Moses had been transformed into a wholly spiritual essence, and his real self was therefore beyond death and beyond burial.

†The text in the Talmud has "since you are only interested in receiving a reward" but the Talmudists generally frowned on performing the commandments so as to receive a reward, which was regarded as an ulterior motivation. Zevi Hirsh Hayot in his commentary on the Talmud suggests that the reward alluded to here is the satisfaction the performance of the commandment yields, because "one has been privileged to fulfill the will of God."

portion among the great"—one might assume that this refers to the great of later generations, but not of the earlier generations, therefore does the text add "and he will divide the spoil with the mighty"—this refers to Abraham, Isaac, and Jacob, who were mighty in the study of Torah and the fulfillment of the commandments. "Because he poured out his soul to death"—because he declared his readiness to die as it is written: "And if not [if you do not forgive them], blot me out from Your book which you have written" (Ex 32:32). "And he was numbered with the transgressors" because he was included among those who were condemned to die in the wilderness. "Yet he bore the sins of many"—because he secured atonement for the making of the golden calf. "And he made intercession [*yafgia*] for the transgressors"—because he prayed that the sinners in Israel return in penitence. The word *pegia*, from which the term *yafgia* is derived, means prayer of intercession, as in the verse: "Therefore, pray not for this people, do not offer on their behalf any entreaty or prayer, or make intercession [*tifga*] with Me" (Jer 7:16).

13b–14a

■   THE LOVE OF GOD AND THE FEAR OF GOD   ■

On that day R. Joshua b. Hyrcanus expounded: Job served the Holy One, praised be He, only out of love, for it is written: "Even if He slay me yet will I wait for Him" (Jb 13:15). But this verse is not decisive since a variant reading in the text may yield the meaning: "I will not wait for Him."* We have another text which declares: "Till I die I will not put away my integrity from me" (Jb 27:5). This teaches that he acted out of love. Said R. Joshua [ben Hananyah]: Who will take away the dust from your eyes, Rabban Yohanan b. Zakkai! All your days you taught that Job served God only out of fear, for it is written: "That man [Job] was blameless and upright, who feared God and turned away from evil" (Jb 1:1). And now Joshua, the disciple of your disciple, has taught that he served out of love.

MISHNAH 5:5

---

*The Hebrew *lo* in *lo ayahel* may be spelled with a *vav* or with an *aleph*. In the latter case it would mean: "I will not wait for Him"

163

THE TRACTATE SOTAH

It was taught: R. Meir said: The term "God-fearing" is used to characterize Job (Jb 1:1) and it is used to characterize Abraham (Gn 22:12). As the term "God-fearing" in the case of Abraham referred to a service out of love, so does the term when applied to Job designate a service out of love. How do we know that this is so in the case of Abraham himself? We know it from the verse: "The seed of Abraham who loved Me" (Is 41:8).

Two disciples sat before Rava. One said: In my dream they recited for me: "How abundant is your goodness, which you stored up for them who fear you" (Ps 31:20). The other said: In my dream they recited for me: "Those who trust in you will rejoice, they will always sing, and you will protect them; those who love your name will exult in you" (Ps 5:12). He [Rava] said to them: "Both you scholars are wholly righteous, but one of you is motivated by love and the other by fear."

31a

■ THE LANGUAGE OF PRAYER ■

The Shema [may be read in any language]. How do we know this? Because the verse states: "Hear, O Israel"—in any language that you comprehend.*

The Amidah [may be recited in any language]. Its essence is supplication, and one may offer prayer in any language he chooses.

The Grace after Meals [may be recited in any language]. This is derived from the verse: "And you will eat, and be satisfied, and you shall praise the Lord your God" (Dt 8:10)—in any language in which you offer praise.

32b–33a

■ ON JURIDICAL DECISIONS ■

"My son, fear the Lord and the king, and mingle not with repeaters (Prv 24:21).† Said R. Isaac: This refers to those who merely repeat the

---

*The Hebrew term for "hear," *Shema*, also means to comprehend.

†The Hebrew here rendered as "repeaters" is *shonim*, which is translated as "those given to change" (JPS) or "those who rebel" (Confraternity), but the primary meaning in Hebrew is "repeaters" and it is so used in this Talmudic text.

laws. But is it not obvious that this is what it means? It might have been assumed that it refers to those who repeat their transgressions, and that this text was in accordance with the statement of R. Huna, that if a person repeats his transgression, it becomes for him as though permitted. It is for this reason that he [R. Isaac] offered his interpretation.

It was taught: The repeaters of the teachings destroy the world. Destroy the world! Can one really mean this? Said Ravina: This refers to those who decide cases on the mere knowledge of texts. We have studied similarly: Said R. Joshua: Are such people to be regarded the destroyers of the world? Are they not in truth the builders of the world, as we have been told: The laws are "paths to Him" (Hb 3:6 and cf. Megillah 28b)? But this refers to those who decide cases on the surface meaning of texts [without considering the underlying reasons involved in the text or in the unique particularities of the cases before them].

22a

IX

The Tractate Kiddushin

Kiddushin is the last tractate in the Order of Nashim, or "women." The term means betrothal. The meaning of the term kadosh is "holy," and by the act of betrothal a woman was regarded as having been consecrated to the man as his wife, to be holy to him, set apart for him exclusively. Strictly speaking, betrothal was a preliminary stage to marriage, and the consummation of the marriage generally took place after an interval of twelve months in the case of a maiden, and thirty days in the case of a widow. In many respects, however, the act of betrothal created the essence of a state of marriage. Its dissolution would require a divorce, and unfaithfulness would be regarded as adultery.

The core theme of the tractate is presented in the opening Mishnah. It lists the ways in which betrothal may be effected: a gift by the groom to the bride of any token of value to indicate his readiness to assume the obligations of married life; a written statement of proposal; and cohabitation, when it takes place in a context that establishes it clearly as a prelude to marriage. Two witnesses are required to make these actions public, and mutual consent is presupposed. Betrothal by means of cohabitation was frowned on, and penalties were imposed on anyone who used it, even though the betrothal was deemed valid.

Various other themes are introduced into this tractate, some only tangentially related to the primary subject. The establishment of the relationship between the betrothed couple suggested a discussion of the way in which other relationships are established. The change from free person to slave and the acquisition of property rights are the principal status changes discussed. The Talmud speaks harshly of a person who voluntarily surrenders his freedom and accepts a state of bondage. This was usually done to escape the ravages of poverty, but the Talmud regards any surrender of freedom as a spurning of God's will for human life.

The Mishnah also discusses various blemishes in family status that disqualify a person from marrying into a normal family. The bastard, usually the child of an adulterous cohabitation, is the principal illustration of this. Children of blemished families could intermarry among themselves. The Talmud also discusses ways in which these blemished people might purge themselves of their blemish.

The selections included here present various Talmudic comments on the family, on servitude and freedom, on learning and righteousness, and on the vulnerability of human nature to the assault of passion. The Torah is a source of strength to help a person overcome the potency of temptation, but God himself remains the most viable source of strength to a person assailed by temptation. At the same time the Talmud cautions us not to be overconfident as to our impregnability against temptation's onslaughts, but to steer ourselves with care not to fall into its trap.

The tractate is divided into four chapters, which are spread over eighty-two folio pages.

■   THE RESPONSIBILITY OF AND HONOR DUE A PARENT   ■

The rabbis taught: A father is obligated to circumcise his son, to redeem him,* to teach him Torah, to arrange for his marriage, to teach him a trade, and some say he is also obligated to teach him how to swim. R. Judah says: Whoever fails to teach his son a trade, teaches him to become a criminal. A criminal—can you really mean this? What it means is that it is as though he taught him to be a criminal.

R. Hisda praised R. Hamenuna to R. Huna as a great man. He said to him: When you get the opportunity, bring him to me for a visit.

---

*Exodus 13:13 provides that the first-born son of a nonpriestly family is to be redeemed from a priest to release him from the commitment clinging to him from an earlier period when the first-born sons were the religious functionaries of their family units.

When he came, he [R. Huna] noticed that he did not wear a turban over his head [as was customary for married persons]. He said to him: Why are you not wearing a turban over your head? He replied: Because I am not married. He thereupon turned his face away from him and said to him: See that you do not visit me again until you are married. R. Huna acted in accordance with his view that if a person reached the age of twenty and was not yet married all his days will be spent in sin. Is it conceivable that he really meant in sin? But what he meant was that he would be sinning in his thoughts.

The school of Ishmael taught similarly: Until the age of twenty the Holy One, praised be He, sits and waits, asking: When will this person take for himself a wife? When he reaches the age of twenty and is still not married, He says: Alas, for the deterioration which will set in for that man.

Rava said to R. Nathan b. Ami: While you still have influence over your son, see that he marries between the years of sixteen and twenty-two, and others say, between eighteen and twenty-four.

Said R. Joshua b. Levi: Whoever teaches his grandson Torah is deemed, by a statement in a verse, as though he himself had received it at Sinai. Thus it is written: "And you shall make them known to your sons and your sons' sons" (Dt 4:9), and the next verse reads: "The day you stood before the Lord your God at Horeb" [Sinai].

R. Hiyya b. Abba saw R. Joshua b. Levi throw a covering on his head as he led a child to school. He asked him: Why this hurry [that you were not fully dressed]? He replied: Is it a trivial matter that the verse states: "And you shall make them known to your children," and immediately thereafter the verse adds: "The day you stood before the Lord your God at Horeb" [Sinai]? After this R. Hiyya b. Abba did not have his breakfast* until he had his child recite for him the previous day's lesson and he added to it. Rabba b. R. Huna did not have his breakfast until he had taken his child to school.

[The father is obligated] *to arrange for his marriage.* How do we know this? Because it is written: "Take your wives, and beget sons and daughters and take wives for your sons, and give your daughters to husbands" (Jer 29:6). As for getting a wife for his son—this is within his initiative. But is it within his initiative to get a husband for his

---

*The term used in the Talmud is *umza*, which Rashi defines as: "a small portion of meat gridled on the coals which it was customary to eat at breakfast."

daughter? What it means is this. He is to give her a dowry, clothe her, and adorn her, so that men will be attracted to her.

Some say that he must also teach him how to swim. What is the reason for this? Because his life may depend on it.

29a–30B

The rabbis taught: Three partners share in bringing a person to life: the Holy One, praised be He, the father, and the mother. When one honors his father and his mother, the Holy One, praised be He, says: I regard it as though I dwelt among them and he honored me.

It was taught: Rabbi [Judah Ha-Nasi] said: It was well known to Him who by His word created the world, that a child honors his mother more than his father, because she coddles him with soft words, and for this reason the Holy One, praised be He, placed the honor due to the father before the honor due to the mother (in Ex 19:12). It was also known to Him that he reveres the father more than the mother, because the father teaches him Torah, and it is for this reason that the Holy One, praised be He, asked for the reverence of the mother before that due to the father (Lv 19:3).

The question was asked of R. Ulla: How far is one obligated in honoring one's father and mother? He replied: Go and see how a certain idolator in Ashkelon by the name of Dama the son of Nethinah acted. At one time the Sages sought to purchase from him merchandise on which he would have earned six hundred thousand [golden *denars*] profit. But the key [to the storeroom] was under the pillow on which his father slept, and he refused to wake him. When R. Dimi came he cited this illustration [of the conduct of Dama the son of Nethinah]: Once he was robed in a gold embroidered silken cloak and he sat among the nobles of Rome when his mother came and tore it from him, struck him on the head and spat at him, but he would not shame her.

Said R. Abbahu: My son Abimi is an illustration of how one keeps properly the commandment to honor one's parents. Abimi had five grown sons who were knowledgeable in traditional proprieties during the lifetime of his own father. Yet when R. Abbahu came and announced himself at the door, he himself ran and opened it to him, chanting, I am coming, I am coming, until he got there. One day he [R. Abbahu] said: I would like a drink of water. Before he brought it to him, he fell asleep. He [Abimi] remained bent over him and waited until he awoke. While waiting Abimi succeeded in clarifying to himself why Psalm 79, which describes the destruction of the Temple and the devastation of Jerusalem at the hands of Israel's enemies, bears the title "A Song of Asaph" instead of "A Lamentation of Asaph."*

When R. Joseph heard his mother's footsteps he would say: Let me arise before the divine presence [*shekinah*] that is approaching.

The rabbis taught: What is meant by reverence [*mora*, which is sometimes translated as fear] and what is meant by respect? Reverence means that one does not stand in his parent's place or sit in his seat, that he does not contradict his words, and that he does not tip the scales [in any dispute] against him. Respect means that he is to give him food and drink, clothe him, and assist him in going and coming. The question was raised: At whose expense [is one to render those services to the parent]? R. Judah said: at the son's expense, and R. Nathan said: at the father's. The rabbis instructed R. Jeremiah, and some say R. Jeremiah's son in accordance with the view that it was to be at the father's expense. This was challenged with the following: It is written: "Honor your father and your mother" (Ex 20:12), and it is also written: "Honor the Lord with your substance" (Prv 3:4). Just as the latter involves a financial commitment so does the former involve a financial commitment. But if you say that it is to be at the father's expense, what commitment does the son make? The answer is: It involves a commitment of time.

If a person saw his father transgress a commandment of the Torah he must not tell him: Father, you have transgressed a commandment of the Torah, but he is rather to tell him: Father, thus it is written in the Torah. But this would still grieve him! He is rather to say, Father, there is a verse in the Torah [citing the verse but not implying that it is contrary to his action].

Eleazar b. Mattiah said: If my father should ask me to give him a drink of water, and I have a commandment of the Torah to perform, I would defer the duty to respect my father and I would carry out the other commandment, because my father and I are obligated to carry out the commandment. Isi b. Judah said: If someone else can carry out the other commandment, let someone else carry it out, and let him

---

*The nature of the clarification is not given in the text, and various suggestions are offered by the commentators. Perhaps as Abimi was waiting patiently, confident that his father would wake from his sleep, so did Asaph dare to trust that God would eventually bestir himself and redress the wrong done to his people, and therefore he sang.

attend to the duty of showing respect to his father. Said R. Mattnah: The law is in accordance with the view of Isi b. Judah.

30b–32a

It is forbidden for a person to betroth a woman until he sees her, lest he find something repulsive in her and she will become loathsome to him, whereas the All Merciful One ordained: "You shall love your mate [*reakha**] as yourself (Lv 19:18).

Rabbi Eleazar said: It is forbidden for a person to arrange for his minor daughter's betrothal until she grows up and declares: I desire so and so.

41a

■   SERVITUDE AND FREEDOM   ■

The rabbis taught: [If the Hebrew slave should be unwilling to be liberated in the sabbatical year] "because he is well off with you" (Dt 15:16)—he must be with you in eating and in drinking: You are not to eat white bread and he black bread, you are not to drink old wine and give him new wine, you are not to sleep on a feather bed and he on straw. Hence, it was generalized that whoever purchases a Hebrew slave has acquired a master for himself.

"And his master shall bore his ear with an awl" [if he is unwilling to regain his freedom] (Ex 21:6). Rabban Yohanan b. Zakkai used to expound this verse symbolically. Why was the ear singled out from all the other organs of the body? But the Holy One, praised be He, decreed: The ear heard my declaration at Mt. Sinai: For the children of Israel are servants to Me, they are My servants" (Lv 25:55), which means, not servants to other servants. This man, nevertheless, went ahead and [when he could have been freed, willingly] chose a master for himself, let him be bored in the ear.

R. Simeon b. Rabbi also expounded this verse symbolically: Why were the door and the doorpost singled out from all other parts of the house [to perform before them the boring of the ear of the slave who

---

Reakha is usually translated as "your neighbor," but the term usually designates a much more intimate relationship. In Song of Songs 2:2 and 5:16 it refers to a lover and his beloved. In modern Hebrew the term in the feminine form, *rayah*, designates a wife. In the present context it is obviously the more intimate relationship that is implied.

refuses to be liberated]? Said the Holy One, praised be He, the door and the doorpost served as witnesses when I passed over the lintel and the doorposts (Ex 12:23), and declared that the children of Israel are my servants, and not the servants of servants, and I liberated them from slavery to freedom. This man, nevertheless, went and chose a master for himself, and let him be bored in the ear before them.

22a–22b

■   THE LEARNED AND THE RIGHTEOUS   ■

Once it happened that R. Eliezer and R. Joshua and R. Zadok attended the feast in honor of the wedding of the son of Rabban Gamaliel, and Rabban Gamaliel waited on them. He offered a cup of wine to R. Eliezer but he refused it. He then offered it to R. Joshua, and he accepted it. R. Eliezer said to him: What is this, Joshua, we are sitting and Rabban Gamaliel is standing and serving us drinks! R. Joshua replied: We find that someone greater than he stood and served his guests. Abraham was the greatest man in his generation and yet the verse reports that "he stood by them" [the three strangers and served them, Gn 18:8]. And lest you say that those strangers seemed to him like angels—they only appeared to him like Arab nomads. Shall we then object that the great Rabban Gamaliel stands and serves us? R. Zadok said to them: How long will you ignore the honor of God and concern yourselves with the honor of men? The Holy One, praised be He, causes the wind to blow, and the clouds to rise, and the rain to fall, and He stirs the earth to sprout new vegetation, and He sets a table for everyone. Are we then to object that Rabban Gamaliel stands and serves us?

Rava said: R. Idi explained this to me. The verse states: "Say of the righteous, when they are good, that they will enjoy the fruit of their labors" (Is 3:10). But is there a righteous person who is good and one who is not good? What it means is this: A righteous person who is good is one who is good in his actions toward God as well as in his actions toward people. A righteous person who is not good is one who is good in his actions toward God but not in his actions toward people. Similarly the verse states: "Woe to the wicked who is evil, the recompense for his work will be granted him (Is 3:11). Is there a wicked person who is bad and one who is not bad? But the meaning is: A wicked person who is bad is one who is bad in his actions toward God as well as in his actions toward people. A wicked person who is not bad is one who is bad in his actions toward God but not in his actions toward people.

Said R. Assi: If a person only intended to do a good deed but circumstances prevented him from doing so, the Holy One, praised be He, ascribes it to him as though he accomplished it. But an evil deed which he intended to do and circumstances prevented him from doing it, the Holy One, praised be He, does not ascribe it to him as though he did it, as it is written: "If I cherished inequity in my heart, the Lord would not listen" (Ps 66:18).

The rabbis taught: A person should always see himself as being equally balanced between his good and his evil elements. Fortunate is he when he performs one commandment, for he has tipped the scales in his favor. If he has performed one evil deed, woe unto him, for he has tipped the scales toward his guilt. Thus it is written: "One sinner destroys much good" (Eccl 9:18); by committing one sin he has forfeited much good. R. Eleazar b. Simeon said: Because the world is judged on the basis of the majority, and the individual is judged on the basis of the preponderance of his actions, fortunate is one on fulfilling a commandment, for he has tipped the scales in his own favor and in favor of the world. Woe to him on violating one commandment, for he has tipped the scales against himself and against the world. Thus it is written: "One sinner destroys much good"—because of one sin this person has done he has lost much good for himself and for the world.

R. Simeon b. Yohai said: Even if a person were fully righteous all his life, but in the end became rebellious, he has lost the benefit of his earlier good deeds. Thus it is written: "The righteousness of the righteous shall not deliver him in the day of his transgression" (Ez 33:12). And even if he were wicked all his life, and repented in the end, his earlier evil deeds will not be recalled against him. Thus the same verse continues: "And the wickedness of the wicked will not be for a stumbling to him when he turns away from his wickedness."

32b–39b

One who is knowledgeable in Bible and Mishnah and possesses good manners will not be easily led to sin. Thus it is stated: "A threefold cord is not readily severed" (Eccl 4:12). One who is not knowledgeable in Bible and Mishnah, and is without good manners, is not considered a good member of society.

MISHNAH 1:9

R. Tarfon and the Elders once met in the upper story of the house of Nitzah in Lydda when the following question was raised: Which is greater, study or practice? R. Tarfon answered that practice is greater, but all the others answered that study is greater, because study leads to practice.

40b

It was taught: R. Judah said: Whoever translates a verse in the Bible literally has perpetrated a fraud, and whoever interpolates his own addition to it has perpetrated blasphemy.

49a

If a man says to a woman: Be my betrothed, with the understanding that I am a righteous man, even if it turns out that he is wholly wicked, [if she accepted his proposal] the betrothal is valid, because he might well have resolved in his mind to do penance.

49b

R. Hezekiah R. Kohen said in the name of Rav: It is wrong to live in a city where there is no physician, or a public bath or a court of law that enforces public order. Said R. Yose b. Bun: It is also wrong to live in a city that does not have gardens of vegetation.

R. Hezekiah R. Kohen said in the name of Rav: A person is destined to give an accounting [before the Heavenly Tribunal] for everything he saw but did not enjoy [ignoring God's world which He meant for man's enjoyment].

Yerushalmi 4:12 (66d)

■   RESISTANCE TO TEMPTATION   ■

Man's evil passion renews its assault against him each day, as it is written: "The schemes stirring the thoughts of his heart are nothing but evil each day" (Gn 6:5). R. Simeon b. Levi said: Man's evil passion renews its assault against him each day, and seeks to slay him, as it is written: "The evil one watches the righteous and seeks to slay him" (Ps 37:32). And were it not for the fact that the Holy One, praised be He, is his support, he would be unable to withstand it, as it is written: "God will not leave him in its power" (Ps 37:33). The school of Ishmael taught: My son, if the despicable one [the evil passion] assails you, take it with you to the academy. If it is like iron, it will break into fragments, as it is written: "Is not my word like fire, says the Lord, and like a hammer that breaks rocks in pieces" (Jer 23:29). If it is like stone it will dissolve, as it is written: "Let every one who is thirsty go for water"* (Is 55:1), and it is also written: "Water wears away stone" (Jb 14:19).

A man should not be alone with two women, but one woman may be alone with two men. R. Simeon said: A man may be alone with two women, if his wife is with him.

MISHNAH 4:12

Said R. Judah in the name of Rav: The rule that one woman may be alone with two men applies only in the case of respectable people, but with people of loose morals, a woman should not be alone even with ten men. Said R. Joseph: The proof for this is that ten men team up and steal a beam and are not ashamed of each other.

Said Abin: The worst times of the year [for moral looseness] are the festivals.

Certain women who had been held in captivity and then ransomed were lodged in the house of R. Amram the pious. The ladder [to their quarters in the upper chamber] was removed. As one of them passed, the skylight shone on her. R. Amram [was struck by her beauty and he] grabbed the ladder, which was too heavy for ten to carry, and he put it up by himself, and began to climb on it. After he had climbed half way, he stopped himself and cried out: There is a fire at Amram's! The rabbis came, and reprimanded him: You have put us to shame! He replied to them: It is better that you be ashamed of Amram in this world than that you be ashamed of him in the world to come. He then adjured his evil passion to leave him, and when it left him it was like a column of fire. He said: See, you are fire and I am flesh, but I overcame you.

R. Meir used to mock those who yielded to their evil passion. One day Satan [a personification of the evil passion] appeared to him in the form of a woman on the other side of the river. There was no ferry across, and he seized a rope [which stretched across the river] and began to cross. After he had reached half way, Satan left him, and said: If they had not issued a warning in heaven to be careful with R. Meir and his Torah, I would have made nothing out of you.

Plemo used to say every day: I defy Satan. One day before the Day of Atonement Satan appeared to him in the guise of a poor man.

---

*Water is here a metaphor for the Torah.

He came to the door and called for help. Plemo brought him out a piece of bread. The poor man said to him: On a day like this everyone is inside but I am outside! He took him inside and gave him the bread. The poor man now said: At a time like this everyone eats at the table, but I am alone! He seated him at the table. He feigned that his skin was full of scabs, and he acted repulsively. Plemo said to him: Sit properly. He then said: Give me a cup of wine to drink. He gave it to him. He coughed and threw his phlegm into the cup. Plemo rebuked him, and he [the disguised Satan] pretended he was dead. The rumor began to circulate: Plemo killed a man, Plemo killed a man. Plemo ran away and hid himself in a toilet outside the city. When Satan saw how distressed he was, he revealed himself to him and said: Why did you speak so defiantly of Satan? But how else should I have spoken? he asked. Satan answered: You should say: May the Merciful One rebuke Satan.

80b–82a

X

The Tractate Baba Mezia

Baba Mezia belongs to the fourth Order of the Talmud, Nezikin which means "damages." This Order deals with the various aspects of civil and criminal law. Appended to it is the tractate Avot, or the Ethics of the Fathers, which focuses on the civilities of human relations. The term Baba Mezia means "the Middle Gate." It is distinguished from two other tractates, Baba Kamma, the "First Gate," and Baba Batra, the "Last Gate." Originally one tractate, it was divided into three on account of its excessive length.

The theme of the tractate Baba Mezia is primarily civil law. It discusses the rules governing lost and found objects, the conflicts between claimants, the various types of guardians of property, the forms of property acquisition, fraud in commerce, usury, employer-employee relations, rentals, and partnerships. The discussions presuppose a simple economy, based largely on agriculture. The possession of land is regarded as the chief source of security. It is no doubt because this type of economy forms the setting for these discussions that the taking of any kind of interest on a loan is forbidden. It is even forbidden to charge a higher price for an article when it is sold on credit.

Some general moralistic principles are to be found in this tractate. While the focus is on civil law, we are reminded that a person must not be content with staying within the law, but most go beyond it, to embrace principles of equity and general moral sensitivity. Here is one of the strongest affirmations of human dignity. Even a heavenly voice is ruled irrelevant in deciding a question of law, and it cannot intervene in a majority decision of scholars after due deliberation and weighing of evidence. Here also is an important recognition that ethics must be *situational rather than dogmatic. Thus we are told that for the sake of peace one may even misquote, and God himself is shown to have misquoted for the sake of peace in the family of Abraham and Sarah. The study of the Torah is stressed in this tractate as it is throughout the Talmud, but we are reminded that the study of the Torah cannot be an end in itself, detached from a life of piety. The occasion of Torah study itself must be in a context of reverence for God from Whom it was revealed for the hallowing of all life.*

The Talmud generally avoids direct involvement in the political controversies of the time. Rome was the dominant power and it would have been hazardous to comment directly on Roman oppression. At times however an indirect comment appears through satire and parable. One of the selections included here pictures a visit by Alexander the Great to a King Katzya, in order to learn his ways of government. The story is mythical but one can read between these lines a sharp invective against the rapaciousness of the Roman imperial government. It is to be noted that this selection is from the Palestinian rather than the Babylonian Talmud. Palestine was dominated by Rome. Babylonian rule was much more benign, and the Jews never questioned the legitimacy of its rulers. Roman power, on the other hand, was an illegitimate imposition of foreign rule by the force of conquest.

There are 119 folio pages in this tractate, divided into ten chapters.

■   LOST AND FOUND   ■

The rabbis taught: Originally, whoever found an object would make a public announcement during the three festivals [in the Temple area], and for seven days following the last festival. This was to give the person hearing it three days to return home [and check whether he suffered a loss], and three days to come back and an additional day to announce his loss. After the destruction of the Temple, may it be rebuilt speedily in our time, it was instituted that announcements [about lost and found] be made in the synagogues and academies. When the oppressors increased, it was ordained that information be communicated to friends and neighbors, and that this would suffice. What is meant by "when the oppressors increased"? This refers to those who enforced the ruling that lost property belonged to the king.

R. Ami found a purse of *denarim*. A certain person saw him showing fear, and he reassured him: Go, keep it for youself, we are not Persians who hold that lost property belongs to the king.

The rabbis taught: There was a store for claims in Jerusalem. Whoever lost anything would go there, and whoever found anything would go there. The finder would make announcement, and the loser would offer marks of identification, and receive it back.

The rabbis taught: At first, whoever lost anything would offer marks of identification and take it back. But when deceivers increased, it was ordained that the claimant be asked to bring witnesses that he was not a deceiver, and then he would take it. Thus it once happened that the father of R. Papa lost a donkey, and it was found. The case came before Rabbah the son of R. Huna, and he told him: Go and bring witnesses that you are not a deceiver, and then you will take it. He went and brought witnesses. He [Rabbah] said to them: Do you know him to be a deceiver? They answered: Yes. He [the father of R. Papa] said to them: I am a deceiver? They replied: We said that you were not a deceiver. Rabbah the son of R. Huna said: It stands to reason that a person would not bring witnesses to hurt his case.

28b

■ A SATIRE ON RAPACIOUS GOVERNMENT ■

Alexander of Macedon visited King Katzya, who displayed to him an abundance of gold and silver. Alexander said to him: I have no need of your gold and silver. My only purpose is to see your customs, how you act and administer justice. While they were engaged in conversation, a man came before the king with a case against his fellow from whom he had bought a field with its scrap-heap and in it discovered a bundle of coins. The purchaser contended, I bought the heap but not the treasure hidden in it, and the vendor asserted, I sold the heap and all it contained. While they were arguing thus, the king turned to one of them and asked, Have you a son? Yes, he replied. He asked the other, Have you a daughter? and he answered, Yes. Let them marry and give them the treasure, was the king's decision. Alexander began to laugh, and Katzya inquired, Why do you laugh? Did I not judge well? Suppose such a case came before you, how would you have dealt with it? He replied: I would have put them both to death and confiscated the treasure. Do you, then, love gold so much? said Katzya.

179

Katzya made a feast for Alexander at which he was served with golden cutlets and golden poultry. I do not eat gold, Alexander exclaimed; and the king retorted, A curse on you! If you do not eat gold, why do you love it so intensely? He continued to ask, Does the sun shine in your country? Certainly, was the reply. Does rain descend in your country? Of course, Alexander replied. Are there small animals in your country? Of course, Alexander again replied. A curse on you! You only live, then, by the merit of those animals! Katzya finally retorted.

Yerushalmi 2:5 (8C)

■   USURY   ■

It has been taught: R. Joseph said: Come and see how blind usurers are. If a person should call someone a wicked man, he will retaliate by becoming his enemy for life, while usurers bring witnesses, a notary, pen and ink, and record and attest that so and so [the usurer] has rejected the God of Israel.

It has been taught: Whoever has funds and extends loans without taking interest, concerning him it is written: "He did not put out his money on interest, and he did not take a bribe against the innocent; he who does these things shall never be moved" [Ps 15:5].*

71a

Said R. Yose: Come and see how blind usurers are. If a person should call someone an idolator, or accuse him of having had sexual relations with a woman forbidden to him, or brand him a murderer, he will be his enemy for life, and this one engages a scribe and witnesses, and tells them to come and testify that he rejected God. R. Simeon b. Eleazar said: More than rejecting God, they are guilty of heresy because they declare the Torah a fraud, and our master Moses a fool, saying, If Moses had known the profits it offers, he would not have written [the prohibition].

R. Akiba said: Interest taking is a grievous offense, for even the extension of a favor is interest. Thus if he [the lender] asked him [the borrower] to buy for him vegetables in the market, even if he gave him

---

*In the Talmud as in the Bible there is no distinction between interest and usury; both are forbidden. Loans are conceived to be given as an act of kindness to the person temporarily in need, but the extensive warnings against interest suggest that it was often taken, in defiance of the law.

the money for it, it is interest [if he was not accustomed to doing such favors] for him. R. Simeon says: Interest taking is a grievous offense, for even extending a greeting may be interest. Thus if he never extended greetings to him [the lender], and because he extended a loan to him he is first to greet him—this is interest.

Yerushalmi 5:8 (10d)

■　　WITHIN THE LAW AND BEYOND THE LAW　　■

R. Joseph taught: [Jethro's advice to Moses in Ex. 18:20 is to be interpreted thus:] "You shall show them"—this refers to the practical ways of life; "the way"—this refers to deeds of lovingkindness; "they must walk"—this refers to visiting the sick; "therein"—this refers to burying the dead [of the poor]; "and the work"—this refers to actions in conformity to the law; "that they shall do"—this refers to actions beyond the demands of the law. For R. Yohanan said: Jerusalem was destroyed only because judgments were pronounced there in accordance with the laws of the Torah. But what should they have followed—the rules of the lawless? What it means is that they based their decisions on the laws of the Torah, and did not go beyond the claims of the law.

30b

Porters broke a barrel of wine belonging to Rabbah b. Hanan, and he seized their cloaks. They went and complained to Rav. He said to him: Return their cloaks. He [Rabbah] asked him: Is this the law? He replied: Yes, "so that you may walk in the way of good men" (Prv 2:20). They continued to complain: We are poor, we worked all day and are hungry, and have nothing. He [Rav] said to him [Rabbah]: Go and pay them their wages. He [Rabbah] asked: Is this the law? He [Rav] answered: Yes, "and keep the path of the righteous" (the conclusion of Prv 2:20).*

83a

When R. Dimi came [from Palestine to Babylonia] he said: How do we know that if one entered a claim for the repayment of a loan of a *maneh*, and the debtor does not have the funds to repay, he is not

---

*This is regarded as a decision that goes beyond the letter of the law.

permitted to pass in front of him? From the verse which states: "You shall not be to him as a creditor" (Ex 22:25).

■ LEVELS OF RESPONSIBILITY ■

A student once said to Rava: Would it be correct to say that in the verse: "You shall surely rebuke your neighbor" (Lv 19:17), "rebuke" means once and "you shall surely rebuke" means a second time? He replied to him: "Rebuke" means even a hundred times. As for "you shall surely rebuke," this comes to overrule the assumption that the master is under obligation to rebuke the disciple. How would we know that the disciple is obligated to rebuke the master? This is to be inferred from "you shall surely rebuke."

31a

If the owner [of the donkey that collapsed under its load] sat himself down and said [to the stranger], Since the commandment directs you to help unload, if you wish to unload, he is not obligated to do so, since the commandment ordains [that one is to unload] "with him" (Ex 23:5). But if the owner was elderly or sick, he is obligated to help him. The commandment of the Torah directs one to help unload, but not to help load. R. Simeon says: To load also. R. Simeon the Galilean said: If the owner had put on the animal more than it can bear, one is not commanded to help him, for the commandment to help specified: [If you see the animal lying] "under its burden," which means a burden it can bear.

MISHNAH 2:10

■ SENSITIVITY TO WORDS ■

As one may be guilty of wrongdoing in buying and selling, so may one be guilty of wrongdoing in words. One should not ask: What is the price of this object, when he has no wish to buy. If a person has repented from former wrongdoing, one must not say to him: Recall your former deeds. If he is a descendant of proselytes, one must not say to him: Remember the actions of your ancestors, for it is written: "And a stranger [*ger,* which came to mean a proselyte] you shall not wrong, nor shall you oppress him" (Ex 22:20).

MISHNAH 4:10

The rabbis taught: "You shall not wrong one another" (Lv 25:17). The verse here refers to wrongs inflicted with words. You say "wrongs inflicted with words," but perhaps this is not so, perhaps what is referred to here is wrongs committed in money matters? When in the same passage an earlier verse states: "When you sell to your neighbors, or buy from your neighbors, you shall not wrong one another" (Lv 25:14), then wrongs in money matters are already covered. What then can be the intent of the admonition in this verse: "You shall not wrong one another" (Lv 25:17)? It must refer to wrongs inflicted with words. How are we to understand this? If he is a penitent, one is not to say to him: Remember your earlier deeds. If he is a descendant of proselytes, one is not to say to him: Remember the deeds of your ancestors. If he is a proselyte and has come to study Torah, one is not to say to him: Shall the mouth that ate forbidden foods, forbidden animals, and reptiles now come to study Torah which was uttered by the mouth of the Almighty? If he should be visited with suffering, if he should be afflicted with illness, or if he buried his children, one is not to speak to him as his friends spoke to Job: "Is not your fear of God your confidence, and the integrity of your ways your hope? Think now, who that was innocent ever perished?" (Jb 4:6–7). If donkey drivers approach him to buy grain, he is not to tell them: Go to so and so who sells grain, when he knows that that person never sold grain. R. Judah said: He is not to pretend an interest in buying certain merchandise when he knows he has no money to buy it. A person knows this only in his own heart, and concerning all such matters which are known in the heart, the verse says: "You shall fear your God" (Lv 25:17).

R. Yohanan said in the name of R. Simeon b. Yohai: The wrong done with words is more serious than the wrongs done in money matters, for in the former case there is an explicit admonition against it in the words: "You shall fear your God," but there is no such admonition against the second case. R. Eleazar says: The former affects the victim's person, the latter only affects his money. R. Samuel b. Nahmani says: In the latter case, compensation is possible, but it is not possible in the former case.

A teacher taught in the presence of R. Nahman b. Yizhak: Whoever embarrasses another person in public it is as though he committed bloodshed. He said to him: Your statement is correct, for I have seen that in the case of such a person his reddish color recedes and he turns pale.

Abbaye said to R. Dimi: What are they especially careful about in Palestine? He replied: Putting other people to shame, for R. Hanina said: All wrongdoers will descend to hell, except three. All? Can you really mean it? This is what is meant: All who descend to hell will return from it, except these three, who will descend and not return. They are the following: One who has intercourse with a married woman, one who embarrasses another person in public, and one who refers to his neighbor with a derogatory nickname. But referring to one's neighbor with a derogatory nickname is the same as embarrassing him! This refers to a case where his neighbor has become used to that nickname.

Said Rav: A person should always be careful not to use words which hurt his wife, for she is readily moved to tears. And he is thus easily prone to violate the commandment against wrongdoing.

Said R. Helba: A person should always be careful to show respect for his wife, for the blessings of a home came about only because of one's wife, as the verse suggests: "And he did well with Abraham for her [Sarah's] sake" (Gn 12:16). It is in this light that we can understand the admonition of Rava to his townsmen in Mehoza: Treasure your wives that you may be enriched.

58b–59a

■   MIRACLES ARE NOT DECISIVE   ■

We studied in the Mishnah (Eduyot 7:7) that if a pottery stove was cut into tiles, and cemented over with sand placed between the tiles, R. Eliezer declared it unsusceptible to ritual uncleanliness, while the other Sages declared it susceptible. This was the Akhnai stove.*

---

*The case seems trivial but an important principle in law was involved here. According to biblical law (Lv 15:13), vessels may be contaminated with ritual uncleanliness. This stove had apparently been contaminated, and the owner, to evade the law that calls for its destruction, broke it into tiles, which were separated from each other by sand and plastered over with cement. Objectively the stove was no longer a "whole" vessel, and thus no longer under the biblical law. On the other hand, it could still be used; functionally it was still a vessel, and therefore subject to the biblical law. R. Eliezer generally ignored subjectivity in his interpreta-

THE TRACTATE BABA MEZIA

Why was it called Akhnai? Said R. Judah in the name of Samuel: They surrounded it with arguments as a snake winds its body around an object, and declared it unclean. It has been taught: On that day R. Eliezer marshaled every conceivable argument, but they did not accept them. Then he said: If the law is according to my views, let this carob tree prove it. Thereupon the carob tree was thrust to a distance of a hundred cubits from its place, and some say four hundred. They replied to him: We adduce no evidence from a carob tree. Again he said to them: If the law is in accordance with my views, let the stream of water prove it, and at once the stream of water flowed in the opposite direction. But they said: We adduce no evidence from a stream of water. Again he said to them: If the law agrees with my views, let the walls of the academy prove it, and the walls of the academy began to bend and were about to fall. R. Joshua rebuked them, saying: If scholars argue on a point of law, what business is it of yours? The walls did not fall out of respect for R. Joshua, but they did not become straight again out of respect for R. Eliezer.

Thereupon he said: If the law is in accordance with my views, let them prove it from heaven. A heavenly voice came forth, saying: What have you against R. Eliezer? The law is as he propounds it in all instances. R. Joshua then stood up and quoted: "It is not in the heavens" (Dt 30:12). What did he mean by quoting: "It is not in the heavens"? Said R. Jeremiah: That the Torah has already been given at Sinai, and we pay no attention to heavenly voices, for You have written at Sinai in the Torah: "Incline after the majority" (Ex 23:2).

R. Nathan met the prophet Elijah and he asked him: What did the Holy One, praised be He, do at that time? He replied: He laughed, and He said: My children have won over me, my children have won over me!

59a–59b

■   THE PRIORITY OF THE SELF   ■

It was taught: If two are on a journey [in the desert] and one has with him a container of water, if both drink from it, both will die, but

---

tion of the law, and therefore ruled it clean, while his colleagues countered (i.e., responded) the subjective factors and therefore ruled it in effect a whole vessel, subject to the law of levitical impurity. It has been suggested that Akhnai was the owner of the stove, but the fact that *akhna* means a snake led the Talmud to offer a homiletical interpretation.

if only one drinks from it he will be able to reach a place of habitation— Ben Patura taught that it is better that both drink and die, but one must not witness the death of his companion, until R. Akiba came and taught: "That your brother may live beside you" (Lv 25:36) means that your life has precedence.

62a

R. Joseph taught: "If you lend money to any of My people with you who is poor, you shall not be to him as a creditor, and you shall not exact interest from him" (Ex 22:25)—[if you have to choose in lending between] my people and a heathen, My people come first; if it is between a rich man and a poor man, the poor man comes first; if it is between the poor who are your kinsman and the general poor of the town, your kinsmen come first; if it is between the poor who are your townsmen and the poor of another town, your townsmen come first.

71a

The rabbis taught: The following cry out but there is no redress for them: One who has money and lends it out without witnesses; one who acquires a master for himself; and one who is dominated by his wife. What is meant by "one who acquires a master for himself"? Some say that it refers to a person who transfers his property to a gentile [to escape restrictions of rabbinic property laws], some say that it refers to one who transfers his property to his children in his lifetime, and some say that it refers to one who does not fare well in his own town, and does not move to another town.

75b

■   TORAH WITHOUT GOD   ■

R. Judah said in the name of Rav: What is meant by the verse: "Who is the wise man who can understand this, to whom the mouth of the Lord has spoken, so that he may declare it? Why has the land been destroyed?" (Jer 9:11). This question was discussed by the Sages but they could not explain it, it was discussed by the prophets but they did not explain it, until the Holy One, praised be He, Himself explained it, as the next verse continues: "And the Lord said: Because they have forsaken my Torah which I set before them" (Jer 9:12). Said R. Judah in the name of Rav: Because they did not pronounce a benediction before studying it.*

85a–85b

■　　FOR THE SAKE OF PEACE　　■

It is written: "And my husband is old" (Gn 18:12), and it is also written: ["And the Lord said to Abraham, Why did Sarah laugh, saying, Shall I yet have a child,] and I am old"? (Gn 18:13). The question quoted by God was not as she had asked it! In the school of R. Ishmael it was taught: Great is peace, for even the Holy One, praised be He, misquoted for its sake. Thus it is written: "And Sarah laughed to herself, saying, After I am old, shall I yet have marital pleasure, and my husband is old also" (Gn 18:12). But in the next verse it is written: "And the Lord said to Abraham, Why did Sarah laugh, saying, Shall I yet have a child, and I am old"? (Gn 18:13).

87a

---

*R. Judah Loew of Prague explains this to mean that they had made the study of the Torah a purely intellectual exercise, enjoyable for its own sake, without reflecting on the wisdom and goodness of God from whom it emanated.

XI

The Tractate Baba Batra

Baba Batra means literally the "last gate." This is the name of the third tractate in the Order of Nezikin or Damages. As noted in the introductory note to Baba Mezia, the first three tractates in this Order are designated the "First Gate" (Baba Kamma), the "Middle Gate" (Baba Mezia), and the "Last Gate" (Baba Batra). They originally formed one tractate but because it was so large, this corpus of material was divided into three tractates. There is a certain continuity in the thematic material covered in each of these tractates: They all discuss various aspects of civil law.

The first three chapters of the tractate discuss laws affecting real estate holdings. We are also informed of various restrictions imposed on the use of private property so as not to hurt the public interest, or the rights of neighbors living in the same courtyard.

The tractate continues with a discussion of the proper procedure for disposal of property by sale or by gift, the proper procedure for acquiring title to property, the duties of the seller and the buyer, and the laws of inheritance. As legal documents are of great importance in the subjects treated in these three tractates, the last chapter in Baba Batra is devoted to the regulations governing the writing of such documents. The tractate closes with a discussion of the great value attached to the study of civil law.

The selections included here embrace both legal and general moralistic material, because these legal discussions reflect a moralistic and ethical sensitivity. The subjects treated are the obligations of property owners to respect the rights of neighbors and of the public at large; the importance of charitable deeds both for the beneficiary and for the person bestowing the benefit; the human dimension in the authorship of the Bible; the contribution of Joshua b. Gamala in establishing a system of elementary education, which called for the placement of teachers in each community; and the guidance of the rabbis in moderating the expressions of mourning that emerged among Jews after the destruction of the Temple.

Baba Batra is one of the largest tractates of the Talmud. It consists of 176 folio pages, which are divided into ten chapters.

■ THE PRIVATE AND THE PUBLIC INTEREST ■

A resident in a courtyard may be compelled to share in building a gatehouse and a door for the courtyard. Rabban Simeon b. Gamaliel says: Not all courtyards need a gatehouse. Every townsman may be compelled to share in building a wall for the town and double doors and a bolt. Rabban Simeon b. Gamaliel says: Not every town needs a surrounding wall.

How long is a person to live in a town to become obligated to sharing in the town's expenses? Twelve months. If he bought a residence in the town he becomes obligated immediately.

MISHNAH 1:5

There was a certain pious man with whom Elijah used to converse. But after building a gatehouse [in his courtyard], he ceased to converse with him [because people in need no longer had access to the residents of the courtyard].

R. Eleazar asked R. Yohanan: When they impose a tax for the building of a town wall, is it levied on individuals equally, or is it according to one's means? He replied: It is levied according to means, and Eleazar my son, fix this ruling firmly in your mind. Another version of this is the following: R. Eleazar asked R. Yohanan: When the poll tax is levied, is it according to the proximity of the houses to the wall, or is it according to means? He replied: It is according to the proximity of the houses to the wall, and Eleazar my son, fix this ruling firmly in your mind.

7b

Rabbah b. Bar Hana said in the name of R. Yohanan: If the people of a town desire to close alleyways which lead to another town, the residents of the other town can object. It is so not only in a case where there is no other entrance to the other town, but even where there is another entrance they may also object, because of the principle laid down by R. Judah in the name of Rav, that a path which has been used by the public must not be damaged.

R. Anan said in the name of Samuel: If residents desire to put doors at the entrance to alleyways which lead to a public thoroughfare, the public may object.

12a

If a person opened a shop in a courtyard, a resident of the courtyard may object, claiming that he cannot sleep because of the noise of those who come and go. But one may make utensils and go out and sell them in the market, and a resident in that courtyard cannot object, and claim that he cannot sleep because of the noise of the hammer or of the millstones. Nor can one object to the noise of children [who come to be taught by a teacher living in that courtyard].

MISHNAH 2:3

■   DEEDS OF CHARITY   ■

Rabbi [Judah Ha-Nasi] opened storehouses of grain [to feed the needy] in a year of famine, and he proclaimed: Let those enter who have studied Bible or Mishnah or Gemara or halakha or aggada, but ignoramuses are not to enter. R. Jonathan b. Amram pushed his way in and pleaded: Master, give me food. He [R. Judah Ha-Nasi] said to him: My son, did you study Bible? He replied: No. Did you study Mishnah? He replied: No. If so, he said, how can I give you food? He [Jonathan] said to him: Feed me as the dog and the raven are fed [by God]. He gave him food. But after he left, Rabbi [Judah Ha-Nasi] sat and felt aggravated, saying: Alas, I gave of my food to an ignoramus! R. Simeon his son then said to him: Perhaps this person was your disciple Jonathan b. Amram who has been reluctant all his life to derive any worldly benefit from the honor due to the Torah. It was investigated and ascertained that this was indeed the case. Rabbi [Judah Ha-Nasi] then said: All may now enter.

8a

THE TRACTATE BABA BATRA

Rabban levied a charity tax on the orphans of the house of Bar Maron. Said Abbaye to him: But did not R. Samuel b. Judah rule that we are not to levy a charity tax on orphans, even if it is to liberate captives? He replied: I collect from them to show that they are important.

Iphra Hurmiz, the mother of King Shapur [of Persia], sent a purse of *dinars* to R. Joseph, with the instruction: Let these be used for an important *mitzvah*. R. Joseph sat and pondered what might be defined as an important *mitzvah*. Said Abbaye to him: Since R. Samuel b. Judah ruled that we do not levy a charity tax on orphans, even if it is to liberate captives, it implies that to liberate captives is to be regarded as an important *mitzvah*.

The rabbis taught: The charity fund is collected by two persons, and distributed by three. It is collected by two, because we do not appoint less than two to an office that exercises authority over the community, and it is distributed by three like the adjudication of civil cases which is in the hands of three judges. Food for the soup kitchen is collected by three and distributed by three, for the distribution follows immediately after the collection. Food allotments for the poor are distributed every day, charity funds are distributed every Friday. Food is distributed to all needy, charity funds are distributed only to the poor of the town. Townspeople may treat charity funds as food allotments and food allotments as charity funds, and to divert [such funds] to any other purpose they desire. And the townspeople are also at liberty to fix weights, and measures, and wages, and to penalize those who violate their ordinances.

"Those who are wise shall shine as the brightness of the firmament"—this refers to a judge who tries a case with full integrity, "and those who turn many to righteousness [*Zedakah*] like the stars forever and ever" (Dn 12:3)—this refers to those who collect funds for charity. In a *baraitha* it was taught: "Those who are wise shall shine as the brightness of the firmament"—this refers to judges who judge a case with full integrity and those who collect funds for charity, and "those who bring many to righteousness shall shine like the stars forever and ever"—this refers to teachers of young children. Like whom, for instance? Said Rav: Like Samuel b. Shilat. Rav once found Samuel b. Shilat standing in a garden. He said to him: Have you deserted your calling? He replied: It is now thirteen years that I have not seen it, and even now my mind is with the children.

The rabbis taught: Those who collect for charity must not separate one from another, but one may collect at the gate, while the others collect at a shop. If he found money in the market, he must not put it in his purse, but into the charity box; on returning home he is to take it for himself. Similarly if he reminded another person in the market that he owed him a *maneh*, and the latter paid him, he must not put it into his purse, but into the charity box; on returning home he is to take it for himself.*

The rabbis taught: Collectors of charity who have no poor persons to whom to distribute their funds are to have others exchange the small coins for large ones, but they are not to make the exchange themselves. If the stewards of the soup kitchen have food left over, with no poor people to whom to distribute it, they may sell it to others, but they may not buy it themselves.

It has been taught: R. Joshua b. Korha says: Whoever turns his eyes away from an appeal for charity is as though he worshiped idols. Here [where we are exhorted to help the needy] it is written: "Beware lest there be a base thought in your heart" (Dt 15:9), and elsewhere [where we are warned against seduction to idolatry] it is written: "Base fellows have gone out from among you" (Dt 13:13–14). As the term "base" in the latter verse refers to idolatry, so the term "base" in the former case denotes an offense as grievous as idolatry.

It has been taught: R. Judah says: Great is charity, for it brings nearer the redemption, for it is written: "Thus has the Lord spoken: Keep justice and do charity [*zedakah*, which is often translated as 'righteousness'], for My help is soon to come, and My righteousness is about to be revealed" (Is 56:1).

He also said: Ten strong things were created in the world. The mountain is strong but iron cuts through it. The iron is strong but fire melts it. The fire is strong but water quenches it. The water is strong but the clouds bear it. The clouds are strong but the wind scatters them. The wind is strong but the body endures it. The body is strong but fear crushes it. Fear is strong but wine dissipates it. Wine is strong but sleep wears it off. Death is mightier than all but charity [*zedakah*, often translated as "righteousness"] rescues from it, as it is written: "But deeds of righteousness [*zedakah*] save from death" (Prv 10:2).

---

*These precautions are all to avoid fraud, for the two collectors exercise some watch over each other. If one collector put the found money or the money collected for a debt in his own purse, he might be suspected by a viewer of pocketing public funds.

THE TRACTATE BABA BATRA

The rabbis taught: It was reported that King Munbaz [Munbaz II, who was king of Adiabene in the first century C.E. and was a convert to Judaism] distributed his treasures and those of his ancestors [to feed the hungry] in years of famine. His brothers and members of the royal household protested to him: Your ancestors saved and added to the possessions of their ancestors, but you squander them! He replied to them: My ancestors accumulated earthly treasures, but I have accumulated heavenly treasures, as it is written: "Truth sprouts from the earth, and charity [zedek] looks down from heaven" (Ps 85:12). My ancestors accumulated where a human hand can reach, but I accumulated where no human hand can reach, as it is written: "Charity [zedek] and justice are the foundation of Your throne" (Ps 97:2). My ancestors accumulated things that bear no fruit, but I accumulated something that bears fruit, as it is written: "Tell the righteous [zaddik] that it shall be well with them, for they shall eat the fruit of their deeds" (Is 3:10). My ancestors accumulated money, but I accumulated treasures of souls, as it is written: "The fruit of the righteous [zaddik] is a tree of life, and one who is wise acquires souls" (Prv 11:30). My ancestors accumulated for others, but I accumulated for myself, as it is written: "And charity [zedakah] shall be for yourself" (Dt 24:13). My ancestors accumulated for this world, but I accumulated for the world to come, as it is written: "Your righteousness [zidkeha] shall go before you, the glory of the Lord shall gather you in"(Is 58:8).

8a–11a

If one is half slave and half free, he serves his master one day and and himself one day. This is the view of the Beth Hillel. But the Beth Shammai say: You have solved the problem for his master, but you have not solved his problem. Thus he cannot marry a bondwoman, and he cannot marry a free woman. Shall he remain unmarried? But the world was created for the sake of propagation, as it is written: "He did not create it to be a waste, He created it to be inhabited" (Is 45:18). But we force his master to free him, and he is given a note for half his value. The Beit Hillel finally reversed themselves and accepted the ruling of the Beit Shammai.*

13a

---

*This slave must have belonged to two partners, one of whom freed him. The note given to his second master who is compelled to liberate him was to be paid by the freed slave, from his earnings as a free man.

THE TRACTATE BABA BATRA

The master has said: Joshua wrote the book which bears his name and the last eight verses of the Pentateuch. We have been taught similarly that the last eight verses in the Torah were written by Joshua. Thus it has been taught: "So Moses, the servant of the Lord, died there" (Dt 34:15). Is it possible that after Moses died he wrote: "Moses died there"? But Moses wrote until this statement; from this point on it was written by Joshua. This is the view of R. Judah, or, according to others, of R. Nehemiah. Said R. Simeon to him: Can we think of a scroll of the Torah with a single letter missing, and being told [by Moses]: "Take this scroll of the Torah" (Dt 31:26)? But until the last eight verses, the Holy One, praised be He, dictated, and Moses wrote. The rest, the Holy One, praised be He, dictated, and Moses wrote with tears. Thus we read similarly: "Then Baruch [the scribe of Jeremiah] answered them, he [Jeremiah] pronounced all these words to me with his mouth, and I wrote them with ink in the book" (Jer 36:18).

One of the rabbis sat in the presence of R. Samuel b. Nahmani and expounded: Job never existed, it is all a parable. He said to him: For one such as you we have the verse: "There was a man in the land of Uz, Job was his name" (Jb 1:1). He replied: But according to you, how do we interpret: "The poor man had nothing, save one little lamb which he had bought and raised" (2 Sm 12:3) [this was part of the prophet Nathan's reprimand to King David]. Is it anything but a parable? Here, too, it is all no more than a parable. If so, replied the other, why is his name and the name of his town mentioned?

15a

"Though You know that I am not guilty, yet no one can save me from Your hand" (Jb 10:7). Rav said: Job sought to exonerate everybody from the divine judgment. He said to Him: Sovereign of the universe, You created an ox with parted hoofs, and an ass with closed hoofs. You created the Garden of Eden [paradise] and You created *gehinnom* [hell]. You created righteous men and You created wicked men. Who can thwart You? But what did Job's friends reply to him? "You undo the fear of God, and hinder devotion before God" (Jb 15:4). The Holy One, praised be He, did create the evil impulse but He created an antidote for it in the Torah.

Rava expounded: "The blessing of him who was about to perish came to me, and I caused the widow's heart to sing for joy" (Jb 29:13).

THE TRACTATE BABA BATRA

"The blessing of one who was about to perish came to me"—Job used to take possession of a field belonging to orphans, improve it, and return it to them. "I caused the widow's heart to sing for joy"—wherever there was a widow who could not remarry, he associated his name with her [claiming she was his relative], and suitors came and married her.

16a

"And it came to pass, when men began to increase (*larov*) on the face of the earth, and daughters were born to them" (Gn 6:1).

R. Yohanan said: [With the birth of daughters] increase came into the world. Resh Lakish said: Quarreling came into the world.* Said Resh Lakish to R. Yohanan: According to you, who hold that [with the birth of women] increase came into the world, why were not the number of Job's daughters doubled?† He replied: Granted that they were not doubled in number, but they became twice as beautiful.

A daughter was born to R. Simeon, the son of Rabbi [Judah Ha-Nasi], and he was disappointed. His father said to him: Increase has come to the world. Bar Kapara said to him: Your father offered you an empty consolation. The world cannot survive without males and females, but fortunate is one who has male children, and alas for one whose children are females; the world cannot do without a spice-seller and a tanner. Fortunate is one whose occupation is that of a spice-seller, alas for one whose occupation is that of a tanner.

This divergence corresponds to a divergence among *tannaim:* "The Lord blessed Abraham with everything" [*bakol*] (Gn 24:1). What is meant by the term "everything"? R. Meir said: It refers to the fact that he did not have a daughter. R. Judah said: It refers to the fact that he had a daughter. Others say: Abraham had a daughter whose name was *Bakol* [everything].

16b

---

*The Hebrew *larov* means to increase, but it suggested to Resh Lakish *lariv*, which means "to quarrel." Resh Lakish apparently thought of women as quarrelsome.
†Job 42:10 reports that after Job's reconciliation with God, his fortunes were doubled. Then in 42:12 it reports him as having seven sons and three daughters.

195

THE TRACTATE BABA BATRA

R. Judah said in the name of Rav: Truly, this man, Joshua b. Gamala is his name, is to be remembered for good: Were it not for him the Torah would have been forgotten in Israel, for at first the child who had a father, his father taught him, and one who did not have a father did not study at all. What biblical authority did they go by? By the verse: "You shall teach them to your children" (Dt 11:19)—this was taken literally, *you* shall teach. Then it was ordained that teachers for young children be appointed in Jerusalem, guiding themselves by the verse: "For out of Zion shall go forth teaching [Torah], and the word of the Lord from Jerusalem" (Is 2:3). Even so, however, a child who had a father took him up to Jerusalem and had him taught there, while one who did not have a father did not study. Then it was decided to appoint teachers in provincial capitals. But they brought their children at the age of sixteen and seventeen, and whenever the teacher was angered with a student, the latter would rebel and leave. Then came Joshua b. Gamala and ordained that teachers of children be appointed in every district and every town, and that children be admitted at the age of six or seven.

Said Rava: Since Joshua b. Gamala's ordinance we do not send young children from one town to study in another, but we do send them from one synagogue to another [in the same town]. However, if a river separates one section of the town from another, we do not send them. But if there is a bridge we do; if it is only a plank we do not.

Rava also said: The number of children to be assigned to a teacher is twenty-five. If there are fifty we appoint two teachers; if there are forty, we appoint an assistant teacher, at the expense of the town.

21a

The rabbis taught: When the Second Temple was destroyed, many turned to asceticism, committing themselves not to eat meat and not to drink wine. R. Joshua approached them and said, My children, why do you not eat meat and drink wine? They replied to him: Shall we eat meat which used to be offered on the altar as a sacrifice, and now has been voided? Shall we drink wine, which used to be brought as a libation on the altar, and now it has been voided? He said to them:

If so, then we ought to discontinue eating bread, because the meal offerings have ceased. Shall we be sustained on fruit? But fruit, too, we should not eat, because the firstfruit offerings have ceased. Shall we get by with other fruit? But then we ought not to drink water because the pouring of water on the altar [on the feast of Succot] has ceased. They were silent. He then said to them: My children, come and I will advise you. Not to mourn altogether is impossible, because it [the destruction] has been decreed. But to mourn too much is also impossible, because we must not impose a decree on the community that the majority find unbearable. "You have imposed on yourselves a curse [if you do not bring the tithe], yet you rob Me, the entire nation" [implying that the vow would not have been effective if the entire nation had not assumed it]. But this is what the rabbis ordained: When a person plasters his house, let him leave a little unplastered. A person can prepare a full-course meal, but should omit a small item. A woman is to put on all her ornaments but is to leave out some item. For so is it written: "If I forget you, O Jerusalem, may my right hand wither. May my tongue cleave to the roof of my mouth, if I do not remember you, if I do not bring up Jerusalem on my greatest joy" (Ps 137:5–6). What is meant by "my greatest joy"? Said R. Isaac: This is expressed by placing ashes on the head of a bridegroom.*

It has been taught: R. Ishmael said: Since the Temple was destroyed, by right we ought to decree against ourselves not to eat meat and not to drink wine. But we do not impose measures on the public unless the majority would find them bearable. And since the evil government [Rome] has spread its power, decreeing against us evil decrees, forbidding us to study Torah, and to fulfill the commandments, and it does not allow us to circumcise a child, by right one ought to decree against ourselves not to marry and bring children to the world. But this would only result in the self-destruction of the children of Abraham. But it is best to leave the children of Israel alone. It is better that they do what they do unintentionally, rather than presumptuously.

60b

---

*The present custom is to break a glass at the end of a marriage service.

XII

The Tractate Sanhedrin

The term Sanhedrin *derives from the Greek* synedrion, *meaning a council or assembly. According to Josephus, the Roman procurator Gabinus divided Judea into five provinces, each to be administered by a Sanhedrin (*Antiquities *XIV 5:4). A sanhedrin, presided over by the High Priest, was the administrative body that acted as an auxiliary to the Roman occupation authorities in ruling Palestine. One of its principal functions was to ferret out subversives who might imperil the submission of the Jews to the Roman control of their land.*

In rabbinic sources the term is used primarily to designate a court of law. The tractate Sanhedrin deals with the composition and procedures of the courts that administered Jewish law. The Great Sanhedrin consisted of seventy-one ordained scholars who served as judges, and it met in the chamber of Hewn Stone in Jerusalem. The lesser sanhedrin consisted of twenty-three judges, and it met both in Jerusalem and in other parts of the country. There were also minor courts of three members, which are referred to by the general term beth din. *The description of the court system in this tractate is not always a faithful reflection of the judicial process as it was operative in early Talmudic times. It is often an idealized version of the judiciary as the Sages envisioned it, even though the reality may never have corresponded to it.*

The court of three dealt with monetary matters, while the court of twenty-three dealt with criminal cases, and was competent to inflict the death penalty. The court of seventy-one was a kind of appellate court, and it also dealt with special cases, such as trying a High Priest or a whole city accused of idolatry. Great care was taken as to the kind of persons appointed to the judiciary. Thus gamblers and usurers could

198

not serve as judges or witnesses. Nevertheless, we have echoes of incidents indicating that incompetent judges were sometimes appointed to this august office.

In the later tractate Makkot it is indicated that the rabbis generally frowned on capital punishment, and that it was in effect discontinued, but in the tractate Sanhedrin it is assumed to be the normal retribution for various offenses. Witnesses were examined with great care in capital cases. Circumstantial evidence was not admitted, and close relations could not testify against their kin in such cases.

There is much spiritual and moralistic material in this tractate. In the selections included here there appears an extended discussion on the various prerequisites for a truly just judiciary, and an interesting discussion of the appropriateness of arbitration, as against the administration of strict justice. The tragedy of taking life, even of a gross offender, is stressed, and we are told that while man, created with a limited moral sensitivity, may rejoice when the wicked fall, God does not rejoice. It is in this tractate that we have the statement that recognizes a pre-Sinaitic revelation that forms the basis for a valid religious life, outside of Judaism; one Sage is quoted as saying that a heathen, if he pursues the study of the Torah, is as precious in the sight of God as a High Priest in Israel. At the same time the Talmud quotes refutations of efforts to prove from biblical verses that God may be conceived in terms of plural forms. We have an echo of the Roman persecutions of Judaism during this period, and the rabbis are quoted as counseling their people how to act in such circumstances. The personal life is not ignored in this tractate—there is a touching description of the relationship that should prevail between husband and wife.

Two subjects in these selections illustrate the flexibility with which the rabbis interpreted biblical texts. In many instances a wide divergence had developed between the world of the Bible and the world of the rabbis, and the biblical exegesis developed by them sought to reconcile the tension between these two worlds. There is no explicit reference in the Bible to the resurrection of the dead and there were interpretations of Judaism that did not accept it. The rabbis, however, held it to be a basic element of their faith that when historical time reaches its end, and the world to come is ushered in, the dead deemed worthy by their earthly life would be resurrected to a new plane of existence. Through an ingenious interpretation of certain texts this teaching was read into the Bible.

Another instance of flexibility in the interpretation of the Bible is the rabbinic exegesis of the text setting forth the treatment of the "stubborn and rebellious son" (Dt 21:18–21). It is clear from some of the rabbinic interpretations of those verses that this law, which called for executing the culprit by stoning, seemed excessively harsh. The rabbinic interpretation narrowed the circumstances when this law might be applied to a point where it became practically inoperative. Indeed, one rabbinic pronouncement states categorically: There never was and there never will be an execution under the rule of the stubborn and rebellious son.*

There are 113 folio pages in this tractate, divided into eleven chapters.

■   CHARITY AND JUSTICE   ■

R. Eleazar the son of R. Yose the Galilean said: [Once a case has come before a judge] it is forbidden to arbitrate it, and whoever arbitrates it is a sinner, and whoever praises the arbitrator shows contempt [for God], and to such a person may be applied the verse: "He who praises the arbitrator despises the Lord" (Ps 10:3).† But let the law take its course [lit. "let the law cut through the mountain"], as it is written: "For the judgment belongs to God" (Dt 1:17). And thus was Moses wont to say: Let the law take its course.

But Aaron loved peace and pursued peace, and fostered peace between man and man, as it is written: "The teaching of truth was in his mouth, and no inequity was to be found on his lips, he walked with me in peace and uprightness, and he turned many away from iniquity" (Mal 2:6). R. Joshua b. Korha said: It is a virtuous act to arbitrate, for it is written: "Execute in your cities judgments of truth and peace" (Zec 8:16). Surely where there is stern justice there is no peace [because the litigants remain in discord], and where there is peace there is no stern justice. But what kind of justice goes together with peace? We must assume that it applies to arbitration. Thus it is also written concerning David. "And David used to execute justice and charity [zedakah] toward all his people" (2 Sm 8:16). But a judgment based on justice is not

*Tosefta Sanhedrin 11:6.
†The Hebrew permits this rendition but the half-sentence quoted is clearly taken out of context. The Revised Standard Version of the Bible renders it thus: "The wicked boasts of the desires of his heart, and the man greedy for gain curses and renounces the Lord."

200

charity, and one based on charity is not justice. This can only refer to arbitration, which takes into consideration justice and charity.

The following interpretation of the above verse will agree with the first *tanna* [master] who held that it was wrong to arbitrate. When David rendered a decision, acquitting the innocent and condemning the guilty, and he saw that a poor person was obligated to make restitution, he paid for it out of his own funds. This is what we mean by justice and charity—justice for the one to whom restitution was made, and charity for the other, because he [David] made the payment out of his own funds.

Rabbi [Judah Ha-Nasi] found difficulty with this interpretation, for in that case the verse should have said that David used to "execute justice and charity to the poor," not "to his whole people." His interpretation was that even if he did not pay out of his own funds, it was still "justice and charity," justice for the one and charity for the other— justice for the one to whom restitution was made, and charity for the other because he forced him to surrender inequitably begotten funds.

R. Simeon b. Menasye said: If two litigants come before you for judgment, before you have listened to their cases, or even if you have listened to their cases, but are still unsure which way the case ought to be decided, you may advise them to go and arbitrate. But once you have listened to their cases, and have decided on what decision is to be rendered, you may not advise them to go and arbitrate, for it is written: "The beginning of strife is like releasing a stream of water, so cease *before* the quarrel starts" (Prv 17:14)—before the case has been argued, you may terminate it, but after the case has been argued you may not terminate it.

Resh Lakish said: If two litigants come before you, one of whom is gentle and the other rough, before you have listened to their arguments, or even after you have listened to their arguments, but have not decided which way the decision ought to go, you may decline to judge the case, out of fear that if this rough one should be found guilty, he might persecute you. But once you have heard the arguments and you know which way the decision is to go, you may not decline to serve as their judge, for it is written: "You shall not be afraid of any man" (Dt 1:17).

R. Joshua b. Korha said: How do we know that if a disciple sits before his master who is trying a case and sees a point favorable to a poor litigant and unfavorable to the rich litigant, that he is not to be silent? We know it from the verse: "You shall not be afraid of any man" (Dt 1:17).

R. Hanina said: Do not hold back your words in deference to anyone. And witnesses should know concerning whom they testify, before Whom they testify, and Who will hold them accountable for their testimony. Thus it is written: "The two men [the witnesses] before whom is the controversy shall stand before the Lord" (Dt 19:17). And the judges should know whom they are judging, before Whom they are judging, and Who will hold them accountable for their judgment. Thus it is written: "God stands in the assembly of the mighty, He judges among those who render judgment" (Ps 82:1). Similarly in the case of Yehoshofat it is written: "He said to the judges, Consider what you do, for you do not judge for man, but for the Lord" (2 Chr 19:6). If the judge should say, Why do I need this trouble? The latter verse also adds: "He is with you in rendering judgment"—the judge is to be concerned only with what his eyes behold.

Said Rav: The law is in agreement with R. Joshua b. Korha [who holds arbitration a virtuous act]. Is this correct? Was not R. Huna a disciple of Rav, and when a case came before him, he would always ask the litigants: Do you wish to have the case adjudicated according to the law, or do you wish a settlement based on compromise? This is indeed what R. Joshua b. Korha meant when he said: It is a virtuous act to arbitrate—it is a virtue to ask them whether they wish to have the cases decided according to the law, or to have it settled by compromise.

R. Samuel b. Nahmani said in the name of R. Jonathan: A judge who judges cases with full integrity causes the *Shekinah* [the divine presence] to abide in Israel, as it is written: "God stands in the assembly of the mighty, He judges among those who pronounce judgment" (Ps 82:1), but a judge who does not render judgment with full integrity causes the *Shekinah* to depart from Israel, as it is written: "Because of the oppression of the poor, because of the sighing of the needy, I will now arise [to depart], says the Lord" (Ps 12:6).

When R. Dimi came [from Palestine] he reported a homily by R. Nahman b. Kohen: What is the significance of the verse: "By justice the king establishes the land, but he who loves gifts overthrows it" (Prv 29:4)? If the judge is like the king who is not subservient to anybody, he will establish the land, but if he is like a priest who goes about the threshing floors to collect the tithes due him as his perquisites, he will destroy it.

The officials of the *nasi* [the ruler of Judea under Roman domination] appointed a judge who was uneducated. The rabbis said to Judah b. Nahmani, the interpreter of Resh Lakish, Go and stand by his side and offer yourself to interpret his teaching. He went, and bent down to hear what he said, but he said nothing. R. Judah then began to expound: "Woe to him who says to a wooden thing, Awake, to a dumb stone, Arise. Can this teach? Behold, it is overlaid with gold and silver, and there is no breath at all in it" (Hb 2:19). But the Holy One, praised be He, will hold accountable those who appoint them, as the above verse is continued with this: "But the Lord is in His holy Temple, let all the earth be silent before Him" (Hb 2:20).

Resh Lakish said: Whoever appoints an unqualified judge is as though he planted an *asherah* [a tree used in an idolatrous cult of the ancient Semites] in Israel. Thus it is written: "You shall appoint judges and officers," and this is soon followed with "You shall not plant any tree as an *asherah*" (Dt 16:18, 21). Said R. Ashi: And where there are scholars [available for such appointment] it is as though he planted it beside the altar, for the admonition against planting a tree as an *asherah* adds the phrase "beside the altar of the Lord your God."

It is written: "You shall not make with Me gods of silver or gods of gold" (Ex 20:23). Is it only gods of silver and gods of gold that are forbidden, but those of wood are permitted? Said R. Ashi: This refers to judges appointed because of considerations of silver and judges appointed because of considerations of gold.

"Hear the cases between your brothers and judge righteously" (Dt 1:6). Said R. Hanina: This is an admonition to the court not to listen to a litigant before the arrival of the other litigant, and it is also an admonition to the litigant not to defend his claim before the arrival of his adversary. The latter inference may also be derived from the same verse, for one may not cause the judge to hear one litigant in the absence of the other. R. Kahane derived the latter inference from this verse: "You shall not take up [*tisa*] a false report" (Ex 23:1)—the verb for "take up" may be read in the causative sense, thus warning the litigant not to cause any condition which may falsify the judgment.

"You shall hear the small and the great alike" (Dt 1:17). Resh Lakish said: This means that a case involving a *perutah* [the smallest coin] shall be as important as one involving a hundred *maneh*. Of what significance is this ruling? Is it to require equal investigation and care in reaching a decision? But this is obvious. It is rather to require that all cases alike be taken up in the order in which they have been presented to the attention of the court.

"And I charged your judges at that time" (Dt 1:16), and shortly thereafter Moses is quoted as saying to the people: "And I charged you at that time" (Dt 1:18). Said R. Eleazar in the name of R. Simlai: The people were admonished to respect the judges, and the judges were admonished to be patient with the people. How far is this patience to go? Said R. Hanan, and according to others, R. Shabbetai said it: The measure of this patience is described in the verse: "As a nurse carries the sucking child" (Nm 11:12).

6b–8a

The following are disqualified from acting as judge or witness in a court of law: One who gambles with dice, a usurer, racers of pigeons, and merchants with produce grown in the Sabbatical year.* Said R. Simeon: At first the disqualification was directed at those who harvested the produce of the Sabbatical year, but when the oppressive tax collectors increased, the disqualification was applied only to merchants of the produce of the Sabbatical year. Said R. Judah: The disqualification applies only when these individuals have no other occupation, but when they have another occupation, they are qualified.

MISHNAH 3:5

Those who play with dice also includes those who play with wooden blocks. Whether one plays with wooden blocks or with nut shells or pomegranate peels, he is not to be accepted [as judge or witness] until he will break the blocks, and is checked to make sure that he has undergone a complete reformation. A usurer is not to be accepted until he tears up his notes, and is checked to make sure that he has undergone a complete reformation. Whether they race pigeons, or incite them to fight, or they incite domestic or wild animals or birds to fight, they are not to be accepted until they destroy the setting for their spectacles and undergo a complete reformation.

As for merchants in the produce of the Sabbatical year—a merchant in the produce of the Sabbatical year is one who is idle during the other years of the seven-year cycle, but when the seventh year comes, he begins to busy himself with selling Sabbatical year produce. These people are not accepted until another Sabbatical year arrives, and it is ascertained that they have undergone a complete reformation. It was taught: R. Jose said: Two Sabbatical years must pass with him

---

*According to Leviticus 25:6, the produce that grows by itself during the Sabbatical year was to be used only by the owner of the land and his household, and by the stranger who lived among the Israelites and had no land of his own.

abstaining from such commerce. R. Nehemiah said: There has to be restitution of money, not merely a verbal declaration of change. He must say to them: Here is this sum of two hundred [zuz] which I earned by merchandising fruit, when it was forbidden to do so, and distribute it to the poor.

Yerushalmi 3:5 (21a)

The rabbis taught: "The fathers shall not be put to death because of the children" (Dt 24:16). What does this seek to convey? If it is to teach us that fathers are not to be put to death for the offenses of children or children for the offenses of fathers, this has already been stated in the conclusion of that verse: "Each person shall be put to death for his own offense." What it seeks to convey is this. Fathers shall not be put to death because of children, that is, through the testimony of children, and children shall not be put to death because of fathers, that is, through the testimony of fathers. But do not children suffer for the sins of fathers? Is it not written: "He visits the iniquity of fathers on children" (Ex 34:7)? That applies only where the children follow the ways of their fathers.

28a

Resh Lakish said: One who raises his hand against his neighbor, even if he did not strike him, is called a wicked man. Thus it is written: "And he said to the wicked man, Why would you strike your fellow?" (Ex 2:13). It does not say, "Why did you strike," but "Why would you strike," which shows that even if he did not strike him he is called a wicked man. Zeira said in R. Hanina's name: He is called a sinner. Thus it is written: "But if not, I will take it by force," whereupon there follows this statement: "Wherefore the sin of those youths was very great before the Lord" (1 Sm 2:16).

58b

■　　BETWEEN HUSBAND AND WIFE　　■

R. Eliezer said: Whoever divorces his first wife, even the altar sheds tears because of him. Thus it is written: "And this again you do: You cover the Lord's altar with tears, with weeping and groaning, for He no longer looks with favor at the offerings, or accepts them favorably from you." And the text continues: "You ask, Why does He not? Because the Lord was witness between you and the wife of your youth, whom you have betrayed, though she is your companion and your wife by covenant" (Mal 2:13–14).

R. Yohanan also said: A person who suffered the death of his first wife, it is as though the Temple was destroyed in his lifetime. Thus it is written: "Son of man, behold, I will take away from you the delight of your eyes with a stroke, yet you shall not make lamentation, nor weep, nor shall your tears run down." Then it is written: "I spoke to the people in the morning, and in the evening my wife died." Then in interpreting this vision to the people the verse quotes the prophet as saying: "I [God] will profane My sanctuary, the pride of your strength, the delight of your eyes" (Ez 24:16, 18, 21).

R. Alexandre said: The world is darkened for a person whose wife died in his lifetime. Of such a person it is written: "The light is dark in his tent, and his lamp above him is put out" (Jb 18:6). R. Yose b. Hanina said: Such a person walks with a shorter step. Thus the above verse is followed with: "His strong steps are shortened" (Jb 18:7). R. Abbahu said: His power of counsel declines, for the above verse concludes with: "And his counsel shall throw him down."

R. Samuel b. Nahman said: For everything there is a substitute, except for the wife of one's youth. Thus it is written: "The wife of one's youth—how can one reject her?" (Is 54:6).

A tanna taught: The death of a man is felt primarily by his wife, and a wife's death is felt primarily by her husband. That a man's death is felt primarily by his wife is suggested by the verse: "And Elimelekh died, the husband of Naomi" (Ru 1:3) [showing that the loss was primarily hers], and that a wife's death is felt primarily by her husband is suggested by the verse: "And as for me, when I came from Padan, I suffered the loss of Rachel" (Gn 48:7).

22a–22b

■　　　THE SANCTITY OF LIFE　　　■

How do we impress upon the witnesses to be awed at their responsibility when testifying in capital cases? They were assembled and admonished thus: Perhaps your testimony is based on conjecture or hearsay, or on a report by another witness or on a statement by a person you judge trustworthy. Perhaps you were not aware that we shall finally cross-examine you carefully. You must realize that civil cases differ from capital cases. In a civil case one may gain atonement for testifying erroneously through monetary restitution, but in a capital case the blood of the innocent executed through false testimony and that of his descendants who might have derived from him will haunt him to the end of time. Thus we find in the case of Cain who killed his brother the text states: "The voice of bloods [the Hebrew is *demei*, which is plural] of your brother cry out" (Gn 4:10). It does not say: The blood of your brother, but the bloods. It refers to his blood and that of his descendants. As to the latter, there is another explanation: The text uses the plural bloods, because his blood lay splashed over trees and stones.

All mankind was created from a single ancestor to teach us that whoever takes a single life it is as though he destroyed a whole world, and whoever sustains a single life it is as though he sustained a whole world. It is also meant to foster peace among people, because no one can boast to his neighbor: My answer was greater than yours. It is also meant to negate the claim of heretics who claim that there are many divine powers. It also serves to dramatize the greatness of the Holy One, praised be He, for a person strikes many coins from one mould and they all remember each other, but the King of Kings, the Holy One, forms all mankind from the mould of the first man, and all are unique. Therefore, each one is obligated to say: The world was created for my sake.

If the witnesses should then say: Why do we need all this trouble? The answer to them is already written: "If one be a witness, whether he saw or knew, and he refuse to testify, he shall bear his iniquity" (Lv 5:1). And if they say: Why should we bear the onus of taking the accused person's life? The answer to this has already been stated: "When the wicked perish, there is rejoicing" (Prv 11:10).

MISHNAH 4:9

"And the joyful cry [*rinah*] went up in the camp" (1 Kgs 22:36) [after King Ahab died, and the army could go home]. Said R. Aha b. Hanina: "When the wicked perish there is rejoicing" (Prv 11:10). When Ahab ben Omri [the wicked king of Israel] died there was rejoicing. But does the Holy One, praised be He, rejoice at the downfall of the wicked? Is it not written: "As they went out before the army [before attacking the adversaries of Judea] they were to chant: "Praise the Lord, for His mercy is everlasting" (2 Chr 20:21). And R. Yohanan asked why the phrase "for it is good" is omitted after "Praise the

Lord,"* and he answered: The Holy One, praised be He, does not rejoice in the downfall of the wicked. For R. Samuel b. Nahman said in the name of R. Jonathan: What are we to comment on the verse: "And one did not approach the other [the pursuing Egyptians and the fleeing Israelites] all night" (Ex 14:20). At that time the angels want to join in a hymn of praise to the Holy One, praised be He, but the Holy One, praised be He, said to them: My handiwork is perishing in the sea, and you are going to sing in celebration? Said R. Yose b. Hanina: He does not rejoice, but He causes others to rejoice [because He created them with a lower level of moral sensitivity].

30b

R. Yohanan said in the name of R. Simeon b. Yehozadok: A consensus was reached at a session in the upper chamber in the house of Nitzeh, in Lydda, that every law in the Torah, if a person is given the choice to violate it or be killed, he is to violate it, except the prohibition of idolatry, incest, and murder.

R. Ishmael said: How do we know that if a person is told to serve an idol or he will be put to death, he is to serve the idol, because it is written: ["You shall therefore keep My statutes and my judgments, which, if a man do] he shall live by them" (Lv 18:5)—but not die by them. It might be assumed that he is to do so publically. The verse therefore states: "You shall not profane My holy name, and I shall be hallowed" (Lv 22:32).

A certain person once came to Rabba and told him: The governor of my town has ordered me to kill so and so, or else he will kill me. He answered him: Let him kill you, but you must not kill. Who says that your blood is redder, perhaps the blood of that person is redder.

74a

■   ATTITUDES TOWARD NON-JEWS   ■

The rabbis taught: Seven commandments were assigned to the children of Noah:† the establishment of a system of justice; the prohibi-

---

*The same chant appears in Psalm 107:1 thus: "Praise the Lord for He is good." The Hebrew permits both translations, "for He is good" or "for it is good."

†The law revealed to the Noahides was conceived by the rabbis as a universal law to govern all human behavior. It preceded the revelation at Sinai, which formed the basis for the particular body of law given to the Israelites.

tion of blasphemy, idolatry, incest, murder, robbery; and the eating of flesh cut from a living animal. R. Hanina included the eating of blood drawn from a living animal. R. Hidka also added castration. R. Simeon also added witchcraft. R. Yose said: A Noahide was cautioned against all the evils mentioned in the chapter on witchcraft: "There shall not be found among you one who consigns his son or his daughter as a burnt offering, an augur, a soothsayer, a diviner, a sorcerer, one who casts spells, or consults ghosts or familiar spirits, or holds seances with the dead. Anyone who practices these abominations is abhorrent to the Lord, and it is because of these abhorrent things that the Lord is dispossessing them [the heathen Canaanites] before you" (Dt 18:10–12). Now the Lord does not punish unless He has previously declared such action an offense.

56a–56b

R. Meir used to say: How do we know that even a heathen who pursues the study of the Torah is as a High Priest [in Israel]? Because it is written: ["You shall therefore keep My statutes and judgments] which if a man do, he shall live by them" (Lv 18:5). It does not say "which if a kohen [a priest] or a Levite, or an Israelite do." From this we may infer that even a heathen, if he studies the Torah, is as a High Priest [in Israel].

59a

■   A STUBBORN AND REBELLIOUS SON   ■

"If a man have a stubborn and rebellious son" (Dt 21:18)—a son, but not a daughter, a son but not a full-grown man. But a minor is exempt [from the penalty], since he has not yet become subject to the commandments.*

MISHNAH 8:1

---

*The full text in the Bible is: "If a man has a stubborn and rebellious son, who will not obey the voice of his father or the voice of his mother, and, though they chastise him, he will not give heed to them, then his father and his mother shall take hold of him and bring him to the elders of the city at the gate of the place where he lives and they shall say to the elders of the city, 'This our son is stubborn and rebellious, he will not obey our voice, he is a glutton and a drunkard.' Then all the men of the city shall stone him to death with stones, so shall you purge the evil from your midst; and all Israel shall hear and be afraid" (Dt 21:18–21). The excessive harshness of this provision led the rabbis of the Talmud to a series of interpretations that limited the applicability of this ordinance.

THE TRACTATE SANHEDRIN

R. Keruspedai in the name of R. Shabetai: The law of a stubborn and rebellious son is applicable only during three months in his life cycle.

69a

If his father desires to have him punished as a "stubborn and rebellious son," but his mother does not, or if his father does not desire it, but his mother does—he is not treated as a "stubborn and rebellious son" unless they both desire it. R. Judah said: If his mother is not suitable for his father, he does not become a "stubborn and rebellious son."

MISHNAH 8:4

It has been taught similarly: R. Judah said: If his father is not like his mother in voice, in appearance, and in height he is not treated as "a stubborn and rebellious son." What is the reason for this? The verse states [in the charge brought against him]: "He will not listen to our voice" (Dt 18:20)—since there has to be a similarity in voice, there also has to be a similarity in appearance and height. With whom does the following teaching accord: There never was a "rebellious son" and there never will be. Why then was it written in the Torah? To give us the benefit of study. It will obviously agree with the view of R. Judah. But if you wish it, we may say that it is in agreement with R. Simeon. For it has been taught: R. Simeon said: Because one eats a *tartemar* of meat and half a log of Italian wine, shall his father and mother have him stoned to death? But it never happened and it never will happen. Why then was it written in the Bible? It was to give us the benefit of studying it.

71a

It has been taught: R. Yose the Galilean said: Is it possible that the Torah should teach that because one eats a *tartemar* of meat and drinks half a log of Italian wine he is to be brought to court and sentenced to stoning? But the Torah foresaw the final course of the stubborn and rebellious son's life. For in the end, after dissipating his father's possessions, and wanting to satisfy his lusts and being unable to do so, he will go into the streets and rob people. The Torah therefore said: Let him die while still innocent, rather than die guilty.

72a

210

THE TRACTATE SANHEDRIN

R. Yohanan said: In all the passages cited by the *minim** as grounds for their heresy, their refutation is found shortly thereafter. There is the passage: "Let us make man in Our image after Our likeness" [implying plurality in the deity]. This is followed by: "And God made man in His image" (Gn 1:26, 27). There is the verse: "Let us go down there and confuse their speech." This is complemented by: "And the Lord [singular] came down to see the city and the tower" (Gn 11:7, 5). There is the verse: "Because there God were revealed [plural] to him." This is complemented by: "To God who answers [singular] me in my distress" (Gn 35:7, 3). There is the verse: "And what one nation on earth is like your people Israel, whom God went [plural] to redeem, to make them a nation to Himself" (2 Sm 7:23).

38a

How can the belief in the resurrection of the dead be proven from the Torah? Because it is written: "and you shall contribute from it the Lord's offering to Aaron the priest" (Nm 18:28). Would Aaron live forever? He did not even enter Eretz Yisrael that offerings should be given him. But this indicates that he was to be resurrected and the children of Israel would give him offerings. Thus the resurrection of the dead is implied in the Torah.

It has been taught: R. Similai said: How can we prove the resurrection of the dead from the Torah? From the verse: "And I have established my covenant with them [the patriarchs] to give them the land of Canaan" (Ex 6:4)—it does not say to give you but to give them [the patriarchs]. This proves the resurrection of the dead from the Torah.

The *minim* asked Rabban Gamaliel: How do we know that the Holy One, praised be He, will resurrect the dead? He cited proofs from the Torah, the prophets, and the other writings, but they did not accept them. As proof from the Torah he cited the verse: "And the Lord said to Moses: You shall sleep with your fathers, and rise up [again]" (Dt 31:16). They said to him: Perhaps the phrase "will rise up"

Minim means sectarians, but it often designates the Judeo-Christians, who polemicized against the Jews, trying to show from Scripture that it was legitimate to speak of God in trinitarian terms. See Reuven Kimelman, "*Birkat Ha-Minim* and the Lack of Evidence for an Anti-Christian Jewish Prayer in Late Antiquity," in *Jewish and Christian Self-Definition*, ed. E. P. Sanders, vol. 2 (Philadelphia: Fortress Press, 1981), pp. 226–44.

should be read with the latter part of the verse, thus: "And this people will rise up and go astray." From the prophets he cited the verse: "Your dead shall live, their dead bodies shall rise. You who dwell in the dust awake and sing for joy, for your dew is a dew of light, and the earth shall cast out its dead" (Is 26:19). [Their retort was:] Perhaps this refers to the dead who were restored to life in Ezekiel's vision (Ez 36). From the other writings he cited the verse: "Your words are like good wine, that goes down sweetly for my beloved, causing those who sleep to speak" (Sg 7:10). [They replied:] Perhaps this only means that their lips will move, even as R. Yohanan said in the name of R. Yehozadok: Anyone in whose name a law is quoted in this world, his lips will move in his grave, as it is written: "Your words . . . causing those who sleep to speak." They were finally persuaded when he quoted to them: "The land which the Lord swore to your fathers to give them" (Dt 11:21)—it does not say to give you, but to give them. This proves the resurrection of the dead from the Torah. Others say that he proved it from this verse: "But you who did cleave to the Lord your God, are all alive this day" (Dt 4:4)—as you are all alive this day, so will you be alive in the world to come.

90b

XIII

The Tractate Makkot

The term makkot means flogging, and this tractate deals mostly with various offenses for which the penalty imposed was flogging, but other subjects are treated as well. Thus the second chapter deals with banishment to cities of refuge, where a person guilty of unintentional homicide found refuge.

Included here are some daring illustrations of the independence with which the rabbis reacted to biblical texts. In the Bible capital punishment is often invoked; it is the most common punishment for infraction of the law. Here, however, are a number of rabbis who in effect ruled out capital punishment as a viable penalty, regardless of the crime. It is generally assumed that there is no doctrinal divergence between the teachings of Moses and those of the prophets, but in this tractate we are given at least four instances where such a divergence is discernible. The selections here quoted cite those passages that illustrate this tendency of the rabbinic mind. According to the rabbis, even the prophets did not reach the heights of the divine standard of love and open forgiveness to the straying penitent. A selection from the Palestinian Talmud reflects this by contrasting the treatment of sinners as recommended by wisdom, by prophecy, and by God himself.

The tractate Makkot is one of the smaller tractates of the Talmud. It consists of 24 folio pages, which are divided into three chapters.

■   CAPITAL PUNISHMENT   ■

A Sanhedrin that is responsible for an execution once in seven years is called "tyrannical." R. Eleazar b. Azaryah said: Once in seventy years. R. Tarfon and R. Akiba said: If we were members of the Sanhedrin, no one would ever be sentenced to death. Rabban Simeon b. Gamaliel said: They would thereby have caused an increase of murderers in Israel.

MISHNAH 1:10

■   A SUMMATION OF THE COMMANDMENTS   ■

R. Similai expounded: Six hundred and thirteen commandments were communicated to Moses at Sinai, three hundred and sixty-five negative ones, corresponding to the number of days in a solar calendar year, and two hundred and forty-eight positive ones, corresponding to the number of joints in the human body. David came and reduced them to eleven. Thus it is written: "A Psalm of David. Lord, who shall sojourn in Your tabernacle, who shall dwell on Your holy mountain? (1) He who walks uprightly, and (2) acts righteously, and (3) speaks the truth in his heart; (4) who hears no slander on his tongue, (5) who does no evil to his fellow, (6) nor takes up a reproach against his neighbor, (7) in whose eyes a vile person is despised, (8) but he honors those who fear the Lord. (9) He swears to his own heart and does not change. (10) He does not put out his money on interest, (11) nor does he take a bribe against the innocent. He who does these things will never be moved" (Ps 15).

Isaiah came and reduced them to six. Thus it is written: "(1) He who walks righteously, and (2) speaks uprightly, (3) who despises the gain of oppression, (4) who withdraws his hands from holding a bribe, (5) who stops his ears from hearing of blood, and (6) shuts his eyes from looking on evil. He shall dwell on high" (Is 33:15–16).

Micah came and reduced them to three. Thus it is written: "It has been told you, O man, what is good and what the Lord requires of you: only (1) to do justly, (2) to love mercy, and (3) to walk humbly with your God" (Mi 6:8).

Isaiah came again and reduced them to two. Thus it is written: (1) "Keep justice and (2) do righteousness" (Is 56:1).

Amos came and reduced them to one. Thus it is said: "Thus has the Lord spoken to the House of Israel: 'Seek me and live' " (Am 5:4). R. Nahman b. Isaac challenged this. Perhaps "seek me" means by observing all the prescriptions in the Torah. But it was Habakuk who reduced them to one. Thus it is said: "The righteous shall live by his faith" (Hb 2:4).

24a

■ MOSES AND THE PROPHETS ■

R. Yose b. Hanina said: Our master Moses issued four decrees against Israel, but four prophets came and voided them. Moses said: And Israel shall dwell safely, the fountain of Jacob *alone* (Dt 33:18). Amos came and voided it, as it is said: "Then said I, O Lord our God, cease, I beseech you, how shall Jacob stand *alone*, for he is small"; and then it is said: "The Lord repented concerning this; this also shall not be, says the Lord God" (Am 7:5–6). Moses said: "And among these nations you shall have no repose" (Dt 18:65). But Jeremiah came and said: "Thus says the Lord, The people who survived the sword found grace in the wilderness, I will go to give Israel rest" (Jer 31:1, 2). Moses said: "The Lord visits the sins of fathers on children and on the children's children, to the third and fourth generation" (Ex 34:7). But Ezekiel came and said: "The soul that sins—it [alone] shall die" (Ez 18:3–4). Moses said: "And you shall perish among the nations" (Lv 26:38). But Isaiah came and said: "And it shall come to pass in that day that a great shofar shall be sounded and those who were lost in the land of Assyria and those who were driven out to the land of Egypt will come and worship the Lord on the holy mountain in Jerusalem" (Is 27:13).

24a

■ THE WAY OF PENITENCE ■

They asked wisdom: What is to be the punishment of the sinner? It replied to them: "Evil shall pursue sinners" (Prv 13:21). They asked prophecy: What is to be the punishment of the sinner? Its reply was: "The soul that sins—it shall die" (Ez 18:3–4). They asked the Holy One, praised be He: What is to be the punishment of the sinner? His reply was, Let him repent and he will be forgiven. Thus it is written: "Therefore does He instruct sinners in the way" (Ps 25:8)—He instructs sinners in the way by doing penance.

Yerushalmi 2:6 (31d)

XIV

The Tractate Abodah Zarah

A few brief selections from the tractate Abodah Zarah are included here. Abodah Zarah belongs to the Order of Nezikin, or Damages. The name means "idolatry," and this tractate records various precautions taken by the rabbis to insulate their people from idolatry.

The warning against idolatry is sounded often in the Bible, but here the idolatry was centered in the various cults adhered to by the indigenous population in Canaan. Many of those people remained and lived among the Israelites who settled in the land. The idolatry that troubled the rabbis was the Roman equivalent, which included deification of various forces of nature, as well as the deification of the emperor. What was as reprehensible was a degraded ethical system, in which life was of little value.

The Talmud alludes particularly to the cruel sports of the Romans, centering in the gladiatorial combat in the arena. The scope of these games may be gauged from the following figures: At the inauguration of the colosseum in Rome five thousand wild and four thousand tame animals were killed and to celebrate one of Emperor Trajan's victories eleven thousand animals were butchered—and how many human victims fell in these wild orgies?

Judea was but a province of the larger Roman empire. The rabbis feared that their people would be contaminated by the Roman way of life, and they adopted various measures to insulate their people from the influence of Roman culture, its idolatrous practices and its low standards of morality. The text of the Talmud speaks in general terms about idolators, but it is evident that it is the Romans who are meant here.

There are 76 folio pages in this tractate, divided into five chapters.

THE TRACTATE ABODAH ZARAH

■   AGAINST COLLABORATION WITH THE ROMANS   ■

R. Ishmael says: For three days before their festivals and for three days after them it is forbidden [to do business with the idolators]. But the Sages say: Before their festivals it is forbidden, but after the festivals it is not forbidden.

And these are the festivals of the idolators: the Calends [the first day of the year, eight days after the winter solstice], the Saturnalia [December 17, eight days before the solstice], Kartesis [the date of the capture of Alexandria by Augustus], the anniversaries of emperors, their birthdays and the anniversaries of their deaths. This is the view of R. Meir. But the Sages say: Funeral rites at which the articles of the deceased are burnt are idolatrous [and forbidden], but when there is no such burning it is not idolatrous.

MISHNAH 1:2, 3

One may not sell them [idolators*] bears or lions or anything else which may result in injury to the public. One may not build with them a basilica, a prison house, a stadium and a podium. But one may build with them pedestals and bath houses. However, one must desist when reaching the vaulted area where the idol is placed.

MISHNAH 1:7

It was taught: One who views the sorcerers and charmers or the performances of *bukion* and *mukion, lulion* and *mullion, blurin* and *salgarin*† has violated the prohibition of sitting "in the seat of the scornful," which is implied in the verse: "He did not sit in the seat of the scornful" (Ps 1:1); and all of these distract a person from the Torah, [which should be his goal,] as it is written: "But in His Torah he meditates day and night" (Ps 1:2).

---

*This Mishnah clearly reflects the effort of the rabbis to insulate the Jews from involvement in Roman culture and its brutal way of life. The bears and lions were undoubtedly to be used in the gladiatorial combat in the arena. The basilica was the administrative building of the Roman authority and the location of its courts. The prison was usually near the basilica and it was notorious for the torture of prisoners. The stadium was part of the amphitheater, where the spectators viewed the games; the podium was the platform from which the games and other administrative matters were directed. The problem with the public baths, a characteristic institution of Roman society, was the placement of an idol in a conspicuous vaulted area.

†These are technical names for various popular forms of Roman entertainment.

THE TRACTATE ABODAH ZARAH

It is forbidden to go to the amphitheater of the gentiles, because of idolatry, so says R. Meir, but the Sages say, when they offer sacrifices it is forbidden because it is "a seat of the scornful" (Ps 1:1–2). One who goes to the amphitheater so as to shout for mercy,* if it is for the public welfare, it is permitted, but if he associates with them, it is forbidden. One who sits in the amphitheater is guilty of bloodshed. R. Nathan permits it because of two considerations. As a spectator he may shout for mercy and thus save lives, and he may be able to testify so as to enable a woman to remarry.†

Yerushalmi 1:7 (40a)

It has further been taught: It is forbidden to sell them weapons or accessories to weapons, nor should one sharpen weapons for them. One may not sell them blocks or neck-bands placed on prisoners or ropes or iron chains—neither to idolators nor to Cuthites.‡ R. Nahman said in the name of Rabbah b. Avuha: Just as they ruled that it is forbidden to sell [these items] to an idolator so is it forbidden to sell them to an Israelite who is suspected of selling them to an idolator. The rabbis taught: It is forbidden to sell them shields, but others say that shields may be sold to them. Said R. Nahman in the name of Rabba b. Avuha: The law agrees with the others.

15b–16a

---

*The rules of the gladiatorial combat allowed spectators to shout for mercy, to spare a wounded gladiator.

†The gladiators were often prisoners of war or those the Roman courts had condemned to death. There were frequently Jews among them. One who witnessed the spectacle might be able to testify to a victim's death, thus enabling the Jewish court to declare his wife a widow and permit her to remarry.

‡The Cuthites have sometimes been identified with the Samaritans. They practiced a deviant version of Judaism. The rule against selling them weapons was due to the suspicion that they might sell them to the idolators, here referring undoubtedly to the Romans.

XV

The Tractate Avot

Tractate Avot, commonly called The Ethics of the Fathers, *is one of the most famous parts of the Mishnah. It is distinctive in not containing any legal teaching but in presenting a collection of comments about life, or moral philosophy, submitted in the name of the rabbinic great masters, as parental advice to the people they sought to educate. It is also notable for its chain of tradition setting out how the rabbis envisioned the transmission of Torah from Moses until their own times.*

Reflecting a custom attested as early as the ninth century, the tractate was studied on Saturday afternoons during the summer months. To facilitate this, it was finally incorporated into the Prayer Book. For the latter purpose, a sixth supplemental chapter to the original five was added. No Gemara to Avot was compiled, though there exists a non-Talmudic treatise called The Fathers According to Rabbi Nathan, *which is structured around Avot and expands on its themes.*

■ CHAPTER I ■

1. Moses received the Torah at Sinai. He conveyed it to Joshua; Joshua to the elders; the elders to the prophets; and the prophets transmitted it to the men of the Great Assembly. The latter emphasized three principles: Be deliberate in judgment; raise up many disciples; and make a fence to safeguard the Torah.

2. Simeon the Just was of the last survivors of the Great Assembly. He used to say: The world rests on three foundations: the Torah;

the divine service; and the practices of lovingkindness between man and man.

3. Antigonus of Soḥo received the tradition from him. He was accustomed to say: Be not like servants who serve their master because of the expected reward, but be like those who serve a master without expecting a reward; and let the fear of God be upon you.

4. Yose ben Yoezer of Zeredah and Yose ben Yohanan of Jerusalem received the tradition from them. Yose ben Yoezer of Zeredah said: Let your house be a gathering place for wise men; sit attentively at their feet, and drink of their words of wisdom with eagerness.

5. Yose ben Yohanan of Jerusalem said: Let your home be a place of hospitality to strangers; and make the poor welcome in your household; and do not indulge in gossip with women. This applies even with one's own wife, and surely so with another man's wife. The sages generalized from this: He who engages in profuse gossiping with women causes evil for himself and neglects the study of the Torah, and he will bring upon himself retributions in the hereafter.

6. Joshua ben Peraḥya and Nittai the Arbelite received the tradition from them. Joshua ben Peraḥya said: Get yourself a teacher; and acquire for yourself a companion; and judge all people favorably.

7. Nittai the Arbelite said: Avoid an evil neighbor; do not associate with the wicked; and do not surrender your faith in divine retribution.

8. Judah ben Tabbai and Simeon ben Shataḥ received the traditions from them. Judah ben Tabbai said: Let not the judge play the part of the counselor; when two litigants stand before you, suspect both of being in the wrong; and when they leave after submitting to the court's decree, regard them both as guiltless.

9. Simeon ben Shatah said: Search the witnesses thoroughly and be cautious with your own words lest you give them an opening to false testimony.

10. Shemaya and Abtalyon received the traditions from them. Shemaya said: love work; hate domineering over others; and do not seek the intimacy of public officials.

11. Abtalyon said: Sages, be precise in your teachings. You may suffer exile to a place where heresy is rampant, and your inexact language

may lead your disciples astray, and they will lose their faith, thus leading to a desecration of the divine name.

12. Hillel and Shammai received the tradition from them. Hillel said: Be of the disciples of Aaron. Love peace and pursue peace; love your fellow creatures and bring them near to the Torah.

13. He also said: He who strives to exalt his name will in the end destroy his name; he who does not increase his knowledge decreases it; he who does not study has undermined his right to life; and he who makes unworthy use of the crown of the Torah will perish.

14. He also said: If I am not for myself who will be? But if I am for myself only, what am I? And if not now, when?

15. Shammai said: Set a fixed time for the study of the Torah; say little and do much; and greet every person with a cheerful countenance.

16. Rabban Gamaliel said: Provide yourself with a teacher, and extricate yourself from doubt; and do not habitually contribute your tithes by rough estimates.

17. Simeon his son said: All my life I was raised among scholars and I found that no virtue becomes a man more than silence; what is more essential is not study but practice; and in the wake of many words is sin.

18. Rabban Simeon ben Gamaliel said: The world rests on three foundations: truth, justice, and peace. As it is written (Zech 8:16): "You shall administer truth, justice and peace within your gates."

■   CHAPTER II   ■

1. R. Judah ha-Nasi said: Which is the right course for a person to pursue in life? That which is honorable in his own eyes, and which will bring him honor from his fellow-man. Be careful with the observance of a seemingly minor commandment as with a major one, for you do not know the true merit of each commandment. Learn to balance the loss incurred in the performance of a commandment against the reward thereof, and the gain by a transgression against the loss thereof. Contemplate three facts and you will be spared from the power of sin: Know what is above you—an Eye

that sees, an Ear that hears, and a Book in which all your deeds are entered.

2. Rabban Gamaliel the son of R. Judah ha-Nasi said: It is good to combine the study of the Torah with a gainful occupation. In meeting the commitments of both, one causes sin to pass out of one's mind. Every study of the Torah which is not associated with a gainful occupation must fail, and will engender sin in the end. Those who serve the community—let them do so for the sake of God, and let them ascribe their achievement to the virtues of the people which are their heritage from past generations, and to the charitableness which is an enduring trait of their character. And as for the communal servants themselves, the Lord will grant them an abundant reward, as though they accomplished all by their own efforts.

3. Be circumspect in dealing with public officials. They befriend a person when it suits their own ends. They pose as friends when it is to their advantage, but they do not stand by a man when he is in trouble.

4. He used to say: Make His will your will so that He will make your will His will. Set aside your will before His will so that He will set aside the will of others before your will.

5. Hillel said: Do not separate yourself from the community, and do not be sure of yourself until the day you die; do not judge your fellow-man until you have been put in his position; do not make pronouncements which cannot be understood at once in the confident thought that they will be understood later on; and do not say that you will study when you will have leisure, for you may never attain leisure.

6. He used to say: An uncultured man cannot really fear sin; an ignorant man cannot be truly pious; a bashful man cannot learn and an impatient man cannot teach; he who engages in much commerce does not necessarily become wise; and in a place where there are no men, strive to be a man.

7. He once saw the skull of a man floating on the face of the waters, and recognizing it, said: Because you drowned others, they drowned you. And those who drowned you will in the end be drowned.

8. He used to say: The more flesh, the more worms; the more possessions, the more anxiety; the more women, the more sorcery; the more female slaves, the more lewdness; the more male slaves, the more robbery; the more Torah, the more life; the more contemplation, the more wisdom; the more counsel, the more understanding; the more righteousness, the more peace. One who has acquired a good reputation has acquired it for himself. One who has acquired for himself Torah, has acquired for himself life eternal.

9. Rabban Yohanan ben Zaccai received the tradition from Hillel and Shammai. He used to say: If you have studied much Torah, claim no special credit for yourself, because you were created for this purpose.

10. Rabban Yohanan ben Zaccai had five disciples: R. Eliezer ben Hyrcanus, R. Joshua ben Hananyah, R. Yose ha-Kohen, R. Simeon ben Nethanel, and R. Elazar ben Araḥ.

11. He used to recount their praises: Eliezer ben Hyrcanus is like a cemented cistern which does not lose a drop; R. Joshua ben Hananyah—happy is the mother that gave him birth; R. Yose ha-Kohen is a saintly man; R. Simeon ben Nethanel is a sin-fearing man; R. Elazar ben Araḥ is like an ever-flowing spring.

12. He used to say: If all the scholars of Israel were on one side of the scale, and Eliezer ben Hyrcanus were on the other, he would outweigh them all. Abba Saul, however, quoted otherwise in his name: If all the scholars of Israel, including Eliezer ben Hyrcanus, were on one side of the scale, and Elazar ben Araḥ were on the other, he would outweigh them all.

13. Said Rabban Yohanan to his disciples: Go and reflect on the highest good which a person ought to cultivate. R. Eliezer said: A generous eye; R. Joshua said: A good friend; R. Yose said: A good neighbor; R. Simeon said: Considering the consequences of one's actions; R. Elazar said: A kindly heart. Said he to them: I prefer the opinion of R. Elazar because your views are embodied in his.

14. Said he to them: Go and reflect as to the greatest evil which a person ought to avoid. R. Eliezer said: An evil eye; R. Joshua said: An evil friend; R. Yose said: An evil neighbor; R. Simeon said: Borrowing without repaying, for borrowing from man is like borrowing from God. As it has been said (Ps 37:21): When the wicked

borrows and does not repay, the Righteous One (God) deals graciously and gives back. R. Elazar said: An unkind heart. Said he to them: I prefer the opinion of R. Elazar, because your views are embodied in his.

15. They said three things. R. Eliezer said: Let your friend's honor be as precious to you as your own; be not easily provoked to anger; and repent one day before you die. He also said: Warm yourself before the fire of scholars, but be careful not to be burnt by their glowing coals. The bite of scholars may be as sharp as that of a fox; their sting is as that of a scorpion; their hiss is as that of a serpent. Their words must all be treated as carefully as coals of fire.

16. R. Joshua said: An evil eye, an evil passion, and hate for one's fellow-man—these undermine a man's life in this world.

17. R. Yose said: Respect the possessions of your friend as you do your own; devote yourself to studying the Torah, for it will not come to you by inheritance; and perform all your actions for the sake of God.

18. R. Simeon said: Be meticulous in reciting the *Shema* and the *Amidah;* do not make your prayers a set routine, but offer them as a plea for mercy and graciousness before God, of whom it has been said (Joel 2:13): He is gracious and merciful, patient and abounding in kindness, and relenting of evil. And do not see yourself as evil in your own estimation.

19. R. Elazar said: Be zealous to study the Torah; be skillful in refuting the arguments of a heretic; and consider before whom you toil, and who the Master is that is due to reward you for your labor.

20. R. Tarfon said: The day is short; the task is great; the workmen are lazy; the reward is abundant; and the Master is pressing.

21. He also said: It is not your duty to finish the work, but neither are you free to desist from it. If you have studied much Torah, you will receive much reward. Your Employer may be trusted to compensate you for your labor. And remember that the true reward of the righteous is in the world to come.

CHAPTER III

1. Akavyah ben Mahalalel said: Meditate on three things and you will be spared from the power of sin: Consider whence you came, and whither you are going, and before whom you are destined to give an accounting. *Whence you came*—from a putrid drop; *whither you are going*—to a place of dust, worms and maggots; and *before whom you are destined to give an accounting*—before the King of kings, the Holy One, praised be He.

2. R. Hanina, the deputy High Priest, said: Pray for the welfare of the government. Were it not for the fear of it, men would swallow each other alive.

3. R. Hananya ben Teradyon said: Two men who sit together without exchanging words of the Torah—they are a company of scoffers, of whom it is written (Ps 1:1): (A good man) does not sit in the company of scoffers. But two men who sit together and do exchange words of the Torah—the divine Presence is among them. As it is written (Mal 3:16): Then did those who revere the Lord speak one to another, and the Lord was attentive and He heard, and a record was made before Him of those who revered the Lord and cherished His name. How do we know that even if only one person engages in the study of the Torah, the Lord appoints for him a reward? Because it is written (Lam 3:28): He may sit alone and meditate silently, for he will take a reward for it.

4. R. Simeon said: Three who ate at the same table without speaking any words of the Torah, it is as if they had eaten of the sacrifices to dead idols, of whom it is written (Is 28:8): For all their tables are full of vomit and filthiness, because God is not among them. But if three have eaten at the same table and did speak words of Torah, it is as if they had eaten at a table set before the Lord. To them may be applied the verse in Scripture (Ezek 41:22): And he said to me: This is the table that is before the Lord.

5. R. Hanina ben Hahinai said: He who stays up nights and he who journeys alone upon the road at night, and he who likes to idle away his time—all these are guilty of undoing their own lives.

6. R. Nehunia ben Hakaneh said: He who submits to the yoke of the Torah liberates himself from the yoke of circumstance. He rises above the pressures of the state, and above the fluctuations of

worldly fortune. But he who rejects the yoke of the Torah submits to the yoke of circumstance. He falls prey to the pressures of the state and to the fluctuations of worldly fortune.

7. R. Halafta ben Dosa of the village of Hananya said: Ten who sit together and engage in the study of the Torah—the divine Presence is among them. As it is written (Ps 82:1): God is present in a congregation (the Hebrew *edah* which was assumed to consist of ten) of the Lord. Whence may we infer that this is true of five? Because it is written (Amos 9:6): He established His group (the Hebrew *agudah* which stands for an aggregate held together by the five fingers of the hand) on earth. And whence do we know that this is also true of three? Because it is written (Ps 82:1): In the midst of the judges (the lowest court consisted of three judges) He judges. And whence do we know that this is also true of two? Because it is written (Mal 3:16): Then did the faithful of the Lord speak one to his neighbor and the Lord listened and heeded. And whence do we know that this also is true of one? Because it is written (Ex 20:24): In every place where I will cause My name to be mentioned, I will come to you and bless you.

8. R. Elazar of Bartota said: Give to God what is His, for you and all you possess are His. And thus did David express it (1 Chron 29:14): All things are from Thee, and we have given Thee only what is Thine.

9. R. Jacob said: He who studies while travelling on a journey and in the very midst of his studies interrupts himself to admire the scenery, saying, How beautiful is this tree, how fair is this field, such a person has brought injury upon his own soul.

10. R. Dostai bar Yanai said in the name of R. Meir: He who forgets anything of what he has learnt has brought injury upon his soul. As it is written (Deut 4:9): Beware and guard well your soul lest you forget the things which your own eyes have seen. It might be inferred that a person is to be blamed even if he forgot because the subject was too subtle for him, that verse therefore adds: And lest they be removed from your heart all the days of your life. He is to be blamed only if he forgot because of deliberate neglect.

11. R. Hanina ben Dosa said: He to whom the fear of sin is more important than wisdom, his wisdom will endure; he to whom his

wisdom is more important than the fear of sin, his wisdom will not endure.

12. He used to say: He whose deeds exceed his wisdom, his wisdom will endure; he whose wisdom exceeds his deeds, his wisdom will not endure.

13. He used to say also: He in whom people take pleasure, God will take pleasure in him also. And he in whom people have no pleasure, God has no pleasure in him either.

14. R. Dosa ben Hyrcanus said: Late morning sleep, midday wine, frivolous, childish talk, and frequenting the gathering places of the ignorant—these undermine a person's life.

15. R. Elazar of Modin said: He who desecrates what is sacred, who disparages the festivals, who exposes another person to public embarrassment, who violates the covenant of our father Abraham, who deliberately misinterprets the Torah—though he be learned in the Torah and perform many good deeds, he has forfeited his share in life eternal.

16. R. Ishmael said: Be submissive toward a great person; be gentle toward the young; and receive all people with a cheerful manner.

17. R. Akiba said: Mockery and levity lead a person to lewdness. Tradition is a fence for safeguarding the Torah; tithing is a fence for wealth; vows are a fence for self-restraint; silence is a fence for wisdom.

18. He used to say: Beloved is man for he was created in the divine image. A special boon was conferred on him as he was told of his creation in the divine image. As it is written (Gen 9:6): For in the image of God made He man. Beloved are Israel, for they were called children of God. A special love was shown them in that they were told they were the children of God. As it is written (Deut 14:1): You are children of the Lord your God. Beloved are Israel for they were given a precious object (the Torah). A special love was shown them in that they were told they had been given a precious object. As it is written (Prov 4:2): I have given you good doctrine; forsake not My Torah.

19. Everything is foreseen, yet freedom of choice is given. The world is judged mercifully, yet all is in accordance with the preponderant quality of the work.

20. He used to say: Everything is a loan given against a pledge, and the net is cast over all the living so that none may forfeit paying by escaping. The shop is open; the shop-keeper extends credit; the ledger is spread out and the hand makes entries. Whoever wishes to borrow may come and borrow, but the collectors make their rounds daily, and exact payment, whether or not one is aware of it. They go by an unfailing record, and the judgment is a judgment of truth. And everything is made ready for the final accounting.

21. R. Elazar ben Azaryah said: Without Torah there are no manners; without manners there is no Torah. Without wisdom there is no reverence; without reverence there is no wisdom. Without knowledge there is no understanding; without understanding there is no knowledge. Without bread there is no Torah; without Torah there is no bread.

22. He used to say: He whose wisdom exceeds his good deeds, to what is he like? To a tree of many branches and few roots; and the wind comes and uproots it and overturns it. As it is written (Jer 17:6): He shall be like a lonely tree in the desert, and he shall not see the coming of good; he shall inhabit the dry places in the wilderness, a salty land and uninhabited. But he whose good deeds exceed his wisdom, to what is he like? To a tree of few branches and many roots, so that even if all the winds of the world blow upon it, they will not stir it from its place. As it is written (Jer 17:8): And he shall be like a tree planted by the waters, that spreads its roots by a stream. It does not see the coming of heat; its leaf is ever green. It is untroubled in a year of drought, and does not cease from bearing fruit.

23. R. Elazar ben Hisma said: The rules about bird-offerings and the rules about the purification of women are essential precepts; astronomy and mathematics are the auxiliaries of wisdom.

■   CHAPTER IV   ■

1. Ben Zoma said: Who is wise? He who learns from all men. As it is written (Ps 119:99): From all who taught me have I gained understanding. Who is mighty? He who subdues his passions. As it is written (Prv 16:32): He that is slow to anger is better than the mighty, and he that rules over his own spirit than he that conquers

a city. Who is rich? He who is happy with his portion. As it is written (Ps 128:2): When you enjoy the labor of your hands, happy will you be, and all will be well with you. *Happy will you be* refers to your state in this world; *and all will be well with you* refers to your state in the world to come. Who attains to honor? He who confers honor upon other men. As it is written (1 Sam 2:30): Those who honor me will I honor, and those who disparage me, I will esteem lightly.

2. Ben Azzai said: Run to do even a minor commandment, and flee from any kind of transgression. For one righteous deed inspires another righteous deed, and one transgression, another transgression. The reward for a righteous deed is another righteous deed, and the penalty for a transgression is another transgression.

3. He used to say: Do not despise any man, and do not disparage any object. For there is not a man that has not his hour, and there is not an object that has not its place.

4. R. Levitas of Yavneh said: Let a person be exceedingly humble, for the end of mortal man is but worms.

5. R. Yohanan ben Berokah said: Whoever desecrates the name of God in secret will suffer the penalty for it in public; and this, whether the act of desecration be committed in ignorance, or in wilfulness.

6. R. Ishmael his son said: He who learns so that he may also teach, it will be given him to learn and also to teach. He who learns so that he may also practise, it will be given to learn, to teach, and also to practise.

7. R. Zadok said: Do not dissociate yourself from the community; let not the judge play the part of the counselor; and do not make of the Torah a crown with which to exalt yourself, or a spade to dig with. As Hillel used to say: He who makes unworthy use of the Torah will perish. Thus may you infer that he who uses the Torah for worldly gain undermines his own life.

8. R. Yose said: Whoever accords honor to the Torah will be accorded honor by other men. Whoever dishonors the Torah will be dishonored by other men.

9. R. Ishmael said: He who avoids the office of judge avoids enmity, robbery, and false oaths. And a judge who is overconfident in coming to a decision is a fool, a wicked and an arrogant man.

10. He used to say: Let not one man alone render a decision. None may judge alone except One (the Lord). And let not any one judge say to his colleagues: Follow my opinion. They may say that to him, but not he to them.

11. R. Jonathan said: He who observes the Torah amidst poverty will yet observe it amidst affluence; and whoever neglects the Torah amidst affluence will yet neglect it amidst poverty.

12. R. Meir said: Curtail your business so that you may attend to the Torah; and be humble before all people. If you begin neglecting the Torah, many interferences will arise to keep you from it. But if you toil zealously in the Torah, the Lord has abundant reward to grant you.

13. R. Eliezer ben Jacob said: He who performs a commandment has acquired a champion to protect him; and he who commits a transgression has acquired an adversary against himself. Repentance and good deeds are a shield against adversity.

14. R. Yohanan ha-Sandlar said: A gathering for the sake of God will yield enduring results, but a gathering which is not for the sake of God will not yield enduring results.

15. R. Elazar ben Shammua said: Let the honor of your disciple be as sacred to you as your own; and let the honor of your colleague be as sacred to you as the honor of your teacher; and let the honor of your teacher be as sacred to you as the honor due to God.

16. R. Judah said: Be cautious in teaching others, for even an unintentional error in teaching is tantamount to a deliberate transgression.

17. R. Simeon said: There are three crowns, the crown of the Torah, the crown of the priesthood, and the crown of royalty. But greater than all of these is the crown of a good name.

18. R. Nehorai said: If necessary, go into exile but to a place of Torah, and do not expect the Torah to follow you, for only in the exchange with colleagues will the Torah become fixed as your possession. And do not depend entirely on your own understanding.

19. R. Yannai said: We cannot wholly account for the ease of the wicked, nor for the afflictions of the righteous.

20. R. Mattithyah ben Heresh said: Be the first to extend greetings to every man; and choose to be a tail to lions rather than a head to foxes.

21. R. Jacob said: This world is like a vestibule before the world to come. Prepare yourself in the vestibule so that you may enter into the main chamber.

22. He used to say: Better one hour spent in penitence and in good deeds in this world than all the life of the hereafter. And better one hour of the bliss in the hereafter than all the joys in this world.

23. R. Simeon ben Elazar said: Do not attempt to appease your friend at the time of his anger; do not begin to console him while his beloved one lies dead before him; do not question him for particulars at the time he makes a vow; and do not try to face him in the hour of his disgrace.

24. Samuel the Younger used to quote Proverbs 24:17–18: Do not rejoice when your enemy falls and let not your heart be glad when he stumbles, lest the Lord see it and be displeased and turn away His wrath from him to you.

25. Elisha ben Abuyah said: If one studies in his youth, to what is he like? To writing with ink on clean paper. But he who studies in his old age, to what is he like? To writing with ink on blotted paper.

26. R. Yose ben Yehudah of Kefar ha-Bavli said: He who learns from the young, to what is he like? To one who eats unripe grapes, and drinks fresh wine from his vat. But one who studies from the old, to what is he like? To one who eats ripe grapes and drinks old wine.

27. R. Meir said: Do not judge by the vessel, but by what is in it. A new vessel may be full of old wine, and an old vessel may be devoid even of new wine.

28. R. Elazar ha-Kapor said: Envy, lust, and the seeking after honor, undermine a man's life in this world.

29. He used to say: Those born are destined to die; and those that die are destined to live again; and those that live are destined to stand in judgment. Let men, therefore, know and proclaim and establish the conviction that He is God, He the Maker, He the Creator, He the Discerner, He the Judge, He the Witness, He the Plaintiff. In His judgment, praised be He, there is no unrighteousness; there is no lapse of memory; there is no favoritism and no bribery. But

everything proceeds in accordance with an accounting. And do not imagine that the grave is an escape. For by divine determination are you formed; by divine determination are you born; by divine determination do you live; by divine determination will you die, and by divine determination are you due to stand in judgment before the Supreme King of kings, praised be He.

■　CHAPTER V　■

1. The world was created by ten divine commands. What was the reason for this? Could it not have been created by one command? It is to make grave the judgment that is to fall on the wicked who injure the world that was created by ten commands, and to merit a goodly reward for the righteous who sustain the world that was created by ten commands.

2. There were ten generations from Adam to Noah, which shows the extent of the divine patience, since all those generations continued to provoke Him, until He finally punished them with the flood.

3. There were ten generations from Noah to Abraham, which shows the extent of the divine patience, since all those generations continued to provoke Him, and then came Abraham who was awarded all the good the others had forfeited.

4. Abraham faced ten tests of his faith, and he met them all, which shows the extent of father Abraham's love for God.

5. Ten miracles were performed for our ancestors in Egypt and ten at the Red Sea. Ten plagues did the Holy One, praised be He, bring down upon the Egyptians in Egypt, and ten at the Red Sea.

6. Our forefathers tried the Holy One, praised be He, ten times in the wilderness. As it is written (Num 14:22): And they have tried Me these ten times, and they did not hearken to My voice.

7. Ten miracles were wrought for our ancestors in the Temple in Jerusalem: No woman miscarried from the scent of the sacrifices; the flesh of the sacrifices never became putrid; no fly was seen in the Temple slaughter-house; the High Priest never became impure on the Day of Atonement; the rain never quenched the fire of the woodpile on the altar; nor did the wind subdue the column of smoke that rose from it; no disqualifying defect was ever found in

the offerings of the *Omer* (Lev 23:19, 20), the two loaves (Lev 12:17), and of the showbread (Lev 24:5,6); the closely standing congregation found room to prostrate themselves; never did a serpent or scorpion injure anyone in Jerusalem; and no pilgrim ever complained that the place was too crowded for him to lodge in Jerusalem.

8. Ten things were created on the eve of the Sabbath at twilight: The mouth of the earth which swallowed Korah and his associates; the mouth of the well of Miriam which accompanied Israel in the wilderness (Ex 17:6); the mouth of the ass which spoke to Balaam (Num 22:28); the rainbow Noah saw after the flood (Gen 9:13, 14); the manna that fed Israel in the wilderness; the rod with which Moses performed God's signs in Egypt (Ex 4:17); the *shamir* worm, which hewed the stones for the building of the Temple (Talmud, Sotah 48b); the script on the two tablets of the Law, the tools for writing, and the stone tablets (Ex 32:15, 16). Others also add: The spirits of destruction; the burial place of Moses (Deut 34:16); and the ram father Abraham used as a sacrifice in place of Isaac (Gen 22:13). Others also add: The pair of tongs which held the first pair of tongs while they were being forged.

9. There are seven characteristics of an uncultured man, and seven of a wise man. A wise man does not speak before one who is greater than he in wisdom; he does not interrupt another man's speech; he is not hasty to answer; his answers are on the subject of the discussion, and his replies are to the point of the inquiry; he deals with first things first and last things last; he acknowledges what he does not know; and he affirms the truth. The opposite of these are the characteristics of the uncultured man.

10. Seven kinds of punishment come upon the world, to expiate for seven capital offenses. When some people contribute the tithe and some do not, a famine caused by drought descends on the world, when some go hungry and some enjoy plenty. If all have resolved not to contribute the tithe, a famine ensues caused by panic and drought. If they all resolved not to contribute the portion of the dough-cake to the priest, a famine of extermination ensues.

11. Pestilence comes into the world to exact the death penalties mentioned in the Torah, the execution of which was not entrusted to the human tribunal, and for using the crops forbidden on the Sabbatical year. The sword descends upon the world because of a

delay of justice or a perversion of justice, and because of the deliberate misinterpretation of the Torah. Wild beasts come ravaging the world because of false oaths, and because of a profanation of God's name. Exile comes upon the world because of idolatry, incest, bloodshed, and for denying rest to the soil on the Sabbatical year.

12. During four periods in each cycle of seven years the pestilence increases: in the fourth, the seventh (the Sabbatical year), the post-Sabbatical year, and at the conclusion of the feast of Sukkot. During the fourth year, for failure to contribute the tithe to the poor, due in the third year; in the seventh, for failure to contribute the tithe to the poor, due on the sixth year; in the post-Sabbatical year, for using the forbidden harvest of the Sabbatical year; at the conclusion of the feast of Sukkot, for robbing the poor of various grants (gleanings, forgotten sheaves, and the corner crops) assigned to them in Scripture.

13. There are four types of character among people. He who says: What is mine is mine and what is yours is yours, is a medium type, and some say that his type is of the wicked city of Sodom; he that says: What is mine is yours and what is yours is mine, is an ignoramus; he that says: What is mine is yours and what is yours is yours, is a saintly man; he that says: What is yours is mine and what is mine is mine, is a wicked man.

14. There are four types of tempers among people. He who is easily injured and easily appeased—his loss is compensated by his gain; he who is hard to anger and hard to appease—his gain is cancelled by his loss; he who is hard to anger and easy to appease is a saintly man; he who is easily angered and hard to appease is a wicked man.

15. There are four types among students. He who learns quickly and forgets quickly—his gain is cancelled by his loss; he who learns slowly and forgets slowly—his loss is compensated by his gain; he who learns quickly and forgets slowly—his is a fortunate lot; he who learns slowly and forgets quickly—his is an unfortunate lot.

16. There are four dispositions toward charity. He who desires to give but who would rather that others did not give—he begrudges the good of others; he who desires that others give but is unwilling to give himself—he begrudges his own good; he who gives and is

desirous that others give also—he is a saintly man; he who refuses to give and does not wish others to give—he is a wicked man.

17. There are four types with reference to attending the House of Study. He who attends but does not perform, has a reward for attending; he who performs but does not attend has the reward of performing; he who attends and performs is a saintly man; he who neither attends nor performs is a wicked man.

18. There are four types among those who study with scholars: a sponge, a funnel, a strainer and a sifter. A sponge absorbs everything; a funnel receives at one end and loses it at the other; a strainer loses the wine and keeps the dregs; a sifter eliminates the coarse and retains the fine flour.

19. A love which is for an ulterior motive will end when the motive has ceased. But a love that is not for a transient motive will never end. What manner of love is for an ulterior motive? The love of Amnon for Tamar (2 Sam 13). What manner of love does not depend on a transient motive? The love of David and Jonathan (2 Sam 1:26).

20. A controversy for the sake of God will lead to abiding results. But a controversy that is not for the sake of God will not lead to abiding results. What manner of controversy is for God's sake? The controversy between Hillel and Shammai. What manner of controversy is not for God's sake? The controversy of Korah and his associates (Num 16:3).

21. He who leads a multitude to virtue will not become involved in sin. But he who leads a multitude to sin will be kept from deeds of penitence. Moses was virtuous and he led a multitude to virtue. The virtues of that multitude may be ascribed to him. As it is written (Deut 33:21): He (Moses) performed the righteousness of the Lord and his judgments with Israel. Jeroboam the son of Nebot was a sinner and he led others to sin. As it is written (1 Kgs 15:30): For the sins of Jeroboam which he sinned and caused Israel to sin.

22. He that has these three attributes is of the disciples of father Abraham, but he who has three contrary attributes is of the disciples of Balaam the wicked. A benevolent eye, a humble mind, and a lowly spirit characterize the disciples of father Abraham, but an evil eye, a haughty mind, and a proud spirit are characteristics of Balaam the wicked. What is the difference in the final destinies between the disciples of father Abraham and those of Balaam? The disciples

of father Abraham have abundance in this world, and they will inherit the world to come. As it is written (Prv 8:41): There is abundance to give My faithful as an inheritance, and I will fill their treasure. But the disciples of the wicked Balaam will inherit *Gehinnom* and they will descend to the pit of destruction. As it is written (Ps 55:24): And Thou, O Lord, wilt bring them down to the pit of destruction; bloodthirsty and deceitful men will not live out half their days; but as for me, I will trust in Thee.

23. Judah ben Tema said: Be bold as a leopard, light as an eagle, fast as a deer, determined as a lion in doing the will of your Heavenly Father. He also said: The impudent are for *Gehinnom*, and the self-effacing are for paradise (*Gan-Eden*). May it be Thy will, O Lord our God and God of our fathers, to cause the rebuilding of the holy sanctuary in Jerusalem, speedily, and in our time; and grant that we may have a portion among those who are devoted to Thy Torah.

24. He was also accustomed to say: Five years of age, for the study of the Bible; ten years for the study of the Mishnah; thirteen years for the performance of the commandments; fifteen years for the study of the Talmud; eighteen years for marriage; twenty years for a vocation; thirty years for fullness of strength; forty years for understanding; fifty years for giving counsel; sixty years for old age; seventy years for the hoary head; eighty years for the grace of special vigor; ninety years for the bent back; at a hundred one is as if he were dead and gone from the world.

25. Ben Bag-Bag said: Study the Torah again and again, for everything is in it; yea, contemplate it, grow old and gray over it, but do not swerve from it, for there is no greater virtue than this.

26. Ben Hé-Hé said: The gain is in proportion to the pain.

Postscript

There are two more Orders in the Talmud. The order of Nezikin is followed by the order of Kodashim, which means "holy things," a reference to the cult of Temple sacrifices. Of the eleven tractates in this Order, ten deal with Temple procedure and the rules governing the offering of sacrifices. The eleventh tractate, known as Hullin, deals with the ritual slaughter of nonsacrificial animals, and it offers some regulations concerning kosher and non-kosher food.

This is followed by the Order of Taharot, which means "purities," a reference to the rules of ritual purity, which was also associated with the Temple in Jerusalem, and the cult of sacrifices. Only one tractate in this Order has a general applicability, the tractate Nidah, which deals with the impurity of a woman induced by her menstrual period. That the overall subject of ritual purity did not elicit much interest among the later rabbis may be seen in the fact that only the tractate Nidah has a Gemara supplement to the Mishnah. The other eleven tractates are without such supplements, offering only a series of succinct *mishnayot*.

No selections from the last two Orders are included here because the subjects dealt with are outside the scope of our interest in this volume.

*Tosefta Sanhedrin 11:6.

237

Index

INDEX

Av, fifteenth of, 120
Avot, 22, 219; text, 219–36
Avtalyon, 103, 220–21
Avya, R., 90

Baba Batra, 188–89; selections, 189–97
Baba Mezia, 5, 177–78; selections, 178–87
Balaam, 19, 113
Bar Kapara, 143, 195
Bastards, 50–51, 167
Ben Azzai, 126, 133, 229
Ben Bag-Bag, 236
Ben Hé-Hé, 236
Ben Patura, 186
Ben Zoma, 41, 77, 126, 228–29
Berakhot, 59–61; selections, 61–83
Beraukhya, R., 162
Beroka Hazaah, 119–20
Beth Din, 101, 107, 146, 160
Betrothal, 166, 169, 171; prayers at, 141–42
Bible: authority of, 33; flexibility in interpretation of, 199–200; as literature, 194–95; Talmud and, 9–15
Birth control, 36, 130, 136
Bivi, R., 135, 136
Blasphemy, 104

Capital punishment, 31–32, 51, 198, 199, 213–14
Celebration, days of, 84, 120–21
Character, Torah and, 102–05
Charity, 95, 190–93, 200–01
Chastity, 21
Children. See Parents and children

Circumcision, 167; prohibition against, 117
Circumstantial evidence, 31, 199
Civil law, 177; lost and found, 178–79; property rights, 34, 166–67, 188–89; usury, 180–81
Cleanliness, 47
Commandments, 15, 59; direct encounter with God and, 8; Shema and the Ten Commandments, 61–62; 613 commandments communicated to Moses, 22, 28, 214; summation of, 22, 214–15; Torah and, 18–22
Community, individual and, 32–33, 111, 115–18
Criminal law: capital punishment, 31–32, 51, 198, 199, 213–14; circumstantial evidence, 31, 199; flogging as punishment, 213; intent, 54; sanctity of life and, 206–08

Dama b. Nethinah, 169
David, 137–38, 200–01
Day of Atonement. See Atonement, Day of
Death: confronting, 97; consoling mourners, 142–43
Death penalty. See Capital punishment
Democracy in academy, 72–76
Deuteronomy, 11, 21, 24, 59, 85
Dima of Nehardea, 94
Dimi, R., 90, 129, 152–53, 169, 181–82, 184, 202
Divorce, 35, 140, 145, 205–06
Dosa ben Hyrcanus, 227

239

INDEX

Dostai bar Yanai, 226
Dowry, 44, 169

Education, 36–38, 196; elementary education, 34, 37–38, 49
Eduyot, 74
Eighteen Benedictions, 60, 69–70, 164
Eleazar, R., 51, 54, 63, 64, 66, 68–69, 82–83, 88, 90, 94, 96, 100, 125, 132, 139, 146–47, 149, 157, 171, 183, 189, 204
Eleazar b. Arah, 223, 224
Eleazar b. Azariah, 73, 75–76, 123, 124, 213–14, 228
Eleazar b. Harsom, 100, 103, 104
Eleazar b. Hisma, 123, 228
Eleazar b. Mattiah, 170
Eleazar b. Pedat, 24–25, 68–69
Eleazar b. Shammua, 230
Eleazar b. Simeon, 113–14, 133, 134, 173
Eleazar b. Yose, 200
Eleazar ha-Kappor Beribbi, 114–15, 231–32
Eleazar of Bartota, 226
Eleazar of Modi'in, 49, 227
Eleazar b. Zadok, 70
Eliezer, R., 62, 70, 80, 82, 89, 90, 97, 133, 145, 156, 161, 172, 184, 185, 205–06, 223, 224
Eliezer b. Jacob, 230
Eliezer the Great. See Eliezer b. Hyrcanus
Elijah, 43, 70, 119–20, 129, 154
Elisha b. Avuyah, 122–23, 126–29, 231
Emunah, 22, 23
Erub, 27
Ethics of the Fathers, The. See Avot

Ethics, situational, 177–78
Evil: evil impulse, 17–18; protesting, 88–89; resistance to temptation, 174–76
Exilarchs, 12, 13, 33, 52
Ezra, 9

Faith, 22–23, 24, 29
Family. *See* Marriage: Parents and children
Fasting, 46, 84, 105, 110, 111, 114–15,
Fathers According to Rabbi Nathan, The, 219
Feast of Tabernacles, 39
Feasts, 84, 120–21; pilgrimage festivals, 54, 122; *see also* specific feasts, e.g. Atonement, Day of
Flogging, 213
Funerals, 44

Gamaliel [of Yavneh], 17, 69–70, 72, 73, 74–75, 75–76, 136, 172, 211, 221, 222
Gamaliel the Elder, 135–36
Gemara, 10, 57, 85, 99
Gemilut hasadim, 29, 44
Gibeonites, rejection of, 137–38
Gladiatorial combat, 216
God, 15–17; attributes, 16, 102; faith in, 22–23, 24, 29; as father, redeemer, 91–93; fear of, 85–88, 163–64; humanity's purpose and, 17–18; love of, 79–81, 163; proof of existence, 16; providence of, 76–78; reverence for, 22–27; *see also* specific headings, e.g.: Prayer
Golden rule, 28

INDEX

Goldenberg, Robert, 11–12
Government: rapacious government, 179–80; society and the individual, 32–33; *see also* Law
Grace after meals, 164

Habakuk, 22, 214–15
Habiba, R., 144
Hadrian, Emperor, 17
Haggadah, 13
Hagigah, 122–23; selections, 123–29
Haita, Daniel, 50
Halafta ben Dosa, 226
Halakha, 13; *see also* Law
Halizah, 130
Hama b. Hanina, 107, 157, 162
Hamenuna, R., 63, 67, 93, 96, 115, 167–68
Hamnuna Zuta, 67
Hana b. Adda, R., 137
Hana b. Hanilai, 78
Hanan, R., 204
Hananya ben Teradyon, R., 225
Hanilai, R., 132
Hanina, R., 45, 82, 88, 129, 184, 202, 203, 205, 209, 225
Hanina ben Dosa, 226–27
Hanina ben Haḥinai, 225
Hanina b. Idi, 112
Hanina b. Papa, 65–66, 125
Hannah, 63
Health, 47–48
Helba, R., 184
Heschel, Abraham Joshua, 8–9
Hezekiah, 144
Hezekiah R. Kohen, 174
Hidka, R., 116–17, 209
High Priests, 99
Hillel, 37, 42–43, 47, 85–87,

103, 104, 131, 135, 143, 147, 193, 221, 222, 229
Hisda, R., 70, 78, 96, 115, 145, 167–68
History, stages of, 55
Hiyya, R., 66, 134
Hiyya b. Abba, 69, 90, 142, 157, 161, 168
Hiyya b. Luliana, 120
Hiyya b. Ba, 69, 101–02
Honesty, 45–46
Hospitality to strangers, 44, 94
Humility, 111–14
Huna, R., 70, 108, 118–19, 124–25, 144, 145, 146, 152, 167–68
Huna b. Bizna, 149
Huna b. Hanina, 146, 159
Husband and wife. *See* Marriage

Idi, R., 172
Idi b. Avin, 121
Idolatry, 21, 26, 53, 61, 216, 217–18
Ilai, R., 133, 134, 145, 149
Illegitimate children, 50–51, 167
Immortality, path to, 139
Individual: before God, 15–17; community and, 32–33, 111, 115–18; moderation in living, 46–47; priority of self, 185–86; public welfare and, 34; spiritual development of character, 40–46
Isaac, R., 64, 76, 82, 93, 108–09, 164–65, 197
Ishmael, R., 53, 134, 197, 208, 217, 227, 229
Ishmael, school of, 167
Ishmael B. Yose, 153
Isi b. Judah, 170–71

INDEX

INDEX

INDEX

Papa, R., 88, 148, 153
Pappus, 80, 81
Parents and children: bastards, 50–51, 167; duty to have children, 36, 111, 131–34; elementary education, 37–38; honor and respect due, 62, 136–37, 169–71; maintenance of, 49; responsibilities of, 167–71; stubborn and rebellious son, 209–10; treatment of children, 36; truthfulness to children, 45
Patience, 85–88
Patriarchs, 12–13, 33, 52
Penitence, 53–55, 99, 107–09, 110, 215
Pentateuch, 19
Pesah, 122
Pesia gasa, 27
Pharisees, 9–10, 37, 52
Pilgrimage festivals, 54, 122
Plemo, 175–76
Poor relief, 34, 44, 49
Prayer, 25, 59–71; abbreviated prayer service, 70; at betrothal and marriage, 141; devotion in, 95; evening prayer, 72–73; guidelines, 62–65; language of, 164; liturgy, 59–61; voluntary prayer, 60–61
Prophecy, 18–20
Property rights, 34, 166–67, 188–89
Proverbs, 21
Psalms, 8
Pseudepigrapha, 10
Public welfare, 34–36, 48–49; private and public interest, 189–90
Purification rituals, 98, 123

Qumran scrolls, 10

Rab. *See* Rav
Rabba, 208
Rabbah, 29, 63, 144
Rabbah b. Adda, 141
Rabbah v. Avuha, 144, 218
Rabbah b. Bar Hana, 100, 111–12, 121, 129, 189–90
Rabbah b. Hanan, 181
Rabbah b. Huna, 88, 179
Rabbah b. Shela, 129
Rabbah b. Ulla, 104
Rabbis, 3–4, 8, 10; emergence as distinct group, 10; exemplary teacher, 32; lay leaders and, 12–13; meaning of word, 12
Rafram b. Papa, 118–19
Rav, 35, 66, 70, 72, 78, 80, 88, 94, 108, 139, 149, 174, 175, 181, 184, 186, 191, 196, 202
Rava, 64, 65, 67, 72, 79, 87, 91–92, 94, 104, 107, 118, 119, 129, 131, 135, 148, 153, 157, 164, 168, 172, 182, 184, 194–95, 196
Ravin b. Adda, 141
Ravina, 165
Repentance. *See* Penitence
Resh Lakish, 46, 91, 108, 115, 125, 129, 131, 137–38, 156, 158, 159, 195, 201, 202, 203, 205; death of son, 142, 143
Reuben, R., 29
Rev, 113
Revelation, 14, 16, 18
Righteousness: learned and righteous, 172–74, priority of, 100–02

INDEX

Other Volumes in this Series

Jacopone da Todi • THE LAUDS
Fakhruddin 'Iraqui • DIVINE FLASHES
Menahem Nahum of Chernobyl • THE LIGHT OF THE EYES
Early Dominicans • SELECTED WRITINGS
John Climacus • THE LADDER OF DIVINE ASCENT
Francis and Clare • THE COMPLETE WORKS
Gregory Palamas • THE TRIADS
Pietists • SELECTED WRITINGS
The Shakers • TWO CENTURIES OF SPIRITUAL REFLECTION
Zohar • THE BOOK OF ENLIGHTENMENT
Luis de León • THE NAMES OF CHRIST
Quaker Spirituality • SELECTED WRITINGS
Emanuel Swedenborg • THE UNIVERSAL HUMAN AND SOUL-BODY INTERACTION
Augustine of Hippo • SELECTED WRITINGS
Safed Spirituality • RULES OF MYSTICAL PIETY, THE BEGINNING OF WISDOM
Maximus Confessor • SELECTED WRITINGS
John Cassian • CONFERENCES
Johannes Tauler • SERMONS
John Ruusbroec • THE SPIRITUAL ESPOUSALS AND OTHER WORKS
Ibn 'Abbād of Ronda • LETTERS ON THE SŪFĪ PATH
Angelus Silesius • THE CHERUBINIC WANDERER
The Early Kabbalah •
Meister Eckhart • TEACHER AND PREACHER
John of the Cross • SELECTED WRITINGS
Pseudo-Dionysius • THE COMPLETE WORKS
Bernard of Clairvaux • SELECTED WORKS
Devotio Moderna • BASIC WRITINGS
The Pursuit of Wisdom • AND OTHER WORKS BY THE AUTHOR OF THE CLOUD
    OF UNKNOWING
Richard Rolle • THE ENGLISH WRITINGS
Francis de Sales, Jane de Chantal • LETTERS OF SPIRITUAL DIRECTION
Albert and Thomas • SELECTED WRITINGS
Robert Bellarmine • SPIRITUAL WRITINGS
Nicodemos of the Holy Mountain • A HANDBOOK OF SPIRITUAL COUNSEL
Henry Suso • THE EXEMPLAR, WITH TWO GERMAN SERMONS
Bérulle and the French School • SELECTED WRITINGS